*Liddell Hart and the
Weight of History*

A volume in the series

CORNELL STUDIES IN SECURITY AFFAIRS

edited by
Robert J. Art
Robert Jervis
Stephen M. Walt

A list of titles in the series is available at
www.cornellpress.cornell.edu.

Liddell Hart and the Weight of History

JOHN J. MEARSHEIMER

CORNELL UNIVERSITY PRESS
Ithaca and London

First published 1988 by Cornell University Press
First printing, Cornell Paperbacks, 2010

Printed in the United States of America

A CIP catalog record for this book is available from the Library of Congress.

For my parents,
Ruth and Thomas Mearsheimer

Contents

Contents

Preface

Sir Basil Henry Liddell Hart (1895–1970) was for almost half a century the most important writer on strategy and military matters in the English-speaking world. This book describes and evaluates the military theories he developed in the 1920s and 1930s and reassesses his widely accepted account of how those theories were received in England and Germany before World War II. It therefore deals principally with military history and security affairs. It deals with something else, however: with the origins and development of knowledge and ideas—that is, with the sociology of knowledge.

First, *Liddell Hart and the Weight of History* explores the origins of the ideas of a military thinker. These ideas, still influential today, were developed in response to a specific context that markedly affected their shape. Liddell Hart was of that generation of Englishmen for whom World War I, the Great War, was a watershed, and his ideas changed profoundly as his interpretation of that war shifted. The rise of Hitler and related British military policy problems had their effects as well. In short, although his theories are widely applied today, they were shaped by a unique historical context and should be applied with caution to current security problems.

Second, this book also bears on how history is written and how it can be distorted. After World War II, Liddell Hart played a key role in shaping the conventional wisdom about how military thought had developed in Europe before the war and about his own role in that development. In fact, he had been quite wrong on the basic military questions of the 1930s, and his writings helped lead the British government into serious error. During the war, wide recognition of those errors damaged his reputation badly. After the war, however, he mounted a successful campaign to replace memories of his past mistakes with purported achievements. By the late 1960s he was widely seen as a prophet whose prescient advice had been tragically ignored. My effort here is to correct the historical record and to describe how Liddell Hart was able to resurrect his tarnished reputation.

I became interested in Liddell Hart while doing research on my book *Conventional Deterrence.* I profited greatly from his stimulating writings, and I still consider them essential reading for serious students of strategy and warfare. But it struck me early on that received opinion about Liddell Hart is seriously flawed. I set out to write a short monograph on the evolution of his thought, to better explain his ideas and to make modest corrections in the record, but I soon discovered, as I delved more deeply, that the conventional wisdom is much more in error than I had believed. Moreover, the details of how Liddell Hart had managed to distort the historical record are abundant and remarkably well preserved, so that I could reconstruct the story at some length. This book is the result. I hope that by setting the record straight I will make it possible for other students of military history and strategy to identify what is of permanent value in the writings of a very important thinker.

This book could not have been written without the assistance of several institutions. I am very grateful to the American Philosophical Society, the John D. and Catherine T. MacArthur Foundation, and the University of Chicago's Social Sciences Research Committee for funding this project, which allowed me to make trips to London to do extensive archival research. It also made it possible to take time off from teaching to do research and to write.

Although scholarly writing is largely an individual effort, critical comments from colleagues help improve the final product. In this case, a host of scholars and friends read various drafts and offered important criticisms: Richard Betts, Michael Brown, Audrey Kurth Cronin, Joseph Grieco, Morris Janowitz, Robert Jervis, James Lewis, Robert Litwak, Timothy Lupfer, Michael McCabe, Steven Miller, Robert Pape, Barry Posen, Jack Snyder, Hew Strachan, William Tetreault, Marc Trachtenberg, and Stephen Walt. I deeply appreciate their help. I also gratefully acknowledge the editorial assistance of Janet Mais and Roger Haydon at Cornell University Press.

I owe special thanks to Robert Art, who not only provided detailed comments but also gave me superb advice about the final structure of the book. Brian Bond too deserves special thanks. He provided detailed comments on two drafts of the manuscript and also took the time on a number of occasions to sit and answer my many questions about Liddell Hart. I am especially grateful to my wife, Mary, who helped me in countless ways. She offered extensive comments on successive drafts and provided invaluable assistance with those mundane but very important chores of typing and proofreading. Most important, she understood why I had to set aside large blocks of time on weekends, during evenings, and on vacations to work on this book.

My greatest debt of gratitude is owed to Stephen Van Evera, whose commitment to scholarly excellence is unsurpassed by anyone I know. He provided extensive comments on various versions of the manuscript and forced me to confront issues I would otherwise have overlooked. His editorial hand rests heavy on this book. He was also a constant source of encouragement: his belief in the value of this study, unflagging from the start, helped sustain my momentum when the going got tough. One could not find a better friend and scholar.

Because the argument in this book is heavily dependent on documentation, I needed help from first-rate research assistants: Sean Harte, Ralph Inforzatto, James Marquardt, Kenneth Moore, Rade Radovich, Denny Roy, Ross Weiner, and especially Francis Gavin. Also, Philip McCarty of the Royal United Services Institution helped me on many occasions to find obscure articles. I thank them all for their help.

I spent many hours working in the Liddell Hart Centre for Military Archives, located at King's College, University of London. I express my gratitude to Patricia J. Methven, the archivist, and her staff for being so hospitable and helpful. Finally, I thank the trustees of the centre for giving me permission to quote extensively from Liddell Hart's papers.

JOHN J. MEARSHEIMER

Chicago, Illinois

Liddell Hart and the
Weight of History

It is only common sense to say that we cannot hope to build up a true doctrine of war except from true lessons, and the lessons cannot be true unless based on true facts, and the facts cannot be true unless we probe for them in a purely scientific spirit—an utterly detached determination to get at the truth no matter how it hurts our pride. Not a few military historians have admitted that they feel compelled by position, interest or friendship, to put down less than they know to be true. Once a man surrenders to this tendency the truth begins to slip away like water down a waste-pipe—until those who want to learn how to conduct war in the future are unknowingly bathing their minds in a shallow bath.

Liddell Hart, 1933

[1]

Introduction: The Need
for a Reassessment

When he died in 1970, Sir Basil H. Liddell Hart was the most famous and widely admired military historian and theorist in the world, and he probably remains so today. Scholars, statesmen, and soldiers have showered him with praise: Alastair Buchan, the late Oxford don who was the first director of the International Institute for Strategic Studies, has called him "the most important military thinker of the age of mechanisation in any country, the man who foresaw with the greatest clarity the effect of the internal combustion engine and the aeroplane on the conduct of war"; the English military historian Michael Howard terms him "the greatest thinker about war in this century"; and A. J. P. Taylor has described him as "the most formidable military writer of the age." The American historian Jay Luvaas declared him "one of the most profound, original and influential military thinkers of modern history"; John F. Kennedy, shortly before becoming president, wrote, "No expert on military affairs has better earned the right to respectful attention. . . . For two generations he has brought to the problems of war and peace a rare combination of professional competence and imaginative insight. His predictions and his warnings have often been correct."[1]

Famous German and Israeli military commanders have offered similar accolades and given him credit for their own battlefield achievements. Heinz Guderian, the driving force behind the development of Germany's panzer forces in the 1930s and a commander of those for-

---

[1]Alastair Buchan, "Mechanised Warfare," rev. of *Memoirs*, vol. 1, by LH, *New Statesman*, 4 June 1965: 887; Michael Howard, *War and the Nation State* (Oxford: Clarendon, 1978), 7; A. J. P. Taylor, "Soldier Out of Step," rev. of *Memoirs*, vol. 1, *Observer Weekend Review*, 30 May 1965, 26; Jay Luvaas, LH's obituary, *American Historical Review* 75 (June 1970): 1573; John F. Kennedy, "Book in the News," rev. of *Deterrent or Defense*, by LH, *Saturday Review*, 3 Sept. 1960, 17.

midable forces in World War II, labeled himself among Liddell Hart's "disciples in tank affairs." Another German panzer general, Hasso von Manteuffel, called Liddell Hart "the creator of modern tank strategy." Yigal Allon, a founding father of the Israeli army, referred to him as "the captain who teaches generals"; Ariel Sharon inscribed a photograph for him with the words "the greatest teacher of all of us."[2]

He was born Basil Hart in Paris on 31 October 1895. His father was of a Cornish family, parts of which had left the Church of England for the Methodist movement at its inception. He had chosen Methodist ordination, later accepting the pulpit at a Wesleyan church in France that used Anglican liturgy. When Basil was born, his father had moved to a similar church in Paris that ministered to a wide variety of Protestants. Shortly after the turn of the century the family moved back to England, where Basil's life became that of the typical upper-middle-class Edwardian boy, including public school (St. Paul's, there being no barriers in the family to both Wesleyan and Anglican connections), where he was a good but not an excellent student. He developed early interests in military tactics and history, sports, and aviation. He was approaching his nineteenth birthday and about to start his second year at Cambridge, where he was reading history, when World War I began. He enthusiastically volunteered for the army and in December 1914 became a lieutenant in the King's Own Yorkshire Light Infantry. He never returned to Cambridge to finish his education.[3]

In the fall of 1915 he was sent to fight in France. Over the next year he served in the front lines on three occasions. His first two experiences in the combat zone were relatively uneventful, but his last was as a participant in the famous Somme offensive of 1916, where the British army suffered sixty thousand casualties on the first day. He was badly gassed in the third week of that battle and for the duration of the war was posted back to England, where he was primarily concerned with training infantrymen for the Western Front.

He began writing about military matters soon after the war ended, thus starting a long and distinguished writing career that would span fifty years. He remained in the army until 1924, when he was forced to

[2]Guderian and Manteuffel quotations are from inscribed photographs in *Memoirs*, vol. 2 (London: Cassell, 1965), btwn. 194 and 195. Allon and Sharon quotations are from inscribed photographs displayed in the Liddell Hart Centre for Military Archives, King's College, University of London.

[3]On LH's early years, see his "Forced to Think," in George A. Panichas, ed., *Promise of Greatness: The War of 1914–1918* (New York: John Day, 1968), 98–115; his *Memoirs*, vol. 1, prologue and chap. 1; Brian Bond, *Liddell Hart: A Study of His Military Thought* (London: Cassell, 1977), 12–17. In 1921 he changed his last name from Hart to Liddell Hart (Liddell was his mother's family name); see B. Bond, *Liddell Hart*, 12, 34.

retire because of a heart problem.[4] Shortly thereafter, he became the military correspondent for the *Daily Telegraph,* a position he held until 1935, when he moved to the more prestigious *Times.* He remained with the *Times* until after the start of World War II. In addition to his newspaper columns he wrote many books and magazine articles, including important and innovative works on infantry tactics, armored strategy, and grand strategy.[5]

Through his writing Liddell Hart soon established a towering reputation, becoming the most famous and respected military commentator in interwar Britain. Col. Edward M. House, Woodrow Wilson's close personal adviser, referred to him in 1933 as "the foremost military critic in the world." One year earlier, Sir Ian Hamilton, the well-known World War I general, labeled him "the most far-sighted and thought-stimulating military writer of our time." David Lloyd George, Britain's prime minister in World War I, came to "regard him as the highest and soundest authority on modern war whom it has been my privilege to meet"; the popular novelist and historian John Buchan described him "not only as an historian of campaigns, but as a philosopher who understands the root principles of human conflict. No one has read so courageously and acutely the lessons of the Great War." It was not uncommon in the 1930s for him to be referred to as the most important thinker about war since Clausewitz or sometimes as "this century's Clausewitz."[6]

This reputation gained Liddell Hart ready access to high government officials, giving him an important role in British military policy making. Although he held no official government position in the 1930s, he maintained close contact with key British policy makers, who, after 1933, were deeply concerned about how to deal with Hitler. Specifically, Britons debated whether to raise a large army to help defend France against the Germans. Liddell Hart firmly opposed building a British army that could fight on the Continent, and he did his utmost, and

---

[4]There is no evidence to support LH's claim (*Memoirs* 1:64–65) that he was forced out of the service because he held unpopular views.

[5]The terms *tactics, strategy,* and *grand strategy* are defined below. Parts of this chapter addressed subsequently at greater length are footnoted at those points.

[6]House and Hamilton quotations cited in "Tributes and Testimonies," 13/2; Lloyd George quotation from *Memoirs* 1:362; John Buchan, "General W. T. Sherman," rev. of *Sherman: The Genius of the Civil War,* by LH, *Spectator,* 15 Mar. 1930, 436. J. F. C. Fuller, the other renowned British military thinker of that era, had a different view of the Clausewitz comparison: "It has been said of him that he is the Clausewitz of the twentieth century; surely, if a comparison is to be sought, he is far closer related to Francis Bacon, that empirical philosopher who because he concentrated on the facts and not on fancies was so full of ideas" ("Mechanical Warfare," rev. of *The British Way in Warfare,* by LH, *English Review* 55 [Sept. 1932]: 337).

with considerable success, to ensure that official policy reflected his view. He made his case in columns in the *Times*, in numerous articles and books, and in consultation with top British officials, most notably Leslie Hore-Belisha. When Neville Chamberlain became prime minister in May 1937 he appointed Hore-Belisha secretary of state for war. Liddell Hart shortly thereafter became a personal adviser to Hore-Belisha, who knew little about military affairs. Thus during the period from May to December 1937, when the Chamberlain government was making some of the most important grand strategic decisions of the interwar period, Liddell Hart helped shape the thinking of one of the government's principal policy makers. He had direct access to many other key persons as well.

During World War II, Liddell Hart's reputation suffered a precipitous decline, and it remained in eclipse until about 1950.[7] His military predictions about the opening battles of the war proved utterly wrong: he totally failed to anticipate the success of the German blitzkrieg. His policy advice, as reflected in the Chamberlain government's decision not to build up the British army, also proved disastrous. His standing was further damaged in wartime Britain by his calls throughout the war for a negotiated settlement with Hitler. As a result he was isolated from policy making and endured the darkest period of his life. He was only forty-three years old when Germany invaded Poland, and he should have been, given his prominence during the 1930s, at or very near the center of events in wartime England. Instead, he was relegated to the sidelines. After 1950 his reputation enjoyed a remarkable revival, until by the mid-1960s he was again widely acclaimed as a brilliant strategist and policy adviser. His faulty predictions and policy advice were largely forgotten; instead he was praised as a prophet who had foreseen disaster in the 1930s and warned against it.

He earned his living in the three decades between the Fall of France and his death in 1970 by writing and lecturing. During these years he held no regular position with a newspaper, and he neither consulted much with government officials nor held a formal government position. He did, however, continue to reach a wide and ever-growing audience with his writings on past and current military affairs. He left behind an enormous body of publications dealing with many aspects of military affairs: detailed histories of both world wars,[8] biographies of

[7]For example, see Irving M. Gibson [A. Kovacs], "Maginot and Liddell Hart: The Doctrine of Defense," in Edward Mead Earle, ed., *Makers of Modern Strategy: Military Thought from Machiavelli to Hitler* (Princeton, N.J.: Princeton University Press, 1943), 365–87.

[8]*The Real War, 1914–1918* (London: Faber, 1930); *History of the Second World War* (London: Cassell, 1970). For a complete list of LH's many books, which includes the different editions of each work, see B. Bond, *Liddell Hart*, 277–78.

Marshal Ferdinand Foch and Gen. William T. Sherman,[9] a comprehensive account of the development of armored forces in Britain,[10] and a book on the retrospective views of the German generals of World War II.[11] Furthermore, he edited the personal papers of F.M. Erwin Rommel and wrote a lengthy biography of T. E. Lawrence.[12] He was also an innovative and influential military theorist who wrote extensively about infantry tactics, armored strategy, and grand strategy. Moreover, Liddell Hart was involved in the early development of nuclear deterrence theory.[13] He was, in fact, a prominent critic of massive retaliation during the 1950s. He wrote extensively, too, about NATO strategy.[14] Through these writings Liddell Hart remains an important influence on Western military thought.

This book has four aims. The first is to describe and evaluate the substance of Liddell Hart's military thought. He helped develop five important military ideas during the interwar years. His theory of *infantry tactics*, which he developed immediately after World War I, is similar to the famous infantry tactics—both offensive and defensive—introduced by the German army in the latter part of that war. There is some evidence he borrowed from the German experience. He is often considered the father of the *blitzkrieg*, but he actually wrote remarkably little about that strategy. We also know that J. F. C. Fuller convinced a doubting Liddell Hart that the tank had the potential to revolutionize warfare and that much of Liddell Hart's early thinking about the blitzkrieg was derived from Fuller's writings. His famous theory of the *indirect approach*, articulated between 1925 and 1931, is commonly linked with the blitzkrieg, but Liddell Hart actually intended it to be an alternative to that armored strategy—a formula for defeating a Continental adversary without having to engage his armies. In fact, Liddell Hart initially identified the indirect approach with a Douhet-like notion of bombing an adversary into submission by launching massive air

[9]*Foch: The Man of Orleans* (London: Eyre & Spottiswoode, 1931); *Sherman: Soldier, Realist, American* (New York: Dodd, Mead, 1929).

[10]*The Tanks*, 2 vols. (London: Cassell, 1959).

[11]*The Other Side of the Hill* (London: Cassell, 1948), pub. simultaneously in the United States as *The German Generals Talk* (New York: Morrow, 1948); *The Other Side of the Hill*, rev. and enlarged ed. (London: Cassell, 1951).

[12]*The Rommel Papers*, trans. Paul Findlay (New York: Harcourt, Brace, 1953); 'T. E. Lawrence' in Arabia and After* (London: Cape, 1934), pub. in the United States as *Colonel Lawrence: The Man behind the Legend* (New York: Dodd, Mead, 1934).

[13]See B. Bond, *Liddell Hart*, chap. 7; Lawrence Freedman, *The Evolution of Nuclear Strategy* (New York: St. Martin's, 1981).

[14]LH's principal writings on nuclear strategy and NATO are *The Revolution in Warfare* (London: Faber, 1946); *Defence of the West* (London: Cassell, 1950); *Deterrent or Defence* (London: Stevens & Sons, 1960).

attacks against his homeland. The *British way in warfare*, Liddell Hart's fourth idea, was actually another variant of the indirect approach. It called for using British sea power to blockade a Continental adversary to bring him to his knees. Finally, there are Liddell Hart's arguments about the great *superiority of the defense* in an armored war.[15] Although it is not widely known, he abandoned his theory of blitzkrieg in the mid-1930s and adopted the opposite argument, that even with tanks it was extremely unlikely that an attacker would succeed on the battle-field.

The second aim is to explain how Liddell Hart's ideas developed: what lies behind the formation of his ideas on tactics, strategy, and grand strategy. In the immediate aftermath of the Great War, he viewed that conflict as a noble cause conducted by brilliant British generals. By the early 1930s he was an archcritic of the war and particularly of British generalship. His revised view of Britain's generals as gross incompetents directly influenced his position on the crucial issue of whether Britain, if faced again with an aggressive Continental foe, should commit itself to raising a large army to fight on the European mainland. The more hostile Liddell Hart became toward the British military, the more he opposed what is commonly called a Continental commitment. His thinking about such a commitment, in turn, directly affected his ideas about strategy and tactics, eventually turning him into an extreme advocate of the view that the defense almost always bests the offense on the battlefield. Brian Bond asks in his excellent study of Liddell Hart's military thinking: "How could the outstanding exponent of the theories of armoured warfare and *blitzkrieg* come to be regarded as the champion of the defensive?"[16] This remarkable switch was largely a consequence of the change in his position on the Continental commitment—which was driven in turn by his changed views about the British generals and their conduct of World War I. In short, Liddell Hart's evolving attitude toward the Great War cast a giant shadow over the rest of his military thinking.

The third aim is to describe and assess Liddell Hart's role in the policy-making process during the interwar period. Britain was unsuccessful in its efforts to stop Germany from starting a European conflict. When war did break out, the British suffered a number of egregious

---

[15]In developing his views about the defender's supremacy on the battlefield, LH offered important insights about the concept of *force-to-space ratios*, which might be considered the sixth important military idea he developed during the interwar period. He also relied heavily on the concept of an *offense–defense equation*, another important subject that continues to attract attention.

[16]B. Bond, *Liddell Hart*, 90.

defeats. Most relevant here is the stunning defeat the Germans inflicted on the French and British in May 1940. The failure to deter the Germans as well as the failure to defend against their onslaughts raises three sets of questions about British policy and more specifically about Liddell Hart's policy prescriptions during the 1930s: As for Liddell Hart's particular views at the time, did he appreciate the seriousness of the threat posed by the Third Reich? What advice did he offer about how to deter that foe? Did he foresee the Fall of France and sound an alarm? and To what extent did his policy prescriptions differ from official policy? Regarding his influence, did he have an impact on official British policy? Was he persuasive in policy-making circles? or Were his views largely ignored? Last, what were the consequences of the views Liddell Hart elaborated at the time?

The widely accepted version of Liddell Hart's role in the 1930s is the one detailed in his *Memoirs* (1965): he fully understood the danger represented by Nazi Germany, was an archfoe of appeasement, and called for standing up to Hitler in 1938 during the Czechoslovakian crisis. Moreover, he foresaw the early stages of World War II, when the Wehrmacht knocked France out of the war and drove the British army off the Continent. His warnings were ignored by his fellow countrymen, especially by the national military leaders; hidebound British generals refused his sage advice. He was a prophet without honor in his own country. The German generals, on the other hand—specifically those identified with panzers and the blitzkrieg—followed his advice and achieved a series of stunning victories. The reviews of *Memoirs*, of which there were hundreds, are overwhelmingly favorable and rarely challenge his claims. A. J. P. Taylor, reviewing the second volume, remarked, "His first volume was greeted with almost deafening praise. His second is even more revealing. Now Liddell Hart has been vindicated."[17] Michael Howard's review of the first volume reflects the tenor and the substance of most of the reviews:

> He would be less than human if he did not remind us, at some length, of the remarkable prescience of his writings on tactics, strategy and warfare in general; and he would be more than human if he could conceal his impatience with the men who so disastrously ignored his advice. But . . . there is no rancour. There is frank criticism, but never a trace of malice. As

[17]A. J. P. Taylor, "A Prophet Vindicated," rev. of *Memoirs*, vol. 2, by LH and *The Theory and Practice of War*, ed. Michael Howard, *Observer*, 31 Oct. 1965, 27. Copies of all the reviews in 9/30/38–44. For two of the few critical ones, see Col. Trevor N. Dupuy, "The Selective Memoirs of Liddell Hart," rev. of *Memoirs*, vols. 1 and 2, *Army* 16 (Aug. 1966): 36–38, 81; Barry D. Powers, rev. of *Memoirs*, vols. 1 and 2, *Journal of Modern History* 40 (Dec. 1968): 630–31.

a result, there are few occasions when his judgements are not completely convincing.[18]

These accolades, many by prominent scholars, show that Liddell Hart's version has become firmly entrenched. For example, when the Congressional Military Reform Caucus held its first press conference in December 1981, its principal spokesman said:

> I have a deep unease that we are not prepared to defend our liberty with the sureness that we once had. . . . I sense a lot of the same inertia that was the curse of the French and British military establishments between the two World Wars. They ignored prophets like Liddell Hart, the British strategist who called for major changes in tactics and strategy. But Hart's strategy was picked up by the Germans, who used it with devastating effect in 1940.[19]

But there is an alternative version: Liddell Hart was hardly an outsider to the establishment, as evidenced by his position at the *Times* and his relationship with Hore-Belisha. His policy prescriptions were largely consistent with those of the Chamberlain government. There is no evidence either that he was an archfoe of appeasement or that he called for taking a stand over Czechoslovakia in 1938. After March 1939, when Britain's leaders moved rapidly away from appeasement toward a more confrontational policy, Liddell Hart opposed this shift and argued forcefully for further appeasement. The claim that his ideas on armored warfare were explicitly rejected by the British generals and adopted instead by the German generals is simply not true. He was almost completely wrong in his estimation of what the World War II battlefield would look like and what would happen when the German and Allied forces finally clashed. Finally, his policy prescriptions weakened whatever prospects Britain had of deterring the Third Reich and lessened her chances of defeating the Wehrmacht when war came. In short, his *Memoirs* are a blatant distortion of the historical record, and the accepted version is quite wrong.

This discussion brings us to the fourth aim: to determine how Liddell Hart was able to rescue his reputation. How did he reverse the public perception of his role in the interwar years? How did he convince so many students of military affairs of the correctness of his version? Liddell Hart had little success in the 1940s, but his fortunes began to change in the very early 1950s, when it became apparent that certain German generals would cooperate with him to rewrite the historical

[18]Michael Howard, "Englishmen at Arms," rev. of *Memoirs*, vol. 1, *Sunday Times*, 30 May 1965, 24.
[19]Statement of the Hon. G. William Whitehurst, Washington, D.C., 14 Dec. 1981, 30.

record. Liddell Hart's own writings were, however, even more important to his campaign than the false endorsements of the German generals. Over the course of the thirty years between the Fall of France and his death, he went to great lengths, culminating in the publication of *Memoirs*, to record his version of the interwar period and challenge anyone who offered a different one. Liddell Hart's success was due to many factors, the most important of which were the absence of a body of scholars specializing in military affairs who could challenge his account of the past; his remarkable powers of persuasion; and his efforts to befriend, and thus partially disarm, young scholars who would, he knew, eventually write the history of his times. For many years hardly anyone in Britain or the United States had the inclination or the knowledge to challenge Liddell Hart's interpretation of the 1930s. In the 1960s, when a network of scholars focusing on military issues, especially military history, began to form in England, Liddell Hart put many of them in his debt by helping with their research and in other ways, which perhaps inclined them to accept his arguments and interpretations of the past more uncritically than would otherwise have been the case. Moreover, by that point Liddell Hart had already done a great deal to reshape the record.

There is good reason to examine Liddell Hart's military thinking. His theories continue to interest students of military affairs. Although he died in 1970 and his principal ideas were elaborated decades ago, his books and articles are still widely read and cited, in part because he remains one of the few civilian strategists who wrote about conventional war, an important subject in the age of nuclear parity.[20] The majority of the first-rate civilian strategists, especially the more senior ones, focus largely on nuclear strategy or related subjects. A student seriously interested in learning about conventional war is thus likely to become immersed in Liddell Hart's writings. Liddell Hart was also concerned about grand strategy, another subject now attracting the attention of defense analysts.[21] He was deeply involved in the debate of the 1930s over whether Britain should accept a Continental commit-

[20]For example, take the development of the U.S. Army's controversial AirLand Battle doctrine, explicated in the army's capstone field manual, *Operations: FM 100-5* (Washington, D.C., Aug. 1982); one of that document's principal authors has described how LH's writings markedly influenced the development of the doctrine: Huba Wass de Czege, "Army Doctrinal Reform," in Asa Clark et al., eds., *The Defense Reform Debate* (Baltimore: Johns Hopkins University Press, 1984), 101–20; see also *Operations: FM 100-5*, 8–6, 9–1, A3.

[21]Strategic nuclear parity has led to increased interest in conventional deterrence, while the relative decline of America's position in the world economy, coupled with the increase in U.S. foreign policy commitments (primarily the Persian Gulf), has produced considerable interest in grand strategy.

ment or adopt instead what is frequently referred to as a "blue water strategy." An examination of Liddell Hart's thinking brings interesting insights to a similar debate in the United States on the merits of withdrawing large numbers of American ground and tactical air forces from Europe and relying more heavily instead on the U.S. Navy to deter Soviet aggression.[22] Given this interest in his often misunderstood theories, it is important to clarify them.

An examination of Liddell Hart's military thinking should be of special interest to social scientists who study military affairs. Although he is known as a strategist or historian, certainly legitimate labels, he was also very much a social scientist. He was constantly comparing events, individuals, and situations to find generalizations that would hold across space and time. There is much truth in Sir Samuel Hoare's statement that Liddell Hart possessed "the un-English gift of generalization."[23] He sought general theories that could be used to solve Britain's strategic dilemmas, stated them boldly, and defended them stubbornly. A man of intellectual courage, he relied heavily on his theories as he immersed himself in the controversies of the day.

Another reason for studying Liddell Hart is that the historical record needs to be set straight, especially because scholars so often rely on his account of what happened. The problem of assessing Liddell Hart's own role is part of the much larger issue of the performance of the British and German armies during the first half of the twentieth century. It is widely believed that Britain's military leaders of that period, especially the army leaders, were generally incompetent, whereas Germany's military chiefs, especially her World War II generals, are usually praised. They built a formidable fighting force around panzer divisions and attack aircraft, it is supposed, because they lost the last war and only the losers learn the correct lessons from the previous war.[24] The German generals of World War I are treated less kindly than their

---

[22]Of the voluminous literature, see for example, Keith A. Dunn and William O. Staudenmaier, *Strategic Implications of the Continental-Maritime Debate*. Washington Paper No. 107 (New York: Praeger, 1984); Robert W. Komer, *Maritime Strategy or Coalition Defense* (Cambridge, Mass.: Abt Books, 1984); Christopher Layne, "Ending the Alliance," *Journal of Contemporary Studies* 6 (Summer 1983): 5–31; Earl C. Ravenal, "The Case for Withdrawal of Our Forces," *New York Times Magazine*, 6 Mar. 1983, 58–61, 75.

[23]Quoted in Brian Bond, "Second Thoughts on War: A Conversation with B. H. Liddell Hart," *Military Review* 45 (Sept. 1965): 29. For an interesting exchange where LH defends the value of general theories against a critic who questions their worth, see Lt. Col. L. V. Bond, "The Tactical Theories of Captain Liddell Hart: A Criticism," *Royal Engineers Journal* 36 (Sept. 1922): 153–63; LH, "Colonel Bond's Criticisms: A Reply," ibid. (Nov. 1922): 297–309.

[24]LH began making this argument as early as 1925, when he wrote, "It is an axiom that nations learn more readily from defeat than from victory, and though for the nonce Germany is prohibited from building tanks, her post-war military reviews and text-books bear ample witness to the study that is being devoted to them and their tactics" ("After Cavalry—What?" *Atlantic Monthly* 136 [Sept. 1925]: 415).

successors, largely because they have so few redeeming qualities; yet their treatment is more favorable than that of their British counterparts.[25] This is due in good part to the attention focused on the progressive infantry tactics the Germans developed in the last years of World War I.[26]

These descriptions of the two armies are considerably overdrawn, if not downright wrong. The Germans in World War I should certainly be given credit for developing innovative infantry tactics, but at the same time the British did develop the tank, and Britain's generals were willing to place heavy reliance on that weapon to win the war.[27] Furthermore, the British army was receptive to Liddell Hart's progressive ideas about infantry tactics—which actually bore marked resemblance to German thinking. On the quality of the leadership, even if we do not completely accept the popular historian John Terraine's defense of F. M. Douglas Haig, he was clearly more competent than commonly thought.[28] He certainly compares favorably with the four wartime leaders of the German army: Gen. Helmuth von Moltke, Gen. Erich von Falkenhayn, F.M. Paul von Hindenburg, and Gen. Erich Ludendorff.[29] It is not an insignificant fact that Britain and her allies won the war. Nor during the interwar years was the German military as progressive as commonly believed, a point readily apparent from a quick reading of Guderian's memoirs, which indicate much resistance in the German army to progressive ideas about tank warfare. The British army, on the other hand, was nowhere near as hidebound as commonly held. Abundant evidence to that effect can be found in Brian Bond's fine study of the British army between the world wars.[30]

[25]Consider, for example, the titles of the following popular books: Col. Trevor N. Dupuy, *A Genius for War: The German Army and General Staff, 1807–1945* (Englewood Cliffs, N.J.: Prentice-Hall, 1977); Donald J. Goodspeed, *Ludendorff: Genius of World War I* (Boston: Houghton Mifflin, 1966). It is difficult to imagine an author using the word *genius* in conjunction with the British army and particularly the British military commanders of World War I.

[26]Timothy T. Lupfer, *The Dynamics of Doctrine: The Changes in German Tactical Doctrine during the First World War*, Leavenworth Paper no. 4 (Fort Leavenworth, Kans.: U.S. Army Command and General Staff College, July 1981).

[27]See Robert H. Lawson, *The British Army and the Theory of Armored Warfare, 1918–1940* (Newark: University of Delaware Press, 1984), chap. 2; John Terraine, *Douglas Haig: The Educated Soldier* (London: Hutchinson, 1963), 95, 220–28, 289, 360, 362, 378, 381, 448–49, 453.

[28]See Terraine, *Douglas Haig;* idem, *The Western Front, 1914–1918* (Philadelphia: Lippincott, 1965); idem, *To Win a War: 1918, the Year of Victory* (Garden City, N.Y.: Doubleday, 1981).

[29]On the shortcomings of these commanders, see Correlli Barnett, *The Swordbearers: Supreme Command in the First World War* (Bloomington: Indiana University Press, 1975), chaps. 1, 4.

[30]Heinz Guderian, *Panzer Leader*, trans. Constantine Fitzgibbon (London: Joseph, 1952), esp. chaps. 2–5; Brian Bond, *British Military Policy between the Two World Wars* (New York: Oxford University Press, 1980).

There are also good reasons for doubting some of the accepted truths about World War II. Consider Franco-British failures in the Battle of France. There is no doubt the French and British failed to grasp the impact the tank would have on the battlefield and employed a foolish strategy in May 1940.[31] Indeed the British army was, for the most part, unprepared for war; not, however, because of military obscurantism but principally because the Chamberlain government decided in December 1937 not to build an army for the Continent—a policy Liddell Hart firmly supported. Moreover, many of the problems the British army faced throughout the war were the result of that political decision, which led to a weakening of an already feeble army in the critical period between December 1937 and early 1939. As for the Wehrmacht, there were surely many superb battlefield commanders in that military during World War II, and consequently it often performed brilliantly on the battlefield.[32] Nevertheless, we do not judge commanders simply on battlefield performance; those same generals for the most part willingly supported Hitler's decisions to start and then expand the war.[33] They bear considerable responsibility for the consequences: the destruction and dismemberment of their homeland. While they succeeded as fighters, they failed disastrously as grand strategists.

The Wehrmacht also bears more than a little responsibility for the Nazi government's genocidal policies, although until recently it was seldom implicated. Indeed, its generals were usually depicted as sagacious commanders subordinated to a leader who knew little about military affairs and who constantly forced decisions upon them that they knew would lead to disaster. This is certainly the viewpoint Liddell Hart took in *The German Generals Talk*. Rather, it now seems that in addition to providing Hitler with the necessary instrument for expansion, the Wehrmacht was also deeply involved in the murder of millions of civilians and prisoners of war on the Eastern Front.[34]

This book is not *directly* concerned with examining how the British

---

[31]See John J. Mearsheimer, *Conventional Deterrence* (Ithaca: Cornell University Press, 1983), chap. 3.

[32]For reason to believe the Wehrmacht's reputation for battlefield proficiency is inflated, see John Sloan Brown, "Colonel Trevor N. Dupuy and the Mythos of Wehrmacht Superiority: A Reconsideration," *Military Affairs* 50 (Jan. 1986): 16–20.

[33]The three key decisions were Poland (1939), France (1939–40), and the Soviet Union (1941). There was certainly opposition from some generals to the Polish and French decisions while hardly any to the invasion of the Soviet Union. See, inter alia, Matthew Cooper, *The German Army, 1933–1945* (New York: Stein & Day, 1978), pt. 3; Barry K. Leach, *German Strategy against Russia, 1939–1941* (Oxford: Clarendon, 1973); Mearsheimer, *Conventional Deterrence*, chap. 4; Telford Taylor, *The March of Conquest: The German Victories in Western Europe, 1940* (New York: Simon & Schuster, 1958).

[34]Both German and English-speaking scholars have shown beyond any doubt that in fact the Wehrmacht played a key role in the German killing machine; see, inter alia, Omer Bartov, *The Eastern Front, 1941–45: German Troops and the Barbarisation of Warfare*

and German militaries are perceived. It does say a good deal, however, about many of the issues discussed above simply because Liddell Hart played a central role in shaping those perceptions. His histories of the two world wars are highly regarded, have been very influential, and remain in print. In these and other writings he made a persuasive case that Field Marshal Haig and his fellow British generals in the Great War were incompetents. He also played a major role, with his *Memoirs* in particular, in shaping the common perception of the British military's performance in the interwar period. He probably had more influence than anyone else in shaping the English-speaking world's conception of the Wehrmacht in World War II.

The Liddell Hart case also points up the fragility of history and the importance of being alert to the danger of its manipulation for selfish purposes. Liddell Hart was, after all, able to convince most scholars that his account of the 1930s was correct, and to do so unchallenged, when those with memories of the interwar years were still alive. Furthermore, he wrote not about obscure events but about important ones that continue to receive wide attention. Yet he carried off his deception with nearly complete success.

Indeed, his deception might have gone undiscovered had he not compulsively recorded his own thoughts and activities, leaving in his personal papers an extraordinarily complete record of his actions—which is yet further reason to study this case. Rarely can we trace the development of someone's ideas precisely and determine that person's role in a particular historical episode, principally because people almost invariably leave incomplete records. Liddell Hart wrote constantly and kept copies of almost everything he wrote, even drafts of his articles. Not only did he write numerous books and scores of articles, but he also wrote memoranda for the record and corresponded with hundreds of persons.[35] Moreover, Liddell Hart had a sense of his

---

(New York: St. Martin's, 1986); Christopher R. Browning, "Wehrmacht Reprisal Policy and the Mass Murder of Jews in Serbia," *Militärgeschichtliche Mitteilungen*, no. 33 (1/1983): 31–47; Jürgen Förster, "New Wine in Old Skins? The Wehrmacht and the War of 'Weltanschauungen,' 1941," in Wilhelm Deist, ed., *The German Military in the Age of Total War* (Dover, N.H.: Berg, 1985), 304–22; idem, "The Wehrmacht and the War of Extermination against the Soviet Union," *Yad Vashem Studies* 14 (1981): 7–34; Raul Hilberg, *The Destruction of the European Jews*, vol. 1 (New York: Holmes & Meier, 1985), 273–390; Helmut Krausnick and Hans-Heinrich Wilhelm, *Die Truppe des Weltanschauungskrieges: Die Einsatzgruppen der Sicherheitspolizei und des SD 1938–1942* (Stuttgart: Deutsche Verlags-Anstalt, 1981); Henry L. Mason, "Imponderables of the Holocaust," *World Politics* 34 (Oct. 1981): 90–113; Christian Streit, *Keine Kameraden: Die Wehrmacht und die Sowjetischen Kriegsgefangenen 1941–1945* (Stuttgart: Deutsche Verlags-Anstalt, 1978).

[35]On the vast size and scope of LH's personal papers, see Stephen Brooks, "Liddell Hart and His Papers," in Brian Bond and Ian Roy, eds., *War and Society: A Yearbook of Military History* (London: Croom Helm, 1977), 2:129–40.

own importance that led him to document different aspects of his intellectual development, so it is relatively easy to trace his thinking about military issues during the interwar period and then to follow his efforts in the years after World War II to rescue his reputation. In short, his papers provide a unique window into an important man's life story.

Finally, an examination of Liddell Hart's experiences sheds light on the role of defense intellectuals in the modern nation-state. Although civilian strategists are mainly a phenomenon of the nuclear age, Liddell Hart along with Hans Delbrück, Julian Corbett, and Spenser Wilkinson were the first important civilian defense experts in the Western world. Liddell Hart was the first nonmilitary thinker in England or the United States to develop ideas about military matters that received widespread public attention and were also considered seriously by the military establishment of the day. Furthermore, he was involved in the development of thinking about nuclear deterrence in the post–World War II era.[36] Anyone concerned with the role of the outside expert in the making of national security policy, be it in the nuclear or the nonnuclear age, would be well served to consider Liddell Hart's experience. What is striking about that experience is that it turned out so badly. He went from being an important and highly respected pundit in the 1930s to an establishment outcast with a badly stained reputation in World War II. Two points about his plight are worth noting now: formulation of coherent and viable military theories is a difficult task; and the best instrument we have for minimizing the chances of wrongheaded ideas dominating a strategic debate is intellectual pluralism. A healthy national policy process depends on independent-minded defense intellectuals challenging the government and one another.

---

[36]Delbrück (1848–1929), German scholar and journalist of the period of the Second Reich, was probably the first civilian strategist to have a broad impact on public thinking about military affairs. The two best sources on him in English are Richard H. Bauer, "Hans Delbrück," in Bernadotte Schmitt, ed., *Some Historians of Modern Europe* (Chicago: University of Chicago Press, 1942), 100–129; and Gordon A. Craig, "Delbrück: The Military Historian," in Peter Paret, ed., *Makers of Modern Strategy: From Machiavelli to the Nuclear Age* (Princeton, N.J.: Princeton University Press, 1986), 326–53. Corbett (1854–1923) and Wilkinson (1853–1937) were well-regarded British civilian strategists who predated LH; see respectively Donald M. Schurman, *The Education of a Navy: The Development of British Naval Strategic Thought, 1867–1914* (Chicago: University of Chicago Press, 1965), chap. 7; and Jay Luvaas, *The Education of an Army: British Military Thought, 1815–1940* (Chicago: University of Chicago Press, 1964), chap. 8. Although "civilian strategist" is an apt label for LH, he did spend ten years in the British army. On the role of later civilian strategists in the development of nuclear strategy in the 1950s and early 1960s, see Gregg Herken, *Counsels of War* (New York: Knopf, 1985); Fred Kaplan, *The Wizards of Armageddon* (New York: Simon & Schuster, 1983); Barry Steiner, "Using the Absolute Weapon: Early Ideas of Bernard Brodie on Atomic Strategy," *Journal of Strategic Studies* 7 (Dec. 1984): 365–93.

Liddell Hart's name and ideas are briefly discussed in countless books and articles, and few students of military affairs have not heard of him; yet the literature on him is sparse. Only two scholarly studies deal with his experiences in the interwar years and the development of his military thinking: Jay Luvaas's chapter on Liddell Hart ("The Captain Who Teaches Generals") in his *The Education of an Army* (1964); and Brian Bond's *Liddell Hart: A Study of His Military Thought* (1977). There are also a small number of excellent articles on specific aspects of Liddell Hart's life.[37] His widow planned to authorize a biography shortly after his death in January 1970, but none has been written and apparently there are no plans to commission one.[38]

How does this book go beyond the works of Luvaas and Bond? Luvaas's piece, being a single chapter in a book, cannot offer a comprehensive and detailed examination of Liddell Hart's principal ideas or his role in the policy debates of the 1930s. More important, the chapter is essentially a recapitulation of Liddell Hart's version. Luvaas, who was an extremely close friend of Liddell Hart's, offers little criticism. In following Liddell Hart, he presents distorted accounts of both his military thinking and his policy recommendations. Bond's book, on the other hand, is a first-rate work of scholarship, both comprehensive and insightful, and should be studied carefully by anyone interested in understanding Liddell Hart's military thinking. In fact I have stood on Bond's shoulders in writing my book.

Nevertheless, there are some important points where Bond's history should be amended or revised. I believe, for example, that Bond is wrong when he denies that Liddell Hart used the German generals to rescue his reputation after World War II.[39] I also think he was wrong to

[37]On LH in the interwar years, see Luvaas, *Education of an Army*, chap. 11; see also idem, *The Military Legacy of the Civil War: The European Inheritance* (Chicago: University of Chicago Press, 1959), 216–25. For Bond, see n. 3 and also Brian Bond and Martin Alexander, "Liddell Hart and DeGaulle: The Doctrines of Limited Liability and Mobile Defense," in Paret, *Makers of Modern Strategy*, 598–623. There was a chapter dealing with LH in the original Earle, *Makers of Modern Strategy* (see Gibson "Maginot and Liddell Hart"); this chapter, which has a number of minor factual errors, nevertheless offers some telling observations about LH's views during the interwar period. LH was involved in an extensive correspondence (in 1/255) with Earle over this piece. Ultimately, however, the piece is not particularly useful because it touches upon only a few dimensions of his military thinking and does not adequately deal with his role in the policy-making process of pre–World War II Britain. For articles on other aspects of LH's life, see, for example, Tuvia Ben-Moshe, "Liddell Hart and the Israel Defence Forces: A Reappraisal," *Journal of Contemporary History* 16 (Apr. 1981): 369–91; Brian H. Reid, "T. E. Lawrence and Liddell Hart," *History* 70 (June 1985): 218–31; idem, "British Military Intellectuals and the American Civil War: F. B. Maurice, J. F. C. Fuller and B. H. Liddell Hart," in Chris Wrigley, ed., *Warfare, Diplomacy and Politics: Essays in Honour of A. J. P. Taylor* (London: Hamilton, 1986), 42–57.

[38]Correspondence with Brian Bond, 24 Sept. 1987.

[39]B. Bond, *Liddell Hart*, chaps. 6, 8, esp. 166, 188, 228.

accept Liddell Hart's claim that he was an archfoe of appeasement.[40] Moreover, I disagree with his claim that "it is far from easy to answer the question whether Liddell Hart accurately predicted the trend of military events in 1939 and 1940."[41] These differences and some others notwithstanding, my work should not be seen as a challenge to Bond's book but as an attempt to go beyond his analysis. Bond's book is also not critical enough of Liddell Hart. Although he offers many telling criticisms, he does not push them to their logical conclusion. The ingredients for a powerful indictment are present in his book but not fully developed.[42]

There are as well important issues not discussed or only touched upon in Bond's book. For example, Bond does not address the question of how Liddell Hart rescued his reputation. Although it is evident from his book that the conventional wisdom is flawed, he does not explain how this distortion came about. To cite another example, he does not directly address the important question of what Liddell Hart wrote during the interwar years about deep strategic penetration, the centerpiece of the blitzkrieg. Nor does he systematically examine the consequences of Liddell Hart's policy prescriptions for dealing with the Third Reich. I attempt to address these issues and others that Bond omits.

A core argument of this study is that Liddell Hart's thinking about World War I and British generalship directly influenced the development of his ideas about grand strategy, which in turn substantially influenced his thinking about strategy and tactics. These concepts must be defined as precisely as possible because they are often used in different ways.

Strategy is concerned with how all the major units of an army and its supporting tactical air forces are deployed and moved about the theater of operations to achieve the overall campaign objective. Strategy, in other words, is concerned with the ways in which the different battles that comprise a campaign fit together to produce the desired military outcome. *Tactics* is a more narrowly focused concept: the focus is on the specific battlefield employment of the different elements that comprise an army and its supporting air forces. Tactics deals with questions about how specific military units are used to win particular battles. To illustrate these concepts, consider the case of the Allied armies

[40]Ibid., 102, 112.
[41]Ibid., 114.
[42]Bond is actually more critical of LH in his later book, *British Military Policy*; see my review essay "The British Generals Talk," *International Security* 6 (Summer 1981): 165–84.

that moved across France and into Germany during the last year of World War II. Strategic questions revolved around the issue of how to employ the different armies and army groups that made up the overall Allied force so as to defeat the Wehrmacht as quickly as possible. Tactical issues concerned the individual conduct of the smaller units that comprised the armies, from the platoon to the corps. Strategy, in this study, is linked with the blitzkrieg and armored warfare; tactics is identified with the deployment of small-scale infantry units.

Grand strategy encompasses two important questions. First, what are the principal military threats from abroad and how should they be ordered? In other words, how should a state rank-order its overseas defense commitments? Second, what kinds of military forces should a state develop to support those commitments? Naturally, the available military means influence the size and scope of the commitments. Grand strategy, as used here, is not concerned with how a nation integrates the diplomatic, economic, and military tools at its disposal to support its interests abroad. Although grand strategy is sometimes defined this way, the concept has a narrower definition here: the relationship between military means and international commitments. This is not to say that diplomatic or economic means are any less important than military ones. Actually, as defined here, the broader concept of *foreign policy* is all about the integration of these three instruments to support overseas commitments. Although the focus is on Liddell Hart's thinking about grand strategy, strategy, and tactics, it is necessary to consider his thinking about broader foreign policy questions when analyzing his views on dealing with the Third Reich.

Whether to pursue a *Continental commitment* has been the central issue in Britain's grand strategic debates throughout this century.[43] A Continental commitment has come to mean accepting the need to send a mass army onto the European continent to prevent a rival power from establishing control over it. Before the twentieth century, Britain was able to support a Continental commitment with a modest-sized army. She compensated for her relatively small contribution in ground forces with her powerful navy, her economic strength, and heavy reliance on the armies of Continental allies.[44] By the start of this century, Britain had to raise a mass army to meet the challenge of a Continental

[43]See Michael Howard, *The British Way in Warfare: A Reappraisal,* The 1974 Neale Lecture in English History (London: Cape, 1975); idem, *The Continental Commitment: The Dilemma of British Defence Policy in the Era of the Two World Wars* (Harmondsworth: Penguin, 1974); Paul M. Kennedy, *The Rise and Fall of British Naval Mastery* (London: Lane, 1976).
[44]See Kennedy, *Rise and Fall,* chaps. 1–5; John M. Sherwig, *Guineas and Gunpowder: British Foreign Aid in the Wars with France, 1793–1815* (Cambridge, Mass.: Harvard University Press, 1969).

power. Because Britain had traditionally maintained a small standing army, this development had profound consequences for the size and shape of her national security establishment in general and her army in particular. In short, the core issue underlying the Continental commitment was the size, shape, and purpose of the British army.[45]

The next five chapters describe and evaluate Liddell Hart's military thinking between 1918 and 1945 and explain its development. Chapter 2 focuses on Liddell Hart in the period between 1919 and 1924, when he developed his theory of infantry tactics and formulated his ideas on the blitzkrieg; chapter 3 considers his growing disillusionment with Britain's generals and especially with their conduct of World War I. The years between 1925 and 1932, when he propounded his theory of the indirect approach and outlined his ideas on the British way in warfare, are the subject of chapter 4. Chapters 5 and 6 focus on the crucial years between 1933 and 1940, when Britain was faced with the grim prospect of fighting another major land war against Germany. His ideas about how Britain should deal with the Third Reich are examined there. Chapter 5 concentrates on his military thinking during those years; chapter 6, on his prescriptions in the broader realm of foreign policy. Chapter 6 also includes brief consideration of his plight during World War II. The discussion in these five chapters mixes narrative and analysis. I would have preferred to separate the two, but the subject matter does not lend itself to such a breakdown.

Although chapters 2–6 have much to say about Liddell Hart's role in the policy-making process, it is nevertheless necessary to devote the entire chapter 7 to this subject. Chapter 8 concerns how Liddell Hart restored his reputation in the years after World War II. Finally, the short conclusion draws some lessons from this case.

[45]On how a Continental commitment affects the British army, see B. Bond, *British Military Policy;* also Mearsheimer, "British Generals Talk."

[2]

Infantry Tactics and the
Blitzkrieg, 1918–1924

The period between 1918 and Hitler's coming to power in 1933 was one of intellectual ferment for Liddell Hart. During these years of relative international calm, he developed his important ideas about infantry tactics, the blitzkrieg, the indirect approach, and the British way in warfare. He also began to influence British policy makers, mainly through his articles in the *Daily Telegraph,* but through his books and magazine articles as well. This chapter and the next two concentrate on the development of his military thinking in these years but touch as well on his role in policy making. This chapter is on the first years after the Great War, when Liddell Hart still held a positive view of the British generals and still believed that the British army should seriously prepare for the possibility of another ground war on the Continent. His thinking about how best to fight such a war is the main focus, although it is also necessary to consider his views about the importance of ideas and how he expected his own military theories to affect the course of a future conflict.

In these years severe retrenchment was the order of the day for the British military.[1] The huge military establishment created to fight the Great War was drastically reduced soon after the war ended, and for the next decade and a half each of the services was starved for funds. Britain was willing to maintain a military ill-prepared to fight a major war and barely capable of fighting minor conflicts in its Empire, and

---

[1]For the broad outlines of British military policy in this period, see Norman H. Gibbs, *Grand Strategy,* vol. 1 (London: Her Majesty's Stationery Office, 1976), pt. 1; Michael Howard, *The Continental Commitment: The Dilemma of British Defence Policy in the Era of the Two World Wars* (Harmondsworth: Penguin, 1974), chap. 4; Paul M. Kennedy, *The Realities behind Diplomacy: Background Influences on British External Policy, 1865–1980* (London: Fontana, 1981), pt. 3.

this in spite of the fact the Empire actually grew as a result of Britain's victory in World War I.

The public, which came in the 1920s to have a jaundiced view of Britain's participation in the Great War, was not favorably disposed toward spending money to maintain a powerful military. Lack of reliable data about public opinion makes it difficult to be precise, but a substantial portion of the electorate believed by the late 1920s that World War I had been a tragic mistake and that those who argued for the necessity of thinking seriously about and preparing for another war would ultimately bring one about. The Labour party, for example, which became a powerful force in British politics in the wake of World War I, contained a large element imbued with antimilitary sentiment. Such attitudes were by no means confined to the Labour party, however, a point reflected in the famous February 1933 Oxford Union vote (275–153) proclaiming that it would "in no circumstances fight for its King and Country."[2]

Many British policy makers and a sizable portion of the public believed that peace among the great powers could be maintained by relying on diplomatic instruments like the League of Nations and the 1925 Locarno Treaty. Although this approach seems naive in light of the horrors perpetrated by the Third Reich, Britons of the interwar years placed much hope in devices such as disarmament conferences and agreements to renounce war.[3] Moreover, it was widely accepted in policy-making circles that defense spending was not good for the British economy, which was generally perceived as anemic during the interwar period. The financial crisis of 1931, just as the international political situation was beginning to deteriorate, further complicated Britain's economic problems, making it extremely difficult to secure extra money needed for defense. Thus, on countless occasions throughout the interwar period, the Treasury played a central role in shaping military policy, invariably by sharply curtailing funds for the services.[4]

Finally, there were in the 1920s no significant military threats to British interests around the world. There was no German threat on the Continent, and although there were situations in the Empire that called for the deployment of military forces, there was no threat or combination of threats that could provide a justification for reversing

[2]For the essence of this phenomenon, see Martin Ceadel, *Pacifism in Britain, 1919–1945: The Defining of a Faith* (Oxford: Oxford University Press, 1980); on the Oxford Union vote, ibid., chap. 8.

[3]E. H. Carr's classic, *The Twenty Years' Crisis*, 2d ed. (London: Macmillan, 1962) is especially valuable here.

[4]See G. C. Peden, *The Treasury and British Rearmament, 1932–1939* (Edinburgh: Scottish Academic Press, 1979); Robert P. Shay, Jr., *British Rearmament in the Thirties: Politics and Profits* (Princeton, N.J.: Princeton University Press, 1977).

the spirit of retrenchment that set in after World War I.[5] Britain had adopted the famous Ten Year Rule in 1919, which mandated that policy makers plan on the assumption that Britain would not be engaged in a major war in the next ten years. That rule, not revoked until 1932, was actually put on a daily moving basis in 1928, which meant that with each new day, Britain assumed there would be no war for at least a decade. Securing funds for the military in such an environment was sure to be a difficult task.

The army suffered the most of the three services in this lean decade and a half. Army budget requests, for example, "were reduced every year until 1932."[6] This deprivation worked to stymie the building of independent armored forces as well as the development of progressive thinking about how to employ those forces. Money was not available to develop the tanks and the other weapons of an armored force. Without a substantial number of up-to-date tanks it was difficult to conduct the realistic training exercises essential for determining how best to employ armor on the battlefield. Especially in the first years after the war, there was also significant turbulence in the personnel system, stemming from the vast peacetime reductions in the army's size. According to Brian Bond, "Four and a half years after the Armistice more than two hundred officers were waiting for vacancies to command battalions, quite half of whom had already commanded brigades in the field for over two years."[7] The personnel system eventually settled down, although older, senior officers long occupied key positions, making it difficult for younger talent to reach the top and surely working to mitigate the development of progressive thinking about armor doctrine.

There was another circumstance that worked against the creation of armored forces capable of fighting against a Continental foe. The British army had traditionally been concerned with two very different missions, fighting on the Continent and policing the Empire, and each required a different type of army. As Bond notes, "The Army's whole organization, recruiting system, training, equipment, and—not least—

---

[5]Instructive on this subject is Keith Jeffrey, "Sir Henry Wilson and the Defence of the British Empire, 1918–22," *Journal of Imperial and Commonwealth History* 5 (May 1977): 270–93.

[6]The best work on the British army in this period is Brian Bond, *British Military Policy between the Two World Wars* (New York: Oxford University Press, 1980), 91 and chaps. 1–5; see also Correlli Barnett, *Britain and Her Army, 1509–1970: A Military, Political and Social Survey* (Harmondsworth: Penguin, 1974), chap. 17; Harold R. Winton, *To Change an Army: General Sir John Burnett-Stuart and British Armored Doctrine, 1927–1938* (Lawrence: University Press of Kansas, 1988).

[7]*British Military Policy*, 45; also 44–55 and *Memoirs* 1:50–51.

tradition were strongly oriented towards imperial defence." Not surprisingly, that bias was the source of much of the resistance to developing an army comprised of large armored units that could engage the German army but would not be useful on India's northwest frontier.[8] Thus there were legitimate reasons for opposing an army largely comprised of armored divisions trained to fight in Europe. Only a definite decision to prepare for a war on the Continent could reverse that bias, and there was none.

Nonetheless, the British army of the 1920s and early 1930s did pay serious attention to the question of how to employ armored forces in a major conventional war (chap. 3). In fact, the British army was widely considered to be in the forefront of experimentation with armored forces during this period, and other European militaries carefully examined what transpired at the British army's annual training exercises. In Bond's view, "Indeed, when all the adverse conditions are taken into account, it is surely remarkable that the British Army did so much to remain in the vanguard of military development in the 1920s and early 1930s."[9] That lead would be lost in the late 1930s, and Britain would go into World War II largely unprepared to engage the Wehrmacht. Nevertheless, between 1918 and 1932, when Liddell Hart was writing about blitzkrieg and other subjects, the British army was paying serious attention to the question of how to employ armor on the battlefield.

Liddell Hart, however, was not interested in armored strategy in the first years of peace. He focused his attention then on infantry tactics, and his views on this subject, as on virtually all other military topics, were deeply affected by his thinking about World War I.

EARLY VIEWS ON THE GREAT WAR
AND THE CONTINENTAL COMMITMENT

Liddell Hart first recorded his views about the war and Britain's military leaders while the conflict still raged. He was remarkably enthusiastic about the British effort in light of his later, bitter criticism, but such zeal was hardly surprising for an impressionable young man

---

[8]B. Bond, *British Military Policy*, 188. LH was well aware that India was a brake on efforts to modernize the army; see, for example, his "The Army and the 'Future,'" *Daily Telegraph*, 25 Sept. 1928, 8; "Memorandum on the Indian Military Problem," 17 Aug. 1929, 11/1929/13c; *When Britain Goes to War* (London: Faber, 1935), 113; also chap. 3 in this book.

[9]*British Military Policy*, 34. See also Barnett, *Britain and Her Army*, 415; Winton, *To Change an Army*, 133. On the Germans' close attention to British maneuvers, see Williamson Murray, *The Change in the European Balance of Power: The Path to Ruin* (Princeton, N.J.: Princeton University Press, 1984), 34–35.

in the service of a state relying heavily on propaganda and value infusion to maintain support for the war, all this against a backdrop of nineteenth-century romanticism.

Consider his contemporary views on the British generals. While waiting for the Somme offensive to begin, he wrote in a small notebook: "In the first half of the war our leadership was flawless, and it may be noted that our generalship alone of all the nations engaged, was perfect."[10] He maintained after the battle that "the British G.H.Q. [General Headquarters] . . . under the Haig regime comprise the most brilliant collection of brains in the world."[11] He was particularly impressed with the generalship of Douglas Haig, the commander of British forces in France, as the following quotation, written after the Somme campaign, reflects:

> Never has any military operation been so wonderfully and minutely organized or so brilliantly executed as this offensive. . . . The chief credit of all must go to Sir Douglas Haig, who worked all through the winter and spring with his genius for efficiency. . . . Every branch and department was overhauled and worked up to the highest pitch of efficiency, until finally at the outset of the offensive, Sir Douglas Haig, the greatest general Britain has ever owned, had created the finest fighting machine the world has ever known.[12]

He also had high praise for Gen. Lord Henry Horne and Gen. Sir Archibald Montgomery-Massingberd. He felt Horne was "undoubtedly [a] military genius of a very high order," while Montgomery-Massingberd was one of "the brilliant Chiefs of Staff of the two armies on the Somme."[13] Liddell Hart retrospectively summarized his early views of the generals in a 1936 diary note: "I intensely admired many of my superiors, and even hero-worshiped a number."[14]

Also especially interesting in light of his later severe criticism are Liddell Hart's thoughts on British strategy in the war, summarized in a 1917 article written for the *Saturday Review*:

> It is possible that the glorious vision of our troops being poured torrent-like through a gap in the enemy's front may at some future time be seen, but that time is not yet. As long as he [German army] has the reserves

[10]Small, untitled notebook in 7/1916/21a. See also the quotations in Brian Bond, *Liddell Hart: A Study of His Military Thought* (London: Cassell, 1977), 18.

[11]LH, "Impressions of the Great British Offensive on the Somme," 1916, 96; copy in 7/1916/22.

[12]Ibid., 84.

[13]The quotation on Montgomery-Massingberd is from ibid., 95; that on Horne, from the small notebook (n. 10).

[14]"Thoughts Jotted Down—To Be Expanded," memorandum for the record, entry for 17 July 1936, 11/1936/2–25c; see also his comments in *Memoirs* 1:26.

with which to make counter-attacks, the correct strategy is to wear down the enemy by constant heavy blows prepared and supported by our massed artillery. . . . The strategy of genius is to wear him down to the breaking point by a constant succession of heavy blows at varying points in his far-flung line and then, when that decisive moment has arrived, the coup de grace will be given. . . . We must not expect one gigantic and decisive blow, but rather a decisive campaign consisting of a constant succession of blows.[15]

Liddell Hart of course endorsed the heavy emphasis the British placed on artillery fire. In a 1917 notebook, under a section titled "Things of Which I Am Proud," he wrote, among other things: "Being present at the introduction of the creeping barrage and knowing of its invention in June 1916." The creeping barrage was a barrier of artillery fire that slowly moved forward at somewhat less than a hundred yards in front of the advancing infantry.[16] Describing the first use of the creeping barrage in the Somme offensive, he wrote,

This wonderful wall of bursting shells, which searches every inch of ground as it creeps forward over the German lines, and yet is so marvellously accurate that our infantry can follow within fifty to one hundred yards of it, is the outstanding tactical innovation of the war. . . . This creeping barrage proved so successful that shortly after the British Army as a whole adopted it . . . the French copied it from us.[17]

In the war's later stages, a number of British commentators criticized the British generals' conduct of the conflict. Liddell Hart staunchly defended the generals and roundly criticized their civilian detractors on the home front. "It is absurd," he argued, "to run down British generalship. We have two of the greatest generals in history in Haig and Robertson, and we have at least a dozen really brilliant higher generals."[18] The dissatisfied civilians back in England were, for him, "armchair critics," men who "have no real understanding" of modern warfare. For Liddell Hart, "only those who have attacked and conquered that wonderful fortress line which stretches across France . . . can realize the magnitude of the British achievement and the difficul-

[15]Apparently never published, although a copy of the galleys, titled "The Somme and Its Sequel," is in 7/1917/5.
[16]Copy of "Pocket Notebook with Jottings" in 7/1917/2. On the creeping barrage, see Shelford Bidwell and Dominick Graham, *Fire-Power: British Army Weapons and Theories of War, 1904–1945* (London: Allen & Unwin, 1982), 83–85, 111–15.
[17]"Somme and Its Sequel."
[18]Small notebook (n. 10). F. M. Sir William R. Robertson was chief of the Imperial General Staff 1915–18.

ties overcome."[19] This theme is reflected in most of his writings from the war years.

This enthusiasm should not obscure the fact that Liddell Hart still felt the war was "horrible and ghastly beyond all imagination of the civilian."[20] He had no illusions about the price the Allies were paying to defeat Germany. His admiration for the generals' conduct of the Somme offensive notwithstanding, he wanted very much to avoid battles of that kind in the future. Thus, he saw his principal mission in life as working "to ensure that if war came again there should be no repetition of the Somme and Passchendaele."[21] Liddell Hart had, however, few doubts at this point about the validity of the British cause and the wisdom of the decision in 1914 to send ground troops to fight against Germany. In short, he considered a Continental commitment a principal tenet of British grand strategy.

There was no perceptible change in Liddell Hart's thinking about the Continental commitment in the period immediately after World War I. He accepted as a matter of course that Britain might again have to fight with a large army on the Continent.[22] His position on this critical issue was due in part to a lack of interest in grand strategic issues; he simply did not concern himself about them in the first years after the war. He was still just a young officer who was almost exclusively concerned with developing infantry tactics and training infantrymen. Furthermore, with Germany defeated, there was no prospect of another Continental war in the foreseeable future, so a Continental commitment was very much a hypothetical issue, although Britain did maintain a small occupation force in the Rhineland until 1930. Most important, he naturally accepted a Continental commitment given his views at the time about the Great War and Britain's military leadership. Believing the war a wholly legitimate cause fought by noble warriors, he had no reason to doubt the original commitment that led Britain to send a mass army to fight the Second Reich. Moreover, as the generals who led Britain's armies in the years immediately after the war were essentially the same men who directed them in World War I, he had every reason to believe they would employ those armies wisely in a future conflict.

Liddell Hart's principal aim in the years right after the fall of the Second Reich, when he took the Continental commitment as a given, was to find a way for Britain and her allies to win the next war quickly

[19]"Somme and Its Sequel."
[20]"Impressions of the Great British Offensive," 84.
[21]*Memoirs* 1:33.
[22]See, for example, his comments in his *The Remaking of Modern Armies* (London: Murray, 1927), 27–28.

and with a minimum of bloodshed. As he noted in an article written shortly after the Great War, "It should be the duty of every soldier to reflect on the experiences of the past, in the endeavour to discover improvements, in his particular sphere of action, which are practicable in the immediate future. Such attempts must be based on the great doctrine of the economy of force; seeking methods which will achieve a greater force behind the blow at a reduced cost in personnel."[23] In essence, Liddell Hart had to find a way to ensure that the offense occupied the dominant position on the battlefield. As he surely recognized, a successful defense, no matter how brilliantly executed, was most unlikely to produce a rapid and decisive victory. Only offense could guarantee that outcome. So Liddell Hart "devoted" himself "to the task of discovering means of renewing the power of the offensive—the accepted military method of deciding the issue of a conflict between nations."[24] His efforts toward this end first focused on the study of infantry tactics.

INFANTRY TACTICS

Liddell Hart settled into the job of training infantrymen for the Western Front after being posted back to England in 1916. He soon began developing his own ideas about tactics, and when the war ended, his "tactical thinking was on the boil."[25] He published two short articles in 1919 that contained his incipient ideas on infantry tactics.[26] In the fall of that year the librarian at the prestigious Royal United Services Institution suggested he give a talk there on that subject. This prospective lecture forced him to organize his thoughts carefully and ultimately to come up with a theory of infantry tactics.[27]

Liddell Hart believed mobility and maneuver had to be restored to

---

[23]"Suggestions on the Future Development of the Combat Unit," *Journal of the Royal United Services Institution* 64 (Nov. 1919): 666.

[24]"Those Whom the Gods Wish to Destroy They First Make Mad," memorandum for the record, 10 Sept. 1939, 11/1939/105.

[25]*Memoirs* 1: 34, 28–33.

[26]"Suggestions"; "The 'Ten Commandments' of the Combat Unit: Suggestions on Its Theory and Training," *Journal of the Royal United Services Institution* 64 (May 1919): 288–93.

[27]On the invitation, see *Memoirs* 1:37. For a copy of his talk (which took place on 3 Nov. 1920), see "The 'Man-in-the-Dark' Theory of Infantry Tactics and the 'Expanding Torrent' System of Attack," *Journal of the Royal United Services Institution* 66 (Feb. 1921): 1–22, where his theory is clearly and comprehensively presented. He had actually developed the ideas in this lecture in three articles published before the talk: "The Essential Principles of War and Their Application to the Offensive Infantry Tactics of To-day," *United Service Magazine* 61 (Apr. 1920): 30–44; "The 'Man-in-the-Dark' Theory of War," *National Review* 75 (June 1920): 473–84; "A New Theory of Infantry Tactics," ibid. (July

the battlefield to avoid another war of attrition. World War I seemed to indicate this could not be done at the strategic level. There was no apparent way to move large-scale units like corps and armies rapidly about the battlefield to produce a quick and decisive victory. Modern armies, so it seemed, were too cumbersome, and moreover, with the broad fronts between them, there were no flanks to turn.[28] The solution to this problem, Liddell Hart argued, was to focus attention on the platoon, one of the smallest units on the battlefield: "The sector of a platoon is a complete battle in miniature. Within its narrow compass we see the eternal principles of great war fulfilled."[29] Specifically, the aim was to encourage the individual platoon to employ maneuver in its own narrow tactical sphere. Maneuver would be restored to the entire front by relying on the tactical maneuvering of many small units. To quote Liddell Hart, "The giving of the power of manoeuvre to the smallest infantry units, even when forming a segment only of the fabric of a large-scale offensive, is an epoch-making change."[30] The principal assumption was that thousands of platoon-sized successes would add up to an overall success. The key to victory on the battlefield, so Liddell Hart argued, could be found "by working out our principles of tactics upwards from the elementary, instead of downwards from the complexities of large operations."[31] In effect, numerous tactical successes would produce a strategic success.

How would the platoon use maneuver to achieve success? Liddell Hart's starting assumption was that the defender's Achilles' heel was his rear area, perhaps reaching back 5–10 miles behind his defensive front, which itself could be several miles deep. There would be few

---

1920): 693–702. LH also wrote other articles and books about infantry tactics: "The Soldier's Pillar of Fire by Night: The Need for a Framework of Tactics," *Journal of the Royal United Services Institution* 66 (Nov. 1921): 618–26; "A Science of Infantry Tactics," pt. 1, *Royal Engineers Journal* 33 (Apr. 1921): 169–82; "A Science of Infantry Tactics," pt. 2, ibid. (May 1921): 215–23; "Are Infantry Doomed?" *National Review* 79 (May 1922): 455–63; "Infantry—'the New Model,'" ibid. (July 1922): 712–22; "The Future Development of Infantry," ibid. 80 (Oct. 1922): 286–94; *The Framework of a Science of Infantry Tactics* (London: Hugh Rees, 1921); *A Science of Infantry Tactics Simplified* (London: Clowes, 1923); *The Future of Infantry* (London: Faber, 1933). See also Lt. Col. L. V. Bond, "The Tactical Theories of Captain Liddell Hart: A Criticism," *Royal Engineers Journal* 36 (Sept. 1922): 153–63; LH, "Colonel Bond's Criticisms: A Reply," ibid. (Nov. 1922): 297–309; Ivor Maxse, "Infantry," *Encyclopaedia Britannica*, 12th ed. (London, 1922), 31:469–79. LH wrote more than half of the latter for Maxse (*Memoirs* 1:54); it is an excellent summary of LH's thinking about infantry tactics, esp. 472–79.

[28] See John J. Mearsheimer, *Conventional Deterrence* (Ithaca, N.Y.: Cornell University Press, 1983), 30–33; also LH, "Essential Principles of War," 40; LH, "Infantry—'the New Model,'" 714–16.

[29] "Infantry—'the New Model,'" 718.

[30] "Essential Principles of War," 40.

[31] "'Man-in-the-Dark' Theory of Infantry Tactics," 20.

combat forces in this rear area, but there would be a widespread network of lines of communication that provided essential support for the fighting forces deployed at or near the front. Destroying that network would render the opponent's fighting forces along the front helpless. To accomplish this the attacking platoons should therefore seek to pierce the defender's front and drive into his rear area, avoiding enemy strongpoints as they progress and instead continually exploiting the opponent's soft spots. Liddell Hart placed special emphasis on the need to maintain the momentum of the attack and not get bogged down in protracted set-piece battles with the defender's forces. This is especially important, he argued, because "modern . . . armies are distributed in great depth, and the attackers are faced with the problem of breaking through a series of positions extending back in layers to a depth of several miles." Thus, the offender must seek to achieve "an automatic and continuous progressive infiltration by the combat units . . . with a constant intention to get forward as rapidly as possible."[32]

The attacking platoons would obviously have to fight some set-piece battles. To make the initial breakthroughs, Liddell Hart called for "infiltration into the crevices of the defensive position."[33] This he believed possible because "modern destructive weapons have enforced a wide dispersion of the combatants on the battlefield."[34] Still, he recognized that to effect a breakthrough it might be necessary for an attacking unit to engage the defender's forces directly. He also believed the attacker's leading units would probably have to fight some battles in the depths of the defense. For example, there would probably be certain defensive positions impossible to bypass because they blocked the only path forward. He believed, however, that the small units, which were at the heart of his tactical theory, could use maneuver to win those battles. His solution, which he called "the man-in-the-dark formula," was straightforward and time honored: a small part of the platoon would fix or pin down the defender, while the rest would maneuver around the flank of the enemy and deliver the decisive blow.[35] The attacking platoons would then concentrate on avoiding further battles of this kind on their drive into the defender's rear to destroy his vulnerable lines of communication.[36] Thus, although the attacker was striking across a broad front, he was actually avoiding (at least in theory) the

[32]Ibid., 12; LH, " 'Ten Commandments' of the Combat Unit," 292–93.
[33]Maxse, "Infantry," 475.
[34]LH, " 'Man-in-the-Dark' Theory of Infantry Tactics," 7.
[35]Ibid., 2–12.
[36]Ibid., 12–15.

bloody frontal assaults of World War I. It was a frontal attack in "outward appearance" only.[37]

Maneuver is thus used in two quite different but complementary ways in Liddell Hart's theory of infantry tactics. One is maneuver around strong points to drive deep into the defender's rear; here, it is employed to facilitate what Liddell Hart called the "expanding torrent." The other is maneuver in support of the "man-in-the-dark formula," where the aim is to eliminate points of resistance that cannot be bypassed; in other words, it is used to win those set-piece battles that must be fought.

Liddell Hart was concerned about the role discipline would play in his tactical scheme. For him discipline was not synonymous with "unthinking obedience." Instead, he called for individual soldiers up and down the chain of command to exercise judgment and initiative in their conduct of the battle:

> Each soldier must move as an individual, think as an individual. Instead of unity of movement, we require unity of purpose. Each individual moves and acts independently, using the ground to the best personal advantage, but combining with his fellows to attain a common objective. In the past this mental discipline was the province of the principal subordinate commanders alone. Now it is shared by every man.[38]

Moreover, he stressed the need for intelligent soldiers, arguing that the officer ranks of the infantry should be filled with "the pick of the nation's candidates for commissions."[39] This emphasis on smart officers capable of demonstrating initiative was undoubtedly because his theory was built around the actions of myriad small units not tightly controlled by higher commanders. With those units operating largely as independent entities, initiative and good judgment would be in great demand as small-unit commanders made rapid-fire decisions to maintain the attacking forces' pace of advance on what promised to be a fluid battlefield.

Liddell Hart's writings on infantry tactics show considerable enthusiasm for employing tanks with infantry. As early as 1919 he predicted, "The tank is certain to play an increasingly important part in future war."[40] He also advocated that tanks and infantry be "trained together

[37]LH, "Essential Principles of War," 40.
[38]"Are Infantry Doomed?" 461.
[39]"Infantry—'the New Model,'" 713.
[40]"Suggestions," 666–69, provides a comprehensive view of LH's thinking about the tank during the period he was working on infantry tactics.

as a permanent part of the same combat unit." Nevertheless, he remained convinced that infantry was the "decisive arm" and that "the infantrymen will still be the only true winner of victory."[41] In contrast to his enthusiasm for tanks, he placed little emphasis on artillery. He had apparently lost his earlier enthusiasm for the creeping barrage and, more generally, for the heavy reliance the British had placed on artillery during World War I. Artillery was closely identified with the protracted attrition battles he was so anxious to avoid in a future war.

Liddell Hart also devised infantry tactics that would enable a defender to thwart an attack. These defensive tactics, which he labeled "the contracting funnel," called for placing only a small portion of the defender's forces on the front line; the majority were to be located directly behind the front. "The role of forward bodies," he argued, "is stationary defence by fire."[42] The forces in the rear, on the other hand, were to function as "manoeuvre bodies." The attacking forces were actually to be "encouraged to penetrate" into the defender's rear, although the "forward bodies" would exact a price from them.[43] Once the attacking forces were in the defender's rear, the defender's "manoeuvre bodies" would converge on their flanks and destroy them. The defender was, in effect, enticing the attacker to move into a killing zone, where the defender's knowledge of the terrain would give him a decisive advantage over the attacker.[44] Liddell Hart believed that such a use of maneuver would allow the defender to avoid the bloody slugging matches of World War I, while still providing the means to inflict a devastating defeat on the attacking forces.

Liddell Hart's theory of infantry tactics bears a marked similarity to the highly regarded infantry tactics, both offensive and defensive, the Germans employed in the last two years of the Great War. In fact, it is difficult to distinguish his tactics for the offender from the famed infiltration tactics the Germans employed in their 1918 offensives against the Allies.[45] Liddell Hart claims in his *Memoirs* that there was a basic

---

[41]Ibid., 667.

[42]"'Man-in-the-Dark' Theory of Infantry Tactics," 19, 15–20; see also *Memoirs* 1:43–46.

[43]"'Man-in-the-Dark' Theory of Infantry Tactics," 17.

[44]LH was *not* calling for a classical mobile defense; he was calling for Britain to employ his prescribed defensive tactics in the context of a strategy of forward defense like that used by both sides on the Western Front in World War I. On mobile defense, see Col. J. R. Alford, *Mobile Defense: The Pervasive Myth* (London: King's College, Dept. of War Studies, 1977); John J. Mearsheimer, "Maneuver, Mobile Defense, and the NATO Central Front," *International Security* 6 (Winter 1981/82): 104–22.

[45]On infiltration tactics, see esp. Timothy T. Lupfer, *The Dynamics of Doctrine: The Changes in German Tactical Doctrine during the First World War*, Leavenworth Paper No. 4 (Fort Leavenworth, Kans.: U.S. Army Command and General Staff College, July 1981), chap. 2; see also Correlli Barnett, *The Swordbearers: Supreme Command in the First World War* (Bloomington: Indiana University Press, 1975), chap. 4; Brig. Gen. James E. Ed-

difference between the two: German infiltration tactics "did not ensure that the momentum of the advance was maintained right through the whole of the enemy's system of defence." Thus, the attacking forces would not effect a clean break of the defender's forward positions, which is, of course, what happened when the Germans employed those tactics against the British and the French in the spring of 1918. He clearly implies in his *Memoirs* that he solved this problem by developing "a method of attack in which exploitation would become a semiautomatic process."[46] But in the early 1920s, Liddell Hart stopped arguing that infantry provided the key to battlefield success and instead became a champion of the tank, in good part because he did not think infantry, even following his tactical prescriptions, could exploit a penetration before the defender sealed the opening shut.[47] More generally, it is difficult to see from his writings how his ideas about exploitation differ from the earlier German concept; they appear to be congruent. Finally, when Liddell Hart wrote about infiltration tactics in the 1920s and 1930s he did not mention any difference between his and the Germans' views on exploitation.[48]

There also appears to be little difference between Liddell Hart's defensive tactics and those of the Germans.[49] The only meaningful difference, in fact, between his theory of infantry tactics and that of the Germans is one that Liddell Hart apparently never mentioned: that he

---

monds, *Military Operations: France and Belgium, 1918*, Official British History of World War I (London: Macmillan, 1935), 1: chap. 7, esp. 155–60; Donald J. Goodspeed, *Ludendorff: Genius of World War I* (Boston: Houghton Mifflin, 1966), 242–45; Lt. Gen. Hermann von Kuhl (German army), *Genesis, Execution, and Collapse of the German Offensive in 1918*, pt. 1: *The Preparation of the Offensive* (Washington, D.C.: Army War College, Dec. 1933); Lt. Col. Pascal H. M. Lucas (French army), *The Evolution of Tactical Ideas in France and Germany during the War of 1914–1918*, trans. P. V. Kieffer (Fort Leavenworth, Kans. 1925), chap. 6, esp. 234–43; Erich Ludendorff, *Ludendorff's Own Story, August 1914–November 1918* (New York: Harper, 1919), 158–325.

[46]*Memoirs* 1:43–44. See also B. Bond, *Liddell Hart*, 26–27; Jay Luvaas, *The Education of an Army: British Military Thought, 1815–1940* (Chicago: University of Chicago Press, 1964), 380–81.

[47]He writes, for example, in *Future of Infantry*, "Infantry, even the best light infantry, cannot replace the need for a modernized cavalry *because they cannot strike quick enough or follow through soon enough* for decisiveness in battle" (emphasis in the original) (34).

[48]See, for example, LH, *The Real War, 1914–1918* (London: Faber, 1930), 390–92; *Future of Infantry*, 27–28.

[49]On German defensive tactics, see Lupfer, *Dynamics of Doctrine*, chap. 1; Capt. G. C. Wynne, *If Germany Attacks: The Battle in Depth in the West* (London: Faber, 1940); also Gen. William Balck, *Development of Tactics: World War*, trans. Harry Bell (Fort Leavenworth, Kans.: General Service Schools Press, 1922), chap. 6; Capt. Cyril Falls, *Military Operations: France and Belgium, 1917*, Official British History of World War I (London: Macmillan, 1940), 1:401–4, 552–53; Goodspeed, *Ludendorff*, 206–10; Ludendorff, *Ludendorff's Own Story*, 1–112; Capt. Wilfrid Miles, *Military Operations: France and Belgium, 1916*, Official British History of World War I (London: Macmillan, 1938), 2:577–79.

emphasized cooperation between infantry and tanks, whereas the Germans paid little attention to the tank and focused instead on infantry-artillery cooperation. The Germans relied heavily on accurate artillery fire to suppress enemy strong points. Liddell Hart, though he did not completely ignore artillery, emphasized it much less than the Germans.

Liddell Hart admitted borrowing from the Germans when he wrote in 1968: "In the course of recasting the *Infantry Training* manual in 1920, I had evolved a method of attack that I christened the expanding torrent. *It was a development of the infiltration tactics of 1918,* based on the ideas of deep penetration and of maintaining the momentum by sustained pressure along the line of least resistance."[50] There is insufficient evidence from the period, however, to detail how the German experience influenced his thinking about infantry tactics.[51] He surely was aware by the war's end of at least the broad outlines of German tactics, for anyone deeply involved in training infantry and later in developing infantry tactics would know how the Germans employed their infantry between 1917 and 1918. The rival armies, after all, paid careful attention to each other's tactics, and those the Germans used in the final years of the war attracted great attention in British military circles, both during and after the war.[52]

There were two major problems with Liddell Hart's theory of infantry tactics that bear mentioning, although he apparently never discussed them. One stems from the fact his theory was comprehensively explained in a series of lectures and widely disseminated articles and books. Such widespread exposure meant that an opponent could easily adopt his tactics and use them against the British army. The second problem is closely linked with the first. Liddell Hart's ultimate aim was to avoid refighting World War I. His defensive tactics, however, provided an excellent antidote to his offensive tactics. Liddell Hart did not claim that an offender who adopted his tactics had an advantage over

[50]LH, "Forced to Think," in George A. Panichas, ed., *Promise of Greatness: The War of 1914–1918* (New York: John Day, 1968), 113, emphasis added. He implicitly acknowledges that he was aware of German infantry tactics in *Memoirs:* "In the course of writing the 'Attack' chapter [in 1920] I came to see that the methods developed in 1918, first by the Germans and then by the Allies" (1:43–44). See also his 1925 memorandum cited in B. Bond, *Liddell Hart,* 26–27.

[51]LH never directly addressed this matter in later years. Given his attempt to convince others after World War II that the German generals of the interwar period had been his pupils—specifically, that German thinking about the blitzkrieg had its genesis in his writings—it is understandable that he should not choose to provide evidence of how German thinking during World War I had influenced the development of his early thinking about war.

[52]See, for example, various volumes of the Official British History of World War I, ed. Brig. Gen. James E. Edmonds, as well as Wynne, *If Germany Attacks.*

an opponent who followed his defensive tactics; in fact he expected the defender to prevail. Consider these comments from his *Memoirs:*

> The problem of defence, as I saw it, was to provide a suitable and effective answer to the new attack method. . . . I accordingly worked out an improved system . . . calling it 'the contracting funnel.' . . . After discussion and trial, [Gen. Winston] Dugan agreed that an attacker employing the infiltration or 'soft spot' tactics of 1918 *would be likely to fail* against an astute defender who adopted the 'contracting funnel' method. (1:44–45, emphasis added)

Thus if Britain were launching an attack against an opponent that had adopted Liddell Hart's defensive tactics, Britain's offense would be thwarted, reproducing the stalemate of World War I. Because he was widely advertising his views, and Germany—the most likely foe in a future war—had already employed essentially the same defensive tactics in World War I, such an outcome was probable. Liddell Hart appears never to have dealt with this dilemma, possibly because he did not recognize it, possibly because his focus of interest was shifting from infantry tactics to armored strategy when the problem became evident. Nevertheless, this predicament would appear again.

THE BLITZKRIEG

Liddell Hart was not Britain's only military thinker writing for a wide audience in those first years after the war. He was in the company of J. F. C. Fuller, an army brevet colonel who had been the chief general staff officer of the British tank corps in World War I. Fuller firmly believed the tank would be the dominant weapon on future battlefields and, if properly employed, would revolutionize land warfare. Liddell Hart was first exposed to Fuller's ideas when he read the colonel's prize-winning essay in the May 1920 issue of the *Journal of the Royal United Services Institution.*[53] Fuller argued in this article that fast-moving tanks would so dominate future battlefields that land warfare

[53]J. F. C. Fuller, "The Application of Recent Developments in Mechanics and Other Scientific Knowledge to Preparation and Training for Future War on Land," Gold Medal [Military] Prize Essay for 1919, 65 (May 1920): 239–74. Fuller's principal works on armored war from the interwar years are *The Reformation of War* (London: Hutchinson, 1923); *The Foundations of the Science of War* (London: Hutchinson, 1926); *On Future Warfare* (London: Sifton Praed, 1928); and esp. *Lectures on F.S.R. III* (London: Sifton Praed, 1932), also pub. as *Armored Warfare* (Harrisburg, Pa.: Military Service, 1943). On Fuller's thinking about armored strategy, see Brian H. Reid, "J. F. C. Fuller's Theory of Mechanized Warfare," *Journal of Strategic Studies* 1 (Dec. 1978): 295–312; also Luvaas, *Education of an*

would approximate naval warfare, with tanks fighting among themselves in a manner similar to ships engaged in battle at sea.

Liddell Hart wrote to Fuller after reading his essay, introducing himself and providing Fuller with copies of his articles on infantry tactics. Fuller replied promptly and thus began a fruitful, although sometimes contentious, correspondence that lasted until Fuller's death in 1966.[54] Fuller liked Liddell Hart's ideas about infantry. He thought, however, that Liddell Hart underestimated "the enormous difficulty of supplying attacking infantry who have effected a penetration."[55] Fuller believed that an armored force was ideally suited for exploiting a breakthrough.

Fuller spent the next year and a half trying to convince Liddell Hart that infantry was no longer the decisive arm on the battlefield and that the tank had the potential to revolutionize warfare. Liddell Hart did his best to counter Fuller's arguments but finally acknowledged defeat in a letter of 31 January 1922: "Your arguments are so convincing on the tank v other arms as they exist, that I am fain to become a disciple." Liddell Hart, who was still in the army, then asked Fuller if it would be possible for him to transfer to the tank corps. Although he was never reassigned and in fact was forced to leave the service in 1924 for medical reasons, he and Fuller became widely known champions of the tank and today are generally considered the intellectual fathers of the blitzkrieg.[56]

Liddell Hart maintained in later years (chap. 8) that there were important differences in their early views on armored war and that his views, not Fuller's, represent the true formula for the blitzkrieg. There

---

Army, chap. 10; Brian H. Reid, "Colonel J. F. C. Fuller and the Revival of Classical Military Thinking in Britain, 1918–1926," *Military Affairs* 49 (Oct. 1985): 192–97; idem, *J. F. C. Fuller: Military Thinker* (London: Macmillan, 1987), chap. 7; Anthony J. Trythall, *'Boney' Fuller: The Intellectual General, 1878–1966* (New Brunswick, N.J.: Rutgers University Press, 1977).

[54]*Memoirs* 1:87–90; correspondence in 1/302.

[55]Fuller to LH, 25 Aug. 1920, 1/302.

[56]LH to Fuller, 1/302. Neither LH nor Fuller, nor the Germans for that matter, used the term *blitzkrieg* in the 1930s. In fact, there was no common term or phrase used to describe the body of ideas about armored war that later came to be called the blitzkrieg. For an etymology of the word, see Len Deighton, *Blitzkrieg: From the Rise of Hitler to the Fall of Dunkirk* (New York: Knopf, 1980), 102–3. LH strongly hints in *Memoirs* that the Germans borrowed the term from him during the interwar period: "Unfortunately, active minds in the new German Army grasped the concept more fully than did the heads of the British Army, and were the first to put into practice the new technique of what I called 'lightning war'—*Blitzkrieg* in German" (1:164). LH did not use the term *lightning war* with any frequency in the interwar period, and there is very little evidence that German thinking about blitzkrieg was based on his writings. Nor is it clear the Germans invented the term *blitzkrieg*, much less derived it from his purported concept of "lightning war."

appear, however, to be hardly any substantive differences in their early views, and the historical record shows Fuller throughout the 1920s influencing Liddell Hart's thinking about armored war, not the other way around.[57] Our concern here, however, is with the relationship between Liddell Hart's early thinking on the use of tanks and the blitzkrieg as we now understand it.

It is not easy to detail Liddell Hart's early thinking about blitzkrieg because he wrote surprisingly little on that subject during the interwar period, especially in the 1930s. The reasons soon become apparent. Most of his principal writings on the subject date from the 1920s, but no one article, speech, or book lays out his views systematically and comprehensively. He deals only cursorily with the subject in a few articles and books.[58] In this regard, his writings on armored strategy stand in marked contrast to those on infantry tactics. Still, it is possible to draw a composite picture of his early views on blitzkrieg from his scattered and scanty writings on that subject, running a risk, of course, of creating an impression of much more coherence than was actually the case.

Liddell Hart was a vocal advocate of mechanization throughout almost all of the interwar period. He argued often in his writings about the need to mechanize the British army. He had decided, in fact, when joining the *Daily Telegraph* in 1925 to use his position as a "platform for

[57]LH acknowledged Fuller's preeminence as well as his own intellectual debt to Fuller in private correspondence; see LH to Fuller, 11 Mar. 1928, 1/302; LH, untitled note, 14 July 1932, 11/1932/24; B. Bond, *Liddell Hart*, 30; Trythall, *'Boney' Fuller*, 156–57. A careful reading of the subsequent discussion of LH's ideas about armored war along with a close examination of Reid's *J. F. C. Fuller* (esp. chap. 3 and 224–26) shows that many of LH's principal ideas on blitzkrieg were *first* propounded by Fuller. There is no evidence, however, that LH ever publicly acknowledged the debt; LH's description in *Memoirs* (1:86–91) of his relationship with Fuller is instructive on this point.

[58]LH's principal writings on blitzkrieg are contained in two books, four journal articles, and a handful of *Daily Telegraph* articles he wrote mainly between 1925 and 1929: *Paris, or The Future of War* (New York: Dutton, 1925), esp. 62–83; *Remaking of Modern Armies*, esp. the preface and pt. 1; "The Development of the 'New Model' Army: Suggestions on a Progressive, But Gradual Mechanicalization," *Army Quarterly* 9 (Oct. 1924): 37–50; "The Next Great War," *Royal Engineers Journal* 38 (Mar. 1924): 90–107 (both reprinted in somewhat shortened form in LH, *The Current of War* [London: Hutchinson, 1941]); "Mind and Machine: I. Tactical Training in 1932," *Army Quarterly* 25 (Jan. 1933): 237–50; "Mind and Machine: II. Tank Brigade Training, 1932," ibid. 26 (Apr. 1933): 51–58; copies of *Daily Telegraph* articles in sec. 10 of his personal papers. Fortunately, at some point after he left the *Daily Telegraph*, he drew up a memorandum that included his key writings on armored strategy from the *Daily Telegraph*; see "Suggestions and Forecasts: Salient Points from Captain Liddell Hart's Articles in The Daily Telegraph, 1925–1934," undated memorandum for the record, 13/3. LH liked to imply in later years that *The Decisive Wars of History: A Study in Strategy* (Boston: Little, Brown, 1929; reissued in revised form as *Strategy: The Indirect Approach* [London: Faber, 1954]) contained some of his key writings on blitzkrieg; this is not the case (see chap. 4 in this book).

launching a campaign for the mechanisation of the Army."[59] Nevertheless, espousing mechanization, however worthy a goal, is not the same as outlining an armored strategy.

Liddell Hart often asserted during the 1920s, but *not* the 1930s, that the tank had the potential to revolutionize land warfare. He championed the view that the tank provided the means to restore mobility to the battlefield and make it possible, once again, to win quick and decisive victories, as in this quotation from a *Daily Telegraph* article of 8 September 1926:

> My conviction is that the Army's most urgent need today is inoculation with the serum of mobility, both in its body and its mind. This motor-power is the main ingredient of this serum in its bodily form, its mental form is best compounded from the wideness of vision, the quick eye for openings, and the swiftness of decision and action which are the essential elements in the true cavalry spirit. The bodily form is subject to change, but may the spirit remain, otherwise our military future is bleak, and a cure for the paralysing "stickiness" of trench warfare hopeless of attainment.[60]

He frequently made the point that the tank is an offensive weapon and that its employment on a large scale would dramatically shift the offense–defense equation in favor of the former.[61] He argued, for example, in the *Daily Telegraph* on 24 September 1926, "The result of the triumph of the machine-gun is to hasten the coming of tank armies. Improving upon the legendary phoenix, a new-born offensive power will rise from the ashes of the defensive mistress of the battlefield."[62]

To acknowledge that Liddell Hart was widely identified in the 1920s as an advocate of mechanization, who believed the tank, with its inherent mobility, provided an offender with the striking power necessary to avoid another war of attrition on the European continent, is not to say that he had articulated his views on how a blitzkrieg works and made these views widely known.[63] To make broad claims about the

---

[59]"Diary Notes. 1926," 11/1926/1b.

[60]"Suggestions and Forecasts," 5.

[61]Throughout this book, I refer to LH's shifting views of the offense–defense equation. His military thinking was predicated on the assumption of a recognizable balance between offense and defense that is principally determined by the nature of available military technologies. I do not think weapons can be usefully categorized as either offensive or defensive, nor do I think it possible to measure the balance between offense and defense; so I have serious reservations about the usefulness of this concept of an offense–defense equation. See Mearsheimer, *Conventional Deterrence*, 25–26; idem, "Offense and Deterrence" (University of Chicago, 1 August 1987).

[62]"Suggestions and Forecasts," 6; this theme is reflected throughout *Remaking of Modern Armies*.

[63]B. Bond (*Liddell Hart*), commenting on LH's writings from this period, remarks that they "had a decidedly *offensive* ring about them" (6).

potential inherent in armored forces is one thing; to provide a detailed discussion to back up such claims is another. What did Liddell Hart say about how a blitzkrieg works? Specifically, what did he say about the relationship between the tank and the other combat arms? Did he call for creating independent armored forces, or did he favor integrating tanks into existing cavalry and infantry units? What were his views on how armored units should be employed on the battlefield to produce the collapse of the defender's forces? These are the questions crucial to an evaluation of Liddell Hart's early thinking about the blitzkrieg.

Liddell Hart wrote remarkably little about the important issue of battlefield employment and only somewhat more about how to organize an armored force. In his 1965 *Memoirs* he based his discussion of blitzkrieg largely on his writings about infantry tactics, on a key piece he wrote about the blitzkrieg *after* World War II, and on his early writings about the indirect approach, which was not intended to be synonymous with the blitzkrieg.[64] In fact he envisioned the indirect approach as an alternative to engaging an opponent's armies. He twice points to a 1924 article from the *Army Quarterly*, emphasizing that it contains some of his key ideas on blitzkrieg and moreover that it had a significant influence on German thinking.[65] This piece, which deals with how to organize an armored force, has hardly anything to say about battlefield employment. Moreover, the discussion of organizational issues, while interesting, offers no important insights and hardly furnishes a blueprint for how future armored forces were organized. Thus the piece provides no quotations for his discussion of the blitzkrieg in his *Memoirs*, which are otherwise filled with lengthy quotations suggesting his prescience in the two decades before World War II. It is evident, however, from the few pieces Liddell Hart wrote during the 1920s that he grasped many of the essentials of the blitzkrieg. Let us examine this matter in greater detail, focusing first on how a blitzkrieg works and then on how Liddell Hart's early views compare with the actual strategy

A blitzkrieg assumes the defender has deployed the majority of his forces at or near the battlefront, and there is a vulnerable communications network in the defender's rear.[66] When this network is dis-

---

[64]His discussion of the blitzkrieg is mainly in 1: chaps. 4, 5, 7, esp. 159–68, where he quotes from only two of his pre–World War II works: *Decisive Wars of History* and *The British Way in Warfare* (London: Faber, 1932). These two books have virtually nothing to say about tank warfare per se, which is clear from a careful reading of the two quotations he excerpts in *Memoirs*. Instead, both books deal with the indirect approach, a concept so elastic it can be used to imply discussion of blitzkrieg, whereas it was offered in these books mainly as an alternative to fighting a major ground war; more on this in chap. 4.

[65]*Memoirs* 1:35, 91–92. For the original article, see "Development of the 'New Model' Army"; the other article he cites on 92 is "Next Great War."

[66]For a more detailed explication, which this discussion draws heavily upon, see

rupted, it becomes impossible for the defender's forces to continue fighting. Hence the attacker aims to mass his armored forces at one or more points along the defender's front, pierce that front, and then drive *deep* into the defender's rear. The campaign has two phases: the breakthrough battle and the exploitation phase. As the attacking forces move forward, they sever lines of communication and overrun key nodal points in the defender's communications network. The defender is paralyzed not only because he is physically unable to coordinate the actions of his forces but also because of psychological dislocation. The attacking forces must concentrate on avoiding the defender's strongpoints once they have made the initial breakthrough. It is the deep strategic penetration that is the key to the blitzkrieg's success.

A blitzkrieg demands that the tank be treated as the principal weapon on the battlefield and that infantry and artillery be assigned subordinate roles. Tanks must not be dispersed among infantry units and used as infantry support weapons.[67] They must be concentrated in large-scale armored units employed together to make the initial breakthrough and effect the deep strategic penetration. There remains a definite need for infantry and artillery within these large armored units, however. Some in Britain argued during the interwar years that infantry and artillery would disappear from the battlefield, leaving massive all-tank armies to do battle. This never happened, and usually in those cases where an army has approximated that ideal it has performed poorly.[68] Armored units need infantry and artillery support, especially for the initial breakthrough battles and those subsequent pitched battles the armored forces cannot avoid. It is imperative, how-

---

Mearsheimer, *Conventional Deterrence*, 35–43; see also Barry R. Posen, *The Sources of Military Doctrine: France, Britain, and Germany between the World Wars* (Ithaca, N.Y.: Cornell University Press, 1984), 85–94, 205–8, 213–15.

[67]Not a major problem today in the armies of modern industrial states; most of their infantry units are mechanized and differ little from standard armored units. Interwar infantry units were usually not mechanized, so there invariably were strong pressures to disperse an army's tanks among those foot-borne infantry divisions. There was, for example, a bitter dispute over this issue in the U.S. army hierarchy during World War II. See Mildred Hanson Gillie, *Forging the Thunderbolt: A History of the Development of the Armored Force* (Harrisburg, Pa.: Military Service, 1947); Kent R. Greenfield, Robert R. Palmer, and Bell I. Wiley, *The Organization of Ground Combat Troops: United States Army in World War II: The Army Ground Forces* (Washington, D.C.: GPO, 1947); correspondence between LH and Maj. Gen. John S. Wood, an American armored commander disenchanted with Allied employment of armored forces against Germany, 1/763.

[68]Fuller leaned heavily at times in this direction, especially with his argument that future armored battles would look much like naval warfare on land; see, for example, *Reformation of War*, chap. 8; idem, "The Development of Sea Warfare on Land and Its Influence on Future Naval Operations," *Journal of the Royal United Services Institution* 65 (May 1920): 281–98. Fuller was not the only military thinker propounding this view; see

ever, that the armored forces not rely too heavily on infantry and artillery support because the command and control as well as the logistical problems associated with combined arms operations can only work to slow down the attacking forces, which would strike at the heart of the blitzkrieg.

Given these problems with artillery, attacking forces in a blitzkrieg prefer to rely on close air support, or what is sometimes referred to as "flying artillery" for fire support. Not only is there great flexibility inherent in attack aircraft, but they also place few logistical demands on the ground forces. Although close air support is a key ingredient of the blitzkrieg, the need for artillery support remains, for there are often times when air support is unavailable.

Finally, a blitzkrieg places a high premium on individual initiative and a flexible command-and-control structure. A blitzkrieg is not based on a rigid plan; in fact the opposite is true. Before launching the attack, an overall objective is established, and detailed plans for the breakthrough battle are prepared. There are, however, no rigid guidelines for the commanders to follow as they conduct the deep strategic penetration. The underlying assumption is uncertainty as to how the battle will develop. In what Clausewitz called "the fog of war," commanders will often be required to make decisions with only a modicum of information at hand. Uncertainty will be commonplace, and therefore risks will have to be taken. A high premium is placed on commanders' ability to make rapid-fire decisions that enable the armored columns to maintain a high attack speed. Boldness is essential, even when information is incomplete, if the attacking forces are to maintain momentum. Furthermore, the command-and-control structure must be flexible enough to encourage command boldness at all levels.

Liddell Hart's early (i.e., pre–World War II) views on armored war have much in common with this description of the blitzkrieg, although there are differences. Regarding organizational issues, he recognized the tank would have to be the dominant weapon on the battlefield.[69] He warned that tanks should not be considered "an adjunct to the infantry"; they should not be "intermingled with infantry and frittered

Trythall, *'Boney' Fuller*, 101–2; LH also tended in this direction. Two often-cited cases of an armored force having difficulties because of neglect of infantry and artillery support are the British army in the early years of World War II and the Israeli army in the 1973 war; see Richard M. Ogorkiewicz, *Armoured Forces: A History of Armoured Forces and Their Vehicles* (New York: Arco, 1970), 55–61; Maj. Gen. Chaim Herzog, *The War of Atonement, October 1973* (Boston: Little, Brown, 1975), 182–92, 270–73.

[69]LH, it should be noted, was a very strong proponent of developing one-man tanks (*Remaking of Modern Armies*, chap. 5), an idea that proved impracticable.

away in driblets on unsuitable ground." Instead, they should be "concentrated and used in as large masses as possible for decisive manoeuvre against the flanks and communications of the enemy."[70]

His views about the role infantry and artillery would play in these large armored formations are difficult to pinpoint, although he came close, on occasion, to arguing that tanks would eventually so dominate the battlefield that there would be no need for infantry and artillery. The argument (identified with Fuller) occasionally heard at the time—that future land battles would approximate naval battles, with tanks functioning like ships—implied there would be no place for infantry and artillery. Liddell Hart often made reference to this same analogy in his early writings, as in September 1927: "Today . . . the conflict of mechanised forces lies still on the border-land of imagination, although when it becomes reality the likelihood is that this conflict will be akin to naval warfare, with the land fleets operating from pivotal bases."[71]

Liddell Hart's writings about the future of infantry and artillery seem to follow a particular pattern. He makes a statement that either clearly implies or directly says these arms will eventually disappear from the battlefield. He then qualifies his argument somewhat and assigns them a minor battlefield role. In *Paris* (1925), for example, he writes:

> A business which retained the aged and infirm as the bulk of its employees would soon be bankrupt; it may find use for a few as caretakers—and that is the only feasible *rôle* for infantry in mobile warfare of the future. . . .
>   Then, with regard to field artillery—though moderately effective against the sluggish tanks of the Great War, its chances would be infinitely less against a modern tank zigzagging at over 20 m.p.h., and infinitesimal against them if launched in masses. If it cannot hit, it will be hit . . . its *rôle* thus becomes purely defensive. (69)

He then notes that in some distant future, tanks will "swallow the older arms completely" (79). Nevertheless, he admits that in the immediate future, artillery and infantry will have minor roles on the battlefield: reducing and then occupying enemy strong points the tanks cannot neutralize; mopping up in the wake of the armored forces; and fighting in wooded and hilly terrain.[72] This same pattern of argument

---

[70]*Remaking of Modern Armies*, 56, 59. See also LH, *Paris*, 73.
[71]From 27 Sept. 1927 article in the *Daily Telegraph* cited in "Suggestions and Forecasts," 12. See also 26, 30 Sept. 1925 articles, ibid., 1, 4; *Paris*, 81; " 'New Model' Army," 44; "Next Great War," 106.
[72]*Paris*, 69, 81–82.

is found in his 1924 *Army Quarterly* piece, where he claims, "The tank is likely to swallow the infantryman, the field artilleryman, the engineer and the signaller," a position he then qualifies by noting, "The logical sequence of events points to the land, or rather overland forces being composed principally of tanks and aircraft, with a small force of siege artillery, for the reduction and defence of the fortified tank and aircraft bases, and of mechanical-borne infantry for use as land-marines."[73]

It is evident from this quotation as well as his other writings that Liddell Hart assigned an important role to close air support, which he saw largely as a substitute for artillery. His reasoning, which he laid out in an article in the *Daily Telegraph* in June 1926, is impressive: "As to the problems of the mobile force . . . tanks move so fast that the difficulty of normal artillery co-operation is vastly intensified, and for this reason I feel that actual 'offensive' support must come, and can only come effectively, from an even more mobile artillery moving immediately alongside. For this purpose the close co-operation of low-flying aircraft . . . is essential."[74]

Liddell Hart also recognized that a blitzkrieg demands a flexible command structure peopled top to bottom with soldiers capable of exercising initiative in difficult combat situations. He discussed on at least two occasions the command-and-control problems associated with a fast-moving armored force. "Control," he noted, "is the real problem—far more than direct protection—of a mechanized force, because of its very fluidity, the distance it covers, and the speed which marks both its movements and engagements."[75] The problem of controlling rapidly moving forces was not new for Liddell Hart, who had confronted it when developing his infantry tactics. His solution, in both cases, was to call for de-emphasizing rigid forms of discipline and emphasizing flexibility and initiative. As he noted in *Paris*, "With a mobile army, control must be more prompt and flexible than ever" (25).

Let us now consider Liddell Hart's thinking about the mechanics of the blitzkrieg, focusing first on his thinking about the breakthrough battle and then the exploitations phase. He recognized the need to concentrate armor at designated points along the front to effect a

---

[73]"'New Model' Army," 44. See also 46, where he writes, "From the complexity of existing weapons and arms we shall gradually evolve, first, an army in which the weapons of each arm are reduced in variety, and then the arms themselves, until finally we have an army of tanks and aircraft."

[74]From 19 June 1926 article in the *Daily Telegraph* cited in "Suggestions and Forecasts," 5.

[75]From 26 Sept. 1927 article, ibid., 12. See also 29 Sept. 1925 article, ibid., 3.

breakthrough. His theory of infantry tactics called for an attack across a broad front by literally hundreds of small units, each seeking to find soft spots in the defender's front; it placed no emphasis on massing forces for a single breakthrough. If Liddell Hart had merely incorporated tanks into his infantry scheme, the armored forces would have been dispersed, which of course is antithetical to the blitzkrieg. He wisely recognized the need for concentrating the tank forces.[76]

There was considerable interest during the 1920s in the idea of holding the attacker's armored forces in reserve until forces dominated by artillery and infantry had ripped a hole in the defender's front.[77] Tanks would then be moved forward and used to exploit the breakthrough. Armored forces, in other words, would assume one of the traditional roles of horse cavalry, a notion incompatible with the blitzkrieg, which called for armored forces to *make* the critical breakthroughs and then effect the deep strategic penetration. Liddell Hart wisely labeled it an "obviously absurd" idea.[78]

The exploitation phase of the blitzkrieg is particularly important because an opponent's rear is considered his Achilles' heel. Liddell Hart of course recognized this point, for his theory of infantry tactics was predicated on this same assumption. His thinking on this matter is summed up in an August 1927 article in the *Daily Telegraph*: the "guiding star in the handling of a mobile force" should be "getting on the enemy's rear, and thereby paralysing his freedom of action as a prelude to his demoralisation, disorganisation, and destruction."[79]

Given this assumption, a blitzkrieg demands deep strategic penetration as its central element, as Liddell Hart emphasized *after* World War II.[80] The deep strategic penetration stands in marked contrast to a more limited tactical penetration, where the emphasis is on using armored forces to disrupt the communications network in the defender's immediate rear. This important distinction was not lost on Liddell Hart, who went to some lengths *after* World War II to argue he had advocated the need for deep strategic penetration in the interwar years, while Fuller

---

[76]LH actually gives the impression at times in his *Memoirs* (1: 48–49, 164) that the blitzkrieg was the result of simply marrying the tank to his theory of infantry tactics. Close examination of his ideas on infantry tactics and armored strategy shows otherwise. On concentrating armor, see *Remaking of Modern Armies*, 230.

[77]Ogorkiewicz, *Armoured Forces*, chap. 2.

[78]From 24 Sept. 1927 article in the *Daily Telegraph* cited in "Suggestions and Forecasts," 11. Nevertheless, LH does once come very close to embracing this "absurd" idea; see *Remaking of Modern Armies*, chap. 4, esp. 44–46.

[79]From 30 Aug. 1927 article in the *Daily Telegraph* cited in "Suggestions and Forecasts," 11; see also *Paris*, 73.

[80]*Memoirs* 1:164–65. This key memorandum was written after World War II, after he had spoken at length with the German generals.

had called for a deep tactical penetration. Fuller, he argued, "favoured the armoured forces being used for a manoeuvre against the opposing army's immediate rear, rather than against its communications far in the rear. Thus he preferred an advance by fairly long but limited bounds, instead of driving on as fast and as far as possible—which became my concept when developing for armoured forces the 'expanding torrent' method" (*Memoirs* 1:91).

There is no evidence, however, that Liddell Hart understood the importance of the deep strategic penetration *before* World War II. Specifically, there is no evidence that the distinction between a tactical and a deep strategic penetration figured in his thinking before the war. He simply did not address the issue of how far into the defender's rear the attacker's forces had to reach to cause his collapse; but then, this was not a central issue among British armor advocates at the time. There is no discussion of the concept in his writings on blitzkrieg from the 1920s, which is not surprising because he claims his thinking about the deep strategic penetration did not crystallize until after he began studying the American Civil War campaigns of William T. Sherman and Nathan Forrest in 1928, after most of his principal works on armored strategy had been written. Yet there is no evidence in his book about Sherman or in any of his subsequent writings from the interwar years that he recognized the concept of a deep strategic penetration, much less called attention to it.[81]

One might argue this concept is implicit in his writings.[82] There is

[81]For LH's writings on the blitzkrieg, see n. 58. On the crystallization of his views on deep strategic penetration, see *Memoirs* 1:166; also LH, Foreword, *Memoirs of General William T. Sherman* (Bloomington: Indiana University Press, 1957), xiii. For further discussion, see chap. 4 in this book. During World War II, LH collected many lengthy quotations from his past writings in *Thoughts on War* (London: Faber, 1944); were there evidence of early advocacy of the deep strategic penetration, it would be there or in *Memoirs* (esp. 1:159–68), where he presents no evidence that he had discovered the importance of the deep strategic penetration *before* World War II. See also "Mind and Machine," pt. 1, 237–50, and "Mind and Machine," pt. 2, 51–58, two key post-*Sherman* articles on blitzkrieg; neither has any discussion of deep strategic penetration. In *When Britain Goes to War*, 71–72, 209–11, LH indicates that an attacking army should consider the defending army's immediate rear as its key target. The only evidence from the interwar period that might possibly indicate LH recognized the concept of deep strategic penetration is a short memorandum he wrote in 1935 about cavalry operations in the American Civil War; in Luvaas, *Military Legacy of the Civil War*, 237–44; see esp. 243–44. He briefly raised the question of whether "long-range moves" or "close-range moves" were most effective against the enemy's rear. His conclusion is equivocal, although he seems to favor the "long-range moves": "Long-range moves seem to have been more effective than close-range. . . . In general, the nearer to the force that the cut is made, the *more immediate* the effect; the nearer to the base, the *greater* the effect. In either case, the effect is much greater and more quickly felt if made against a force that is in motion" (243–44). See also *Memoirs* 1:270.
[82]Luvaas makes this argument in *Education of an Army*, 405.

possibly some truth in this claim. When Liddell Hart talked about the exploitation phase of a campaign, he often spoke in terms of an "expanding torrent." That term can certainly be taken to imply he believed in the need to drive deep into the enemy's rear.[83] He was never explicit on this point in the interwar period, however, and moreover, he did not often use the term *after* the point at which he claims his ideas on the deep strategic penetration crystallized.[84] He first introduced the term *expanding torrent* in his writings on infantry tactics, where, by his own admission, he was not talking about a deep strategic penetration. In short, Liddell Hart apparently did not address the scope of the blitzkrieg's exploitation phase in the years before World War II, nor does he seem to have recognized its importance.

Liddell Hart's theory of infantry tactics included a discussion of both offense and defense, the offense enjoying no special advantage in the scheme. This was not the case with his writings from the 1920s about armored strategy. He wrote hardly anything about how a defense operates on an armored battlefield and almost exclusively about offensive operations. Furthermore he maintained that the tank clearly favored the offender over the defender. His writings suggest that an army that adopts his ideas on armored strategy is almost sure to win a quick and decisive victory. He was, however, aware of the argument that an intelligent defender could use the mobility inherent in tanks to increase his prospects of thwarting an attack, so that increased mobility might not favor the attacking forces. Spenser Wilkinson made this very point in a 1927 review of Liddell Hart's *The Remaking of Modern Armies*. Liddell Hart, however, rejected his argument:

> Next, he argues that any attempt of a tank force to strike at the command and communications centres in the enemy's rear "will hardly be practicable in the next war, because" it "will immediately be met by the enemy's tanks. . . ." I would reply that the more mobile an instrument the greater is its power of evasion, as has been proved by cavalry in the remoter past and by aircraft in the recent past.[85]

Liddell Hart's writings about blitzkrieg convey the impression that he was so committed to finding a way to make offense an attractive option that he either ignored or dismissed out of hand all counterarguments, a point reflected in another comment he made in *The Remaking of Modern*

---

[83]*Memoirs* 1:48–49.

[84]LH wrote little about the blitzkrieg in the 1930s; by the mid-1930s, in fact, he was arguing that the defense had a great advantage over the offense, so he had little reason to expound on deep strategic penetration.

[85]LH, letter, *Army Quarterly* 15 (Jan. 1928): 398; Spenser Wilkinson, "Killing No Murder: An Examination of Some New Theories of War," ibid. (Oct. 1927): 14–27.

Armies. After dismissing the latest developments in antitank weaponry, he remarked:

> This eager and ever-buoyant hope for an antidote to the tank comes curiously from the lips of soldiers who sincerely desire a return to moving warfare, wherein the art of command and the keen eye for an opening can again find scope. I wonder if they realise that the discovery of an antidote must quench all chance of a renaissance of mobility and doom us to a perpetual reign of machine-made slaughter. . . . If the tank should be laid low, the machine gun would be left undisputed master of the battlefield, and the possibility of attack [would] decay and perish before an immovable defence. (7–8)

Three further points about Liddell Hart and defense are in order. First, he was simply wrong in his conclusion that the tank axiomatically favors the offender; that is much too simple a conclusion about a complex subject. Actually, a strong case can be made that the tank favors the defender.[86] This argument assumes, of course, that the defender is adept at using his armored forces. Liddell Hart himself in the mid-1930s replaced his belief that the tank decisively shifts the offense–defense equation in favor of the former to the diametrically opposed but equally extreme belief that the defender enjoys an overwhelming advantage on the battlefield. Second, Liddell Hart seems not to have considered that an opponent of Britain in some future war might pay careful attention to his ideas and use his theory of blitzkrieg to Britain's disadvantage. After all, during the 1920s, Liddell Hart himself was very impressed with the German army, especially its leaders' emphasis on mobility. The Germans could as well have adopted his theory for use against Britain and her allies.

The final point, which is related to the previous one, concerns deterrence. Specifically, does it enhance deterrence to announce that the tank promises to create a situation where offense pays big dividends? Does it make sense to say to a potential aggressor that the blitzkrieg is an excellent tool for overrunning other countries? This issue was of central importance to Liddell Hart in the 1930s, but in the 1920s he paid it hardly any attention, concentrating instead on finding a formula for winning battles in the next war. He did, nevertheless, address the matter of offense and deterrence on at least one occasion. His discussion is worth quoting at length because it shows how deeply committed he was to making the offense more powerful than the defense:

> Armies to-day have become mass minus velocity . . . the outbreak of another war will doom us to a repetition, but more complete, of the paralysis

[86]See n. 61.

of the last war, ruinous alike to the human and economic strength of the nation.

The pacifist might be disposed to welcome such a condition, holding that if armies are incapable of offensive action, offensive war is also impossible. He might thus argue for the maintenance of armies in this present state on the ground that, with their teeth drawn but their mass remaining, they ensure the defence of a country but cannot lend themselves to aggression against another country.

In adopting this argument he would delude himself. Armies merely capable of defence are only a useless channel of expenditure when the power of offence is lost.[87]

Liddell Hart would completely change these views in the 1930s.

In conclusion, what about the fit between Liddell Hart's early thinking about armored strategy and the blitzkrieg as we now understand it? Liddell Hart did not carefully develop his ideas on blitzkrieg. He did not have a fully developed theory of offensive armored war. Instead, he was principally concerned with waging a public campaign to mechanize the British army. To this end, he argued that the tank would be the principal weapon on future battlefields and armies would have to be organized for rapid movement of large-scale armored units. He was widely identified with this view.[88]

Despite the paucity of his writings on blitzkrieg, he seems to have grasped many of the essential elements of that strategy. Although he did not recognize the importance of the deep strategic penetration in these early years, he did understand that the defender's key vulnerability was the command-and-control network located in his rear. Furthermore, he recognized that destruction of that complex network required the attacking forces to maintain a high speed of advance as they drove into the defender's rear. On organizational matters, he was not so foolish as to claim that the more traditional arms, infantry and artillery, had no place on the battlefield, although he does appear to have underestimated the important role combined arms operations would play in a blitzkrieg. Most salient, he grasped the importance of organizational flexibility and individual initiative as well as close air support. His most glaring error in judgment is probably his failure to recognize that tanks do not simply favor the offense but can be effectively used by a competent defender. Such shortcomings aside, one

---

[87]*Remaking of Modern Armies*, v–vi.

[88]If the reviews of *Remaking of Modern Armies* are any indication, LH was widely recognized by the public as an advocate of mechanization, not as a proponent of an explicit blitzkrieg strategy. Although that book contains some of his most important thoughts about blitzkrieg, the reviewers pay them little attention; copies of reviews in 9/3/7.

gets the sense from Liddell Hart's writings that he basically understood the blitzkrieg. This is an impressive achievement when one considers Liddell Hart formulated his ideas when the tank was a relatively new weapon, when there was little empirical evidence about tank warfare, and when no developed body of literature on the subject existed. He was, however, importantly helped toward his discovery by Fuller.

There is one final matter to discuss about Liddell Hart's thinking on armored warfare. He believed that a state could build two very different kinds of armies and that this choice had important implications for the blitzkrieg. Specifically, he maintained that only a relatively small army that eschewed conscription and was dominated by professional soldiers would be capable of effecting a blitzkrieg.[89] A mass army based on conscription would only be capable of engaging in attrition warfare as on the Western Front between 1914 and 1918. There was, he argued, an "essential antithesis between mass and mobility," and in those cases where a small professional force engaged a mass army, the former would almost always win quickly and decisively.[90] The number of forces on each side would not matter in such engagements the way it would if two mass armies fought each other. Mobility, not numbers, would provide the smaller force with the key to victory. The greater the mass of an army or the more men under arms, in fact, the more cumbersome that army would be and thus the more likely to meet defeat in battle.[91]

Liddell Hart maintained in *Paris* there were three reasons a mass army would be incapable of engaging successfully in armored war.[92] First, mass armies because of their size were simply too unwieldy to be rapidly moved about the battlefield. "Mobilizing huge conscript armies," he argued, was likely to result in "self-induced paralysis."[93] There would also be little room for maneuver in a theater of war occupied by mass armies. Second, a mass army, because of its size and slow-moving nature, would be "too vulnerable a target to modern fireweapons." He thought air attacks would be especially effective at disrupting a large army.[94] Third, a mass army "imposed so great a strain on the means of supply" that even if it were possible to overcome the

[89]A frequent theme in his writings throughout the interwar period; see, for example, *Paris*, 62–86; *Remaking of Modern Armies*, chap. 2; *When Britain Goes to War*, chaps. 2, 3, 6, 8, 10; "New Wars or Old?" *Saturday Review of Literature*, 6 Jan. 1934, 389–90. Fuller, however, first introduced this idea; see his *Tanks in the Great War, 1914–1918* (New York: Dutton, 1920), esp. xix, 308–21; also Reid, *J. F. C. Fuller*, 154, 169, 220.

[90]LH, "The Armies of Europe," *Foreign Affairs* 15 (Jan. 1937): 250.

[91]*When Britain Goes to War*, 72; see also 152–53.

[92]This and all quotations in this paragraph, unless otherwise noted, are from 62–63.

[93]*When Britain Goes to War*, 57.

[94]Ibid., 55–56.

problem of sheer unwieldiness, it would be impossible to supply such a force once it got moving.

There was an important fourth reason Liddell Hart believed a mass army could not effect a blitzkrieg. It is apparent from his writings he did not think it would be possible to mechanize a large army—undoubtedly for financial reasons—and therefore such an army would be dominated by infantry and artillery, not tanks.[95] This was a situation sure to lead to repetition of the experience on the Western Front. Only a smaller, nonconscript army led by professionals could be adequately mechanized.

In sum, Liddell Hart's belief in the blitzkrieg was not the only consideration that led him to think Britain could avoid another war of attrition. He also seems to have believed that armies of the future were likely to be relatively small, making it very difficult, even if a blitzkrieg failed and a stalemate ensued, to wage a war on the scale of the Great War. One gets the unmistakable impression from Liddell Hart's writings that he wanted very much to return to the limited wars of eighteenth-century Europe and that he saw mechanization as a powerful inducement to move in that direction.[96] Of course, World War II showed that to be a chimerical vision.

Liddell Hart as a Great Captain

Liddell Hart remained on active duty in the army for six years after the Great War, during which time his principal concern was to find a way to restore the offense to its dominant position on the battlefield. He took it for granted during these years that Britain would accept a Continental commitment; he simply wanted her and her allies to be able to win a future European war quickly and decisively.

Liddell Hart firmly believed that if he set his mind to it he would discover the key to battlefield success. He viewed himself as a supremely rational actor who could solve important military problems by careful study, then communicate his insights to the responsible military leaders, who would implement them. Liddell Hart believed brilliant individuals, or "great captains," were largely responsible for the fate of nations in war. Military history, for Liddell Hart, to use Carlyle's famous phrase, was "the biography of great men."[97] Throughout his

---

[95]His thinking in the late 1930s about sending a small British armored force to France (chap. 6 in this book) reflects this point.

[96]*Remaking of Modern Armies*, chap. 14.

[97]LH's emphasis on great men as the principal force in history reflects a major tenet of the "Whig" or "Liberal" interpretation that was the dominant historical paradigm in the

life he paid little attention to the materiel forces that affect war while placing much emphasis on ideas. "The history of the world, if not entirely the history of its great men," he argued, "is the history of its creative minds."[98] Of course ideas and individuals were inextricably linked in his mind because individuals spawn ideas and ultimately are judged by the quality of them. The following remark from *The Remaking of Modern Armies* nicely captures his view: "War is no different from the other branches of life and knowledge. The great discoveries of science have all been achieved by the solitary research of some individual, whose mind is able to investigate unfettered by the mental grooves characteristic of all types of corporate institution" (183). This emphasis on great men and their ideas is found throughout Liddell Hart's writings.[99] Consider one important example.

Liddell Hart was naturally concerned with determining the root cause of the bloody stalemate that developed in World War I. He concluded that ultimate responsibility rested with Clausewitz, whose wrongheaded theories about war had been enthusiastically adopted by European armies.[100] Clausewitz, he argued, was "the Mahdi of mass and mutual massacre," the philosopher of war who exalted the value of bloody pitched battles.[101] Moreover, he was "the master at whose feet have sat for a century the military students of Europe."[102] It was the students' adherence to the master's teachings that produced the disasters of World War I. He maintained, for example, that the German army's failure in World War I could be directly attributed to its close following of Clausewitz's "theories [which] have ended by bringing

England of his youth; see Herbert Butterfield, *The Whig Interpretation of History* (London: Bell, 1968); Valerie E. Chancellor, *History for Their Masters: Opinion in the English History Textbook, 1800–1914* (New York: Kelley, 1970); Brian Simon and Ian Bradley, eds., *The Victorian Public School: Studies in the Development of an Educational Institution* (Dublin: Gill & Macmillan, 1975), esp. chap. 8.

[98]LH, "'Woman Wanders—the World Wavers' or Woman and the World-quake," *English Review* 59 (Sept. 1934): 311.

[99]Chap. 11 of *Remaking of Modern Armies* has an excellent discussion of his views on the importance of great men and their ideas.

[100]This argument is succinctly stated in *Paris*, 10–18. For an expanded version, see LH, *The Ghost of Napoleon* (London: Faber, 1933); see also *British Way in Warfare*, 16–18. For defense of Clausewitz, see Wilkinson, "Killing No Murder," 14–27.

[101]*Ghost of Napoleon*, 120, 118–29.

[102]*Paris*, 10. This is not the place to discuss Clausewitz's influence in the decades before World War I, but it was nowhere near as great as LH implies. If anyone is to be described as such a "master," it should be Baron Henri Jomini; see John Shy, "Jomini," in Peter Paret, ed., *Makers of Modern Strategy: From Machiavelli to the Nuclear Age* (Princeton, N.J.: Princeton University Press, 1986), 143–85; also Peter Paret, "Clausewitz and the Nineteenth Century," in Michael Howard, ed., *The Theory and Practice of War: Essays Presented to B. H. Liddell Hart on His Seventieth Birthday* (London: Cassell, 1965), 23–41.

his Fatherland into a more impotent and impoverished state even than when it was under the iron heel of Napoleon."[103] The implication was clear: if only there had been no Clausewitz and if instead there had been a wiser man in his place, Europe would have been spared the horror of World War I. Liddell Hart naturally saw himself as the source of wisdom who would counteract Clausewitz's bad ideas. Because, however, he was only a junior officer in an organization dominated by colonels and generals, he could only fulfill his mission if his superiors chose to take him seriously and heed his advice. The young officer, so he argued, had to be made to feel that he had "a marshal's baton in his knapsack."[104] Liddell Hart could only be "the captain who taught generals" if the generals were willing to be taught.

He had good reason to believe this would be the case during the years immediately after the war. His general attitude toward Britain's military leaders, which of course was inextricably bound up with his thinking about World War I, was positive at this juncture. A number of British generals openly applauded and promoted his ideas, and a much larger number of officers paid attention to them—points not lost on Liddell Hart. He remarked, for example, in 1923: "I am deeply grateful for the large measure of courtesy and encouragement I have received in regard to my own military theories; far more probably than any other profession would have shown to a comparatively junior officer." He affirmed the point in 1936, well after his attitude toward the British military had soured, when he wrote that in the early 1920s, "the leading generals treated me as an equal in military knowledge."[105]

The first indication Liddell Hart's ideas would be taken seriously by his superiors came toward the end of World War I, when his writings on infantry training were greeted with much enthusiasm. "It had been an exhilarating experience," he wrote in his *Memoirs*, "to find my tactical ideas greeted so favourably, and the booklets taken up so widely" (1:32). Then, immediately after the war, a handful of influential generals went to considerable lengths to help him secure an audience for his ideas.[106] Liddell Hart's account of his 1922 lecture on infantry

[103]*Paris*, 11.
[104]"Bardell" [LH], "Study and Reflection v. Practical Experience," *Army Quarterly* 6 (July 1923): 330. See LH's comments on this article in *Memoirs* 1:59–60. Most of this article is incorporated in chap. 11 of *Remaking of Modern Armies*.
[105]Letter, *Army Quarterly* 8 (Apr. 1924): 8; "Thoughts Jotted Down—To Be Expanded," memorandum for the record, entry for 4 Aug. 1936, 11/1936/2–25c.
[106]*Memoirs* 1: chap. 2; also correspondence with Gen. Ivor Maxse, 1/499.

tactics at the Royal United Services Institution shows the exposure his ideas received:

> When I entered the lecture-theatre I was staggered by the large and distinguished audience, including numerous generals, who had come to hear me. . . . [A]fterwards . . . the Commandant of the School of Military Engineering [requested] that I should go there to repeat it as soon as possible. Besides being published in both the *R.U.S.I. Journal* and the *R.E. Journal*, two leading military publishers—Gale and Polden, and Hugh Rees—offered to bring it out in booklet form, a course which Maxse [a general officer who was a staunch backer of Liddell Hart] had suggested. (*Memoirs* 1:47)

What makes this all quite remarkable is that Liddell Hart was only a young captain without a distinguished military record. He achieved this notoriety largely on the basis of his fine analytic mind, which had attracted the attention of a few influential generals. His treatment by the military establishment in these early years naturally reinforced his deeply held belief that what the military needed was a supremely rational thinker who could find a way to restore the primacy of the offense and then pass that formula on to the generals.

This discussion should not obscure the fact there were signs in these early years of that deep-seated hostility which would later characterize Liddell Hart's relations with the generals. He wrote in 1923, for example, a very controversial article in the *Army Quarterly* in which he warned against the "professional hack . . . who disparages without examination the views of the outside student." He also cautioned that there was "an increasing tendency for the narrow-minded type of regular soldier to fall back upon this last line of defence of his claims to superior authority on war."[107] Liddell Hart was directly challenged on these points in subsequent issues. He responded by adopting a considerably more moderate line, a pattern he was never to repeat.[108] In the future he would hold his ground. These early signs of disenchantment notwithstanding, Liddell Hart was quite hopeful in the first few years of peace that the generals would welcome his new ideas.

In sum, by 1924 Liddell Hart was confident he had found a way to restore the offense to a dominant position in the offense–defense equa-

[107]"Study and Reflection v. Practical Experience," 320, 321.
[108]For the critical responses to Liddell Hart's original piece, see Bvt. Col. H. R. Headlam, "Scrap the Army?" *Army Quarterly* 7 (Oct. 1923): 97–101; P.S.C., "A Reply To 'Bardell,'" ibid. (Jan. 1924): 382–87. For LH's reply to his critics, see letter, ibid. 8 (Apr. 1924): 7–10.

tion. The blitzkrieg would provide a way for Britain and her allies to win a quick and decisive victory in the next war on the Continent. The question, however, was whether he could convince Britain's generals of the wisdom of his theory.

[3]

Liddell Hart, the Generals, and World War I

Above all else, it was Liddell Hart's assessment of how the British generals would conduct a future war in Europe that shaped his military thinking during the interwar years. During this period he concluded that Britain's post–World War I military leadership was incompetent and almost sure, if confronted with another Continental war, to repeat the experience of the Western Front between 1914 and 1918. This conclusion profoundly influenced his thinking about grand strategy, strategy, and tactics.

Liddell Hart's hostile view of the generals and the next war resulted in good part from contact with Britain's military leaders during the 1920s. It was also shaped in important ways by his thinking about the Great War, which changed markedly during the 1920s and early 1930s. His early view of the war was so positive as to invite some erosion of enthusiasm; he developed an extremely negative view: that Britain's participation was an unmitigated disaster. Her conduct of the war on the Western Front was fundamentally flawed and under no circumstances to be repeated. Liddell Hart had always recognized the horrors of the Western Front—it would have been difficult for a veteran of the Somme offensive not to have been aware of the blood price Britain paid to defeat Germany. But during and immediately after the war he believed Britain's World War I commanders had done their brilliant best in a noble effort under extremely difficult circumstances. When he later came to believe this assessment completely wrong and the generals incompetents who had recklessly led countless British soldiers to their death, he naturally developed a never–again attitude with important consequences for his military thinking.

Liddell Hart's criticism of Britain's World War I leaders is difficult to separate from his criticism of the army's postwar leadership, chiefly because almost all of Britain's senior military commanders in the 1920s and early 1930s had held important command and staff positions in the war. Consider, for example, Montgomery-Massingberd, who became chief of the Imperial General Staff (CIGS) in February 1933, just as Hitler was coming to power in Germany. Montgomery-Massingberd, whom Liddell Hart disliked intensely, had been chief of staff of Gen. Sir Henry Rawlinson's Fourth Army during the Somme offensive. This pattern of promotion is not unusual (promotion in all militaries is invariably linked to seniority), but it was exacerbated in the British case by peculiar personnel policies that resulted in a postwar army led by very senior commanders.[1]

The result of this overlap was that Liddell Hart's view of the generals' performance in World War I became virtually indistinguishable from how he expected them to conduct a future war. More generally, the military commanders of World War I became synonymous with the postwar leaders. Thus, every piece of evidence pointing to misconduct in the Great War served to condemn the interwar leaders, while every negative experience with a senior officer after the war worked to reinforce Liddell Hart's emerging critical view of World War I. He developed an all-consuming distrust of Britain's military leaders, which was to have most important implications for his hope that senior officers would listen to and ultimately adopt his ideas on how to win a major land war. He was in fact left with little hope his ideas on the blitzkrieg would be adopted; World War II would instead be only a replay of World War I. That conclusion then led him to become irrevocably committed to ensuring that Britain never again got involved in a major European land war. This commitment, in turn, had profound implications for all aspects of his military thinking.

Let us first examine the marked change in Liddell Hart's thinking by recounting it from his own perspective, then consider whether the historical record bears out his harsh assessment. Was the picture of the British generals in his mind reasonably accurate? Especially important are their views on mechanization and the employment of tanks on the battlefield, both to an understanding of the broader context in which Liddell Hart developed some of his most important military ideas and to a better understanding of why he became so thoroughly disenchanted with the British army.

---

[1]On LH's dislike of Montgomery-Massingberd, see *Memoirs* 1:19, 70–71, 102–03, 120–21, 213, 227–31; recall that LH had considered Montgomery-Massingberd a brilliant general at the time of the Somme offensive. On the personnel system, see chap. 2, n. 7 and the attendant text in this book.

LIDDELL HART'S PERSPECTIVE ON THE GREAT WAR

Liddell Hart's first doubts about the war grew, ironically, out of the attention senior officers paid his ideas on infantry tactics. If the generals were brilliant strategists, he reasoned, then why did they need to rely "on a novice like me to show them the lessons of the war?"[2] He might even have wondered why the generals did not discover *during* the war the innovative infantry tactics he developed afterward. But the generals' interest in his ideas did little as yet to alter his reverential attitude. An intelligent general officer is expected to take advantage of talented junior officers; and Liddell Hart, after all, was counting on the generals to heed his advice about how to fight the next war.[3] He came to believe, however, that the generals were not very intelligent. The more direct contact he had with them, the more he was struck by "how barren of ideas most of the generals were."[4] Years later, during World War II, he remarked to a friend who had also fought in the Great War: "There is nothing so disillusioning as close contact with generals. That may explain why . . . I was such an enthusiastic young soldier—for I did not see generals 'in undress' until later."[5]

One particularly disturbing experience occurred in 1921 when General Horne, who had been his corps commander during the Somme offensive and who had commanded the First Army during the final two years of the war, visited his army post. Liddell Hart, who had "imagined him to be a superman," was asked "to explain to him the use of the sand-table in tactical instruction." The general proved to be so thoroughly "obtuse" that Liddell Hart was left deeply disturbed by the encounter.[6]

Liddell Hart also had a number of friends—men he respected very much—whose own hostility to the generals contributed to his growing doubts, among them Fuller and Lloyd George. Fuller, who often acted like a misanthrope, was a bitter critic of his fellow officers and often conveyed his views to Liddell Hart. In 1922, for example, Liddell Hart asked Fuller how he had managed to remain an innovative thinker after more than twenty years of military service. Fuller answered, "I think the answer is that it is no way necessary for a Doctor whose work

---

[2]Brian Bond, *Liddell Hart: A Study of His Military Thought* (London: Cassell, 1977), 20.
[3]A point not lost on LH; see, for example, his *The Remaking of Modern Armies* (London: Murray, 1927), 178.
[4]*Memoirs* 1:60; see also his comments quoted in B. Bond, *Liddell Hart*, 32.
[5]LH to Vivian Gaster, 19 July 1941, 1/309.
[6]*Memoirs* 1:58.

compels him to look after lunatics to go mad himself.''[7] When Liddell Hart entered the Royal United Services Institution's Gold Medal essay contest the next year (1923), Fuller told him beforehand that the judges would not accept his progressive ideas: "I am afraid you will not win the essay—you should have proved that men on donkeys armed with bows and arrows will win the next war." When he failed to win the contest, Fuller wrote, "No wonder you did not win the R.U.S.I. Essay—look at the judges!"[8]

The pronouncements of Lloyd George, another acerbic critic of the generals, surely also worked to reinforce Liddell Hart's growing doubts about his country's military leadership. The former prime minister had often clashed with the generals during World War I, and he was especially antagonistic toward Haig, who was to become Liddell Hart's principal bête noir among the World War I generals.[9] The depth of Lloyd George's hostility can be seen in Liddell Hart's description of a talk he had with Lloyd George and Gen. Hubert Gough, who was something of an outcast from the military establishment at the time because he had been blamed for the British army's serious setbacks on the Western Front in March 1918: "It was a very stimulating evening— trying to keep Gough from being swept away by L.G.'s exuberance and charm, and to keep L.G. on the rails, so that he wouldn't go too far in criticism of the 'soldiers' and thus deter Gough from unfolding, and making the necessary contribution to the task of piecing history together." Nevertheless, Liddell Hart went on to note that Lloyd George "overdid denunciation of Haig—stupid etc."[10] Liddell Hart met with the former prime minister on many other occasions during the interwar years, and apparently they almost always talked about the generals.[11]

Liddell Hart's thinking about the Great War also changed because of the emergence of new information that he saw as casting a bad light on the British army's battlefield performance. He wrote a memorandum for the record in November 1936 indicating how his view of the war had changed since the armistice. In it he provided a chart where "R

---

[7]Fuller to LH, 12 Apr. 1922, 1/302; see passim in Fuller's letters to LH, 1/302.

[8]*Memoirs* 1:92.

[9]See David Lloyd George, *The War Memoirs of David Lloyd George*, 6 vols. (London: Nicholson & Watson, 1933–36); David R. Woodward, *Lloyd George and the Generals* (Newark: University of Delaware Press, 1983).

[10]"Talk with Lloyd George and General Sir Hubert Gough (at the Athenaeum)— 28/11/35," memorandum for the record, 11/1935/107.

[11]See, for example, "Talk with Lloyd George at Criccieth," memorandum for the record, 24 Sept. 1932, 11/1932/42a; "Talk with L. G. and Hubert Gough, at Reform Club, dinner—27/1/36," memorandum for the record, 11/1936/31; also *Memoirs* 1:357–75. Finally, it should be noted LH helped Lloyd George write his *War Memoirs*.

represents a number of important facts which have a favorable bearing on the performance of the Higher Command in the war, and L a similar number on the other side":

1919:	1L vs 4R
1927:	10L vs 10R
1930:	24L vs 12R
1933:	30L vs 13R
1936:	45L vs 15R[12]

His early work on strategy and tactics naturally had required him to consider carefully how the war was fought. This undertaking had not led to any faith-shattering discoveries about the high command, although his curiosity about the conduct of the war had been piqued. As the 1920s wore on, there began to reach him theretofore unknown facts and opinions about the war that invariably portrayed the generals in a negative way. Cracks in his positive view soon began to form—cracks that grew larger with the passage of time.

In 1927, for example, the diaries and letters of the late field marshal Sir Henry Wilson were published. He had been a very influential senior officer before and during the Great War, becoming CIGS in February 1918 and holding that position for four years. Liddell Hart had claimed as late as 1922 that, along with G. F. R. Henderson, he was "the only real military genius thrown up by us for the past century." Wilson's diaries and letters were remarkably candid and exposed many of his shortcomings as well as those of other senior commanders.[13] They left Liddell Hart stunned: "Never has any man so condemned himself." The diaries, he argued, destroyed Wilson's reputation and "stamped him as of third-rate judgement."[14]

The person who probably did the most to alter Liddell Hart's view of the war was Brig. Gen. Sir James Edmonds, the army's official historian. These two met often during the interwar years, and at virtually every meeting Edmonds would provide Liddell Hart with information

---

[12]"Explanation by Avoirdupois," memorandum for the record, 29 Nov. 1936; copy in LH's correspondence with J. M. Scammell, 1/622. There is a host of memoranda for the record in LH's files that chronicle his growing disenchantment with the war, for example, "Some Odd Notes for History (1933)," 11/1933/35; "Peccavi—Contra Veritatem: How Opinions Must Yield to Facts," 1935, 11/1935/160; untitled note, 7 Dec. 1935, 11/1935/52.

[13]Quoted in B. Bond, *Liddell Hart*, 54. Maj. Gen. Sir C. E. Callwell, ed., *Field Marshal Sir Henry Wilson: His Life and Diaries*, 2 vols. (London: Cassell, 1927).

[14]Jay Luvaas, *The Education of an Army: British Military Thought, 1815–1940* (Chicago: University of Chicago Press, 1964), 391.

that portrayed the generals' conduct of the war in a negative light.[15] The official historian had few kind words for Britain's wartime leaders and, moreover, seemed to enjoy confirming Liddell Hart's worst suspicions. Edmonds's behavior also helped change Liddell Hart's thinking. After detailing the generals' errors in judgment, he would declare that he could not report them in the *Official History*, maintaining, however, that although he could not tell the complete truth, "it would be evident to those who could 'read between the lines.' "[16] This claim infuriated Liddell Hart, who was not above lashing out at Edmonds when he made this argument. As Liddell Hart became increasingly critical of the high command's performance in the Great War, Edmonds began to change direction and defend the generals. Thus, Liddell Hart remarked in a biting note to Edmonds on 17 May 1934, "No one has given me clearer evidence of the deficiencies of our higher leaders as individuals than you have, yet you are inclined to pretend that, collectively, they were up to the problem they had to face."[17] Edmonds, writing six months later in response to another verbal attack from Liddell Hart, remarked, "I see the divergence between our views increasing as we grow older. I become more and more inclined to lay weight on the difficulties of the fighting soldiers' task and sympathise with them, whilst you are becoming more and more critical and see their blunders larger than their achievements."[18] The official historian's defense of the generals, after he had worked to condemn them with damning evidence, further reinforced Liddell Hart's mounting suspicion that the entire system was rotten.

Liddell Hart's relationship with General Edmonds points to a related factor that bears mentioning. Another general told Liddell Hart in 1936 that Edmonds was "utterly unscrupulous" and "just a spiteful old gossip."[19] There is much information in Liddell Hart's files to support these charges. Moreover, not only Edmonds but many other generals

[15]On Edmonds as official historian, see David French, " 'Official But Not History'? Sir James Edmonds and the Official History of the Great War," *Journal of the Royal United Service Institute for Defence Studies* 131 (Mar. 1986): 58–63; also Jay Luvaas, "The First British Official Historians," *Military Affairs* 26 (Summer 1962): 49–58. LH's memoranda recounting the details of their many meetings are throughout sec. 11 of his papers; for their extensive correspondence filled with information about the Great War, see 1/259.

[16]*Memoirs* 1:211. LH published a book about World War I in 1938 titled *Through the Fog of War* (New York: Random House); it is dedicated to "Archimedes [a pseudonym for General Edmonds], who knows more of the history of the War than he will ever write."

[17]LH was almost always courteous in his personal correspondence. Key exceptions to this rule are found in his correspondence with Edmonds; see esp. their correspondence for 1934 and 1939, in 1/259.

[18]Edmonds to LH, 9 Nov. 1934, 1/259, prompted by a vitriolic letter of 6 Nov. 1934 from LH.

[19]"Cruttwell's Opinions, 2nd Oct. 1936," memorandum for the record, 11/1936/80.

and civilians involved in army-related affairs gossiped with Liddell Hart, as can be seen from the vast array of gossip-filled letters and memoranda in his files, some of them referred to in his *Memoirs*. Col. (later F.M.) Michael Carver remarked in 1965, after reading the galleys of those *Memoirs*, "It is astonishing, really, how much freedom senior officers and others had in those days to discuss matters of real military importance with those outside the machine, and also to gossip about each other. It certainly would not be tolerated these days." And Carver had not examined Liddell Hart's archives. Liddell Hart maintained in later years that he was an outsider to the military establishment. This is simply not true. Throughout almost all of the interwar period, he was keenly aware of and occasionally involved in the bureaucratic struggles of the day. Such direct and constant exposure to the seamier side of organizational life undoubtedly did much to decrease his respect for Britain's military leaders. Little wonder that he claimed, "There is nothing so disillusioning as close contact with generals."[20]

There is a point about Liddell Hart's gossiping that is difficult to prove but still worth noting. Going through his personal papers one has the clear sense that once his disenchantment with the generals was widely known—probably in the latter part of the 1920s—many with whom he corresponded and talked would pass him information showing the generals in a negative light and reinforcing his critical thoughts. At the same time, hardly anyone appears to have been willing to defend the generals before Liddell Hart; he was, after all, a formidable intellect and a skillful debater. This one-sidedness, too, would confirm his critical view.

Liddell Hart's position as a journalist also contributed to his falling out with the military. The relationship between a good journalist and the institution he covers is not purely adversarial but usually has an adversarial dimension. Given his strongly held opinions on many military issues, Liddell Hart was almost certain to clash with the army leadership. In fact, his first major run-in with the army over a news story came in April 1927 when he wrote a *Daily Telegraph* article critical of the army's handling of the experimental armored force. It badly strained his previously quite good relationship with the army's high command. The dispute soon cooled down, but mutual distrust was thereafter a key ingredient in the relationship.

Finally, large segments of the British public changed their view of the Great War in the two postwar decades, reaching the conclusion that British participation had been a terribly costly mistake. Liddell Hart's writings contributed to the growth of this widespread disen-

[20]Col. Michael Carver to LH, 22 Feb. 1965, 1/153. LH to Gaster, 19 July 1941, 1/309.

chantment, which undoubtedly contributed in turn to his growing disillusionment. He was an integral part of that powerful body of forces that shaped the view, still widespread today, that Britain's military leaders in the Great War were incompetent and the war itself a tragic blunder. This point is nicely illustrated by Liddell Hart's close friendships with C. S. Forester and Robert Graves, two of the leading revisionists among the literati. In fact Liddell Hart vetted Forester's classic antiwar novel, *The General* (1936).[21]

Liddell Hart had become by the mid-1930s a bitter critic of the British military's performance in World War I and, more generally, a strong critic of the military profession. His level of bitterness is reflected in his description of Haig in a 1935 diary note: "He was a man of supreme egoism and utter lack of scruple—who, to his overweaning ambition sacrificed hundreds of thousands of men. A man who betrayed even his most devoted assistants as well as the Government which he served. A man who gained his ends by trickery of a kind that was not merely immoral but criminal." Actually, it mattered little to him by this time which generals were in charge; the problem, he believed, was much bigger than specific individuals. As he noted in the mid-1930s, "The men [who led the nation in World War I] have gone; [but] the system remains."[22]

ASSESSING THE BRITISH GENERALS

Liddell Hart's characterization of Britain's generals as incompetents is widely accepted, but it is not accurate. He has bestowed upon us a distorted description. The majority were not troglodytes but intelligent

---

[21]On changing views of the Great War, see, inter alia, Bernard Bergonzi, *Heroes' Twilight: A Study of the Literature of the Great War* (London: Constable, 1965); Paul Fussell, *The Great War and Modern Memory* (New York: Oxford University Press, 1975); Samuel Hynes, *The Auden Generation: Literature and Politics in England in the 1930s* (London: Bodley Head, 1976); Robert Wohl, *The Generation of 1914* (Cambridge, Mass.: Harvard University Press, 1979), chaps. 3, 6. For the correspondence with Forester and Graves, see 1/292 and 1/327 respectively. The vetted copy of Forester's *The General* (Harmondsworth: Penguin, 1936) is in 15/7/17.

[22]Untitled note, 7 May 1935, 11/1935/137; untitled note, 1 Dec. 1935, 11/1935/50. LH muted his deep-seated disenchantment with the conduct of the war in the books he wrote about the conflict. He believed it would be counterproductive to be overly critical in his public writings; see untitled note, 7 Dec. 1935 entry, 11/1935/52; also his comments about *The War in Outline* in his "Explanation by Avoirdupois." His books about World War I are: *The Real War, 1914–1918* (London: Faber, 1930) pub. in rev. and enlarged form as *A History of the World War, 1914–1918* (London: Faber, 1934); *The War in Outline, 1914–1918* (London: Faber, 1936); *Reputations* (London: Murray, 1928), 81–123; *Through the Fog of War.*

and thoughtful officers whose performance looks impressive enough when the problems they faced are accurately assessed. This is not to imply that most were great strategists or brilliant battlefield commanders. They were not, but it would be unrealistic to expect them to meet such a standard. No army in modern history has had commanders close to that ideal. Some armies have performed better than others, so it is possible to make critical judgments about the quality of an army's leadership. On this count Britain's commanders look surprisingly good.

Liddell Hart's case against the generals has three components: they were incompetent in the Great War;[23] after the war they would not listen to his ideas or at least take them seriously (he being an outsider largely ignored by the military establishment); and in the interwar years they were firmly opposed to change, not interested in mechanization, and showed few signs of understanding how the tank should have been integrated into the army and employed on the battlefield.

The literature on the conduct of World War I is generally of poor quality. There are few studies that systematically examine Allied military policy on the Western Front between 1914 and 1918. It is difficult, for example, to trace the development of British, as well as French and American, battlefield tactics. Also, despite the frequent references to alternatives to a strategy of slugging it out with the Germans on the Western Front, there are no studies that systematically consider those alternatives. Furthermore, there are very few good studies of Germany's conduct of the war, either at the tactical or strategic level.[24] Thus, it is not only difficult to evaluate the British generals' performance but hard to consider their conduct of the war from a com-

[23]LH never offered a systematic analysis of the British generals' conduct of World War I but focused mainly on their performance in specific battles, although he sometimes would make sweeping generalizations supported with anecdotal evidence. Thus, it is difficult to challenge this element of his case directly.

[24]Among the best works on Britain's conduct of the war on the Western Front are Shelford Bidwell and Dominick Graham, *Fire-Power: British Army Weapons and Theories of War, 1904–1945* (London: Allen & Unwin, 1982), 59–146; Hubert Essame, *The Battle for Europe, 1918* (New York: Scribner's, 1972); Maj. Gen. E. K. G. Sixsmith, *British Generalship in the Twentieth Century* (London: Arms & Armour, 1970), chaps. 2–8; John Terraine, *Douglas Haig: The Educated Soldier* (London: Hutchinson, 1963); T. H. E. Travers, *The Killing Ground: The British Army, the Western Front, and the Emergence of Modern Warfare, 1900–1918* (Boston: Allen & Unwin, 1987). The multivolume Official British History of World War I, ed. Brig. Gen. James E. Edmonds, is also useful. On battlefield tactics, Bidwell and Graham, *Fire-Power*, and Travers, *Killing Ground*, are useful. On German conduct of the war, two exceptions are Timothy T. Lupfer, *The Dynamics of Doctrine: The Changes in German Tactical Doctrine during the First World War*, Leavenworth Paper no. 4 (Fort Leavenworth, Kans.: U.S. Army Command and General Staff College, July 1981); and Capt. G. C. Wynne, *If Germany Attacks: The Battle in Depth in the West* (London: Faber, 1940).

parative perspective, which is essential for a proper evaluation of their failures and accomplishments. It would take a whole book to address this complex issue; here, I can only offer some points that challenge the conventional assumptions. My aim is not to substitute one over-simplified description for another. The subject is too complex to permit that; moreover the poor quality of the existing literature does not allow for categorical judgments at this juncture. There is, though, ample evidence that the usual description is flawed and that a detailed and systematic analysis of the British generals' performance would show them in a favorable light. This is especially true if one compares the British army's performance with that of the other principal armies, in which case the British generals appear quite competent.

To assess the British generals' conduct of World War I, four sets of questions must be answered. First, what result did they produce? Who won the war, and how does the overall performance of the British army compare with that of other armies? Second, what were the organizational problems they faced in building up their army, and how well did they deal with them? Did they do a satisfactory job of raising and training an army for the Western Front, and did they provide adequate support for those forces? Third, were tactics and strategy wisely chosen? How appropriate were they against the German army? And did the generals actively search for alternatives? Were they receptive to new weapons and novel ideas for employing them on the battlefield? Fourth, does hindsight reveal an alternative grand strategy? In other words, was there any option other than fighting the Germans along the Western Front?

Britain and her allies, *not* Germany, won the war. Any fair-minded assessment must ascribe considerable weight to the fact the British army ultimately prevailed in a war of unprecedented scale against a formidable adversary. Furthermore, of the principal armies engaged in the Great War (the German, the British, the French, and the Russian), the British was the only one that neither collapsed nor was faced with large-scale insurrection.[25] The Russians effectively withdrew from the war in late 1917 when their armies disintegrated from the deadly combination of social upheaval on the homefront and the blows of the German army at the front lines. The Germans sued for peace in the fall of 1918 largely because their military was crumbling in the face of increasingly powerful Allied offensives. The French suffered serious mutinies during the spring of 1917 in the wake of the abortive Nivelle

[25]This is not to imply that the British army faced no problems of unrest; see Douglas Gill and Gloden Dallas, *The Unknown Army* (London: Verso, 1985).

offensive.[26] For the remainder of the war, French commanders, fearing further mutinies, were very cautious when using their army for offensive purposes. The British army, in contrast to these Continental armies, never cracked and became increasingly formidable as the war progressed.

The British army's strength is highlighted by its role in defeating Germany in the war's final year. The German army opened the 1918 campaign in March with a massive offensive on the Western Front.[27] Further German offensives immediately followed. The British army, which absorbed the brunt of those attacks, suffered serious setbacks and came under tremendous pressure. Then the Allies began launching their own offensives in mid-July 1918, which lasted until Germany was knocked out of the war in early November 1918. The British army played the central role in those offensives. Consider that in the final four months of the war the British army captured more German prisoners than the French, American, and Belgian armies combined and that the British army captured 2540 German guns while the French and American forces, respectively, captured 1880 and 1421 guns.[28] The commanders who led those British forces through the difficult years of war and in the great offensives of 1918 surely deserve some credit for their armies' remarkable resiliency and growing fighting power over time.

The British generals had a significant organizational problem the commanders of the other major armies were spared. The pre–World War I British army was very small by Continental standards and was

[26]On the Russians, see Gen. A. A. Brussilov, *A Soldier's Notebook, 1914–1918* (London: Macmillan, 1930); Maj. Gen. Sir Alfred Knox, *With the Russian Army, 1914–1917: Being Chiefly Extracts from the Diary of a Military Attache*, vol. 2 (London: Hutchinson, 1921); Allan K. Wildman, *The End of the Russian Imperial Army: The Old Army and the Soldiers' Revolt (March–April 1917)* (Princeton, N.J.: Princeton University Press, 1980). On the Germans, see Essame, *Battle for Europe*, chaps. 14–15; John Terraine, *To Win A War: 1918, The Year of Victory* (New York: Doubleday, 1981), esp. chaps. 8–9. On the French, Jere Clemens King, *Generals and Politicians: Conflict between France's High Command, Parliament and Government, 1914–1918* (Berkeley and Los Angeles: University of California Press, 1951), chaps. 8–10; Richard M. Watt, *Dare Call It Treason* (New York: Simon & Schuster, 1963).

[27]For a short summary of Britain's contribution, see Brian Bond, *British Military Policy between the Two World Wars* (New York: Oxford University Press, 1980), 1–6. On Britain's role, see also Brig. Gen. James E. Edmonds, ed., *Military Operations: France and Belgium, 1918*, 5 vols., Official British History of World War I (London: Macmillan, 1935–47); Essame, *Battle for Europe*; Terraine, *To Win a War*. Formidable Canadian and Australian forces fought with the British army. On the German offensive, see Martin Middlebrook, *The Kaiser's Battle, 21 March 1918: The First Day of the German Spring Offensive* (London: Lane, 1978).

[28]War Office, *Statistics of the Military Effort of the British Empire during the Great War, 1914–1920* (London: His Majesty's Stationery Office, Mar. 1922), 757.

not designed for rapid expansion in the event of war. The British thus had to face the daunting task of raising and training a large and powerful army while deeply engaged in a major war. This problem was compounded by the fact that the small prewar army, which would have to serve as the foundation upon which the new armies were built, had few experiences—especially in the training process—that prepared it for the large-scale operations that became commonplace in the war. The Germans, the French, and the Russians, on the other hand, had organized and trained their prewar armies for a major European land war. Britain's problem was further compounded by her sizable extra-European commitments, which put demands on her army that complicated the task of raising and training an army for the Western Front. Thus, Britain alone was guaranteed to face special growing pains under fire.[29] Battlefield performance provides substantial evidence the generals overcame these formidable organizational problems.

What can one say about the British generals' willingness to experiment with new weapons and tactical ideas as well as their ability to learn from battlefield experience? The war on the Western Front, often portrayed as a mindless slugging match, was actually surprisingly dynamic at the tactical level.[30] After all, poison gas, the tank, and the airplane were first used in the Great War, not World War II. These weapons had to be incorporated into existing battlefield doctrine. Furthermore, there were constant debates about how to employ the traditional arms—infantry and artillery. These debates were played out on the front lines in the form of frequent tactical adjustments and counteradjustments by the principal combatants.

The British generals responded reasonably well to this dynamic environment. They were certainly willing to use airplanes, poison gas,

---

[29]John Gooch, *Armies in Europe* (London: Routledge & Kegan Paul, 1980), chap. 5. The Americans, who entered the war in April 1917 with a very small army, faced problems similar to Britain's. Unlike the British, however, who were heavily involved in the fighting on the Western Front from the war's outset, the Americans had the luxury of building up their forces at a measured pace while the British and French held the line against the Germans. On problems the Americans nonetheless faced in rapidly building a mass army, see Col. Leonard P. Ayres, *The War with Germany: A Statistical Summary* (Washington, D.C.: GPO, 1919). On problems Britain faced as it expanded its army, see Dominick Graham, "Sans Doctrine: British Army Tactics in the First World War," in Timothy Travers and Christon Archer, eds., *Men at War: Politics, Technology and Innovation in the Twentieth Century* (Chicago: Precedent, 1982), 62–92; Edmonds, *Military Operations: France and Belgium, 1918*, 5:587–602; *Sir Douglas Haig's Despatches*, ed. J. H. Boraston (New York: Dutton, 1920), 311–57.

[30]Bidwell and Graham, *Fire-Power*; Lupfer, *Dynamics of Doctrine*; Hew Strachan, *European Armies and the Conduct of War* (Boston: Allen & Unwin, 1983), chap. 9; Wynne, *If Germany Attacks*.

and the tank for military advantage. The British army actually introduced the tank to the battlefield during the Somme offensive and by mid-1918 was placing marked reliance on it. Still, in the early years of the war the generals were not particularly efficient at making tactical adjustments after important battles.[31] Changing tactics in the midst of a war *is* a very difficult task, especially in the early stages of war when an army is making the demanding transition from a peacetime to a wartime organization. Even the German army, highly regarded for its tactical innovations in the Great War, was slow to make advances in the early years of the conflict. Its major tactical innovations came in the final two years. The British army's problem was probably further compounded by its rapid expansion while under fire, combined with its lack of preparation for a Continental war in the years before 1914. Regardless, the generals had by 1917 become reasonably proficient at learning tactical lessons from previous battles, a skill that surely helps account for the army's achievements in 1918.

One might ask, If the British generals were basically progressive in their tactical thinking, why did the defeat of Germany take so long and involve so many casualties? Intelligent generals surely should have been able to find a more efficient way to victory. The unpleasant truth is that innovative tactics were not going to provide an important advantage against a formidable opponent like the German army, which was always quick to adjust to new British tactics. This is not to deny the desirability of employing smart tactics, only to observe that it would not have led to significant reductions in casualties.[32]

[31]On British use of tanks, see Kenneth Macksey, *The Tank Pioneers* (London: Jane's, 1981), chaps. 2–3; also LH, *The Tanks*, vol. 1 (London: Cassell, 1959), pt. 1. On British receptivity to the airplane, see Malcolm Cooper, *The Birth of Independent Airpower: British Air Policy in the First World War* (Boston: Allen & Unwin, 1986); H. A. Jones and Walter Raleigh, *The War in the Air: Being the Story of the Part Played in the Great War by the Royal Air Force*, 6 vols. and apps. (Oxford: Clarendon, 1922–37). On British willingness to experiment with gas, see Maj. Gen. C. H. Foulkes, *"Gas!": The Story of the Special Brigade* (London: Blackwood, 1936); L. F. Haber, *The Poisonous Cloud: Chemical Warfare in the First World War* (Oxford: Clarendon, 1986). On tactical adjustments, see Bidwell, *Fire-Power*, 59–146; T. H. E. Travers, "Learning and Decision-making on the Western Front, 1915–1916: The British Example," *Canadian Journal of History* 18 (Apr. 1983): 87–97; idem, *Killing Ground*.

[32]The British army's casualty levels for August, September, and October 1917, when it was heavily involved in bloody frontal assaults against German positions at Ypres, compared with British casualty levels for the same three months in 1918, when the German army was beginning to fold and the British army was becoming increasingly involved in mobile operations at the tactical level, illustrate the point: British casualties in those three months of victorious fighting in 1918 were 122,272, 114,831, and 121,046 respectively. The casualty figures for the same three months in 1917, when the army was engaged in the infamous Passchendaele offensives, were 81,080, 81,249, and 119,808 respectively. Winston Churchill, *The World Crisis* (New York: Scribner's, 1927), 3:299.

The argument is sometimes made that although there was no easy way to defeat the armies of the Second Reich, there was an alternative strategy that would have resulted in considerably fewer British casualties but still provided the means to wear down the German army to the point of surrender. British strategy on the Western Front placed heavy reliance on launching major offensives to serve two broad purposes: to wear down the powerful German army, each offensive being one step in a cumulative process of bleeding the Germans white;[33] and to find a desperately desired way out of the war of attrition that had set in on the Western Front. Thus, specific offensives were also designed to crack the German front in the hope of producing a decisive victory. The relative importance of these two goals varied over time and among commanders.

Some critics of this offensive approach maintained that Britain should instead have adopted a defensive strategy that would allow only some limited offensives.[34] They argued a decisive breakthrough was not possible, and in waging a war of attrition, casualty exchange ratios markedly favor the defender, not the attacker, thus obviating both rationales for offensives. The aim should therefore have been to force the German army to exhaust itself by conducting fruitless offensives against a well-entrenched British army. Circumscribed offensives were consistent with this aim. Initiating limited attacks—where British forces achieved surprise, quickly overran the Germans' forward positions, and then assumed a defensive posture—was acceptable because the resulting British casualty levels would be low and because such offensives were well-suited for baiting the Germans into launching fruitless offensives. Moreover, it would be necessary, once the Germans had been worn down by years of failed offensives, to launch a major offensive to knock them completely out of the war. Yet the essence of the critics' strategy was to remain on the defensive for as much of the war as possible.

This alternative strategy was simply not feasible. Adopting a defensive posture on the Western Front would have meant giving up all hope of scoring a rapid victory and accepting instead a protracted war of attrition, an untenable position for Britain's political as well as military leaders, who were under great pressure to end the war on the Western Front quickly. Political expediency required the launching of offensives that might break through the German defenses and produce a decisive defeat. One might argue it should have been clear to the British generals

[33]*Sir Douglas Haig's Despatches*, 319–27.
[34]See F.M. Sir William Robertson, *Soldiers and Statesmen* (London: Cassell, 1926), 1:184. The case for this defensive strategy is well put by Churchill, *World Crisis*, vol. 3, chap. 2.

that a major breakthrough was simply not possible, and thus there was no way to end the war quickly. But the generals could not be sure of this until several attempts to break the German front had failed. What appears obvious with hindsight is seldom so apparent at the time. (Consider, for example, that the Allies' 1918 offensives were not expected to lead to victory, but they did. Allied commanders believed the war would drag on for at least another year.) To complicate matters further, there were sound reasons for thinking offensives might lead to major victories. German offensives on the Eastern Front, for example, usually met with great success, and the Germans did knock the Russians out of the war. Also, both the Schlieffen plan and the 1918 German offensives appear to have come close to knocking the Allies out of the war. Thus it was not entirely clear that offensive strategies were doomed to failure.

The most important reason the British army had to launch major offensives is they were essential for maintaining the integrity of the Triple Entente as well as maximizing the prospects of a German defeat. Although it is not widely recognized, Britain's initial plans for the Western Front actually called for a defensive strategy.[35] The aim was to let the French and the Russians launch powerful offensives that would wear down the Germans. Those two allies, of course, would wear themselves down in the process, leaving Britain in the desirable position of delivering the coup de grace and then dictating the terms of peace. Britain's allies, especially the Russians, would not tolerate this strategy. They insisted the British army launch vigorous offensives and participate fully in the task of wearing down the Second Reich's powerful ground forces. Britain was thus forced to jettison her defensive strategy in the course of 1915.[36]

There was a second reason for assuming an offensive posture, and it too stemmed from Britain's participation in the Triple Entente. To increase the prospects of defeating Germany, each alliance partner had to keep constant pressure on the German forces facing it and at the same time be capable of coming to the rescue of the other armies, should either start to crack under German pressure.[37] This meant all Entente partners would have to launch major offensives. Haig's 1917

[35]See David French, *British Strategy and War Aims, 1914–1916* (Boston: Allen & Unwin, 1986). The discussion in the remainder of this paragraph is based on this book.

[36]British leaders were especially concerned that disagreement among the Allies on this issue would favor Germany's vigorous efforts to split the Triple Entente; see L. L. Farrar, Jr., *Divide and Conquer: German Efforts to Conclude a Separate Peace, 1914–1918* (Boulder, Co.: East European Quarterly, 1978).

[37]Keith Neilson, *Strategy and Supply: The Anglo-Russian Alliance, 1914–1917* (Boston: Allen & Unwin, 1984).

offensive around Ypres, for example, succeeded in taking pressure off the French, who were reeling in the wake of the disastrous Nivelle offensive. Moreover, the decision to launch that offensive was significantly influenced by the belief that it would help the Russian army, which was on the verge of collapse. If the British army had adopted a defensive strategy and stuck to it, the Germans would have been able to reduce the size of their forces opposite the British front and concentrate greater forces than otherwise possible against the French and the Russians. After knocking them out of the war, the Germans could have then turned the full weight of their armies against the British. Germany, in other words, would have been able to deal with its adversaries in turn. Britain's only hope in a war against a powerful opponent like Germany was to have strong alliance partners who, along with her, were willing to launch major offensives against the German army.[38]

Another argument one hears is that the strong case for an offensive strategy is ultimately outweighed by considerations about relative casualties.[39] The offender, so the argument goes, suffers much greater casualties than the defender, making any offensive strategy prohibitively costly. The subject of casualty levels is complicated, and unfortunately the historical record on casualty balances is murky. Nevertheless, the evidence leaves little doubt that offenders do not inevitably suffer greater casualties than defenders, a point illustrated by the fact German offensives against French forces apparently always resulted in greater French casualties.[40] It seems, however, that the attacking British did have higher casualty levels than the defending Germans, although the disparity was not great.

[38]On Haig's offensive, see Terraine, *Western Front*, 152–54; Neilson, *Strategy and Supply*, chap. 7. On the necessity of unity, this same logic applied to the problem of deterring Germany from starting a war in the first place, as became evident in the 1930s.

[39]Haig was apparently sensitive to this argument; see *Sir Douglas Haig's Despatches*, 325.

[40]Churchill, *World Crisis* 3:40–41. Assuming that the relative fighting skills of both sides are roughly equal and that neither side has markedly deficient tactics, one would expect the offender to suffer significantly more casualties than the defender, generally about three casualties for every one inflicted on the defender. It *appears* that this rule of thumb did not hold in World War I because the side usually identified as the defender invariably did considerable counterattacking in the protracted battles, which meant, in effect, that the defender was assuming an offensive role while the side usually referred to as the offender was on the defensive. General Balck, for example, writes in his famous work on German infantry tactics, "The Battle of the Somme led to a complete change of views concerning the conduct of the defense. The passive endurance of the hostile fire ceased. A fresh, offensive spirit was incorporated in the conduct of defense" (*Development of Tactics: World War*, trans. Harry Bell [Fort Leavenworth, Kans.: General Service Schools Press, 1922], 80). The distinction between offender and defender in many of the war's bloodiest battles was less than clear cut. The 3:1 rule seems to hold, but one must be discriminating in applying the terms *offender* and *defender*.

There are two schools of thought on British–German casualty ratios. Winston Churchill argues that the ratio was somewhere between 3:2 and 4:2 in those cases where Britain took the offensive. Brigadier General Edmonds, Sir Charles Oman, and John Terraine contest Churchill's figures and argue that the ratio was about 1:1.[41] It seems clear from a handful of studies on the subject that Churchill's figures are the most reliable.[42] Yet Churchill's numbers require qualification because he does not consider the year 1918, when the ratio was 1:1 with Britain on the offensive, and he uses casualty figures for the entire front rather than the specific battle area, a calculation likely to bias the ratio in the Germans' favor. It seems reasonable to conclude that the British–German casualty ratio was about 3:2. Although this is not an ideal figure, the disparity was not so marked as to make offensives prohibitively costly. It was the Germans, not the British, who lost the war of attrition.[43]

Finally, there was no way Britain and her allies could have defeated Germany by shifting the focus of effort to a peripheral area or employing an indirect approach to produce a sudden German collapse. Pursuing sideshows only worked to increase Germany's chances of winning the war.[44] The reason is simple: a policy of horizontal escalation held no promise of inflicting a decisive defeat on Germany, yet it worked to weaken the Allies' overall position by diverting substantial numbers of British and French forces and very few German forces away from the critical Western Front. No military thinker then or since has provided an alternative grand strategy Britain could have adopted that would have inflicted a rapid and decisive defeat on the Germans.

This includes Liddell Hart, who never explained how the World War I British generals, once faced with war against Germany, could have

[41]Churchill, *World Crisis* 3:41–42; Edmonds, *Military Operations: France and Belgium, 1916*, 1:496–97; Miles, *Military Operations: France and Belgium, 1916*, 2:xiii–xvii, 553; Sir Charles Oman, "The German Losses on the Somme," *Nineteenth Century and After*, 101 (May 1927): 694–705; Terraine, *Haig*, 231–36. See also John Terraine, *The Road to Passchendaele: The Flanders Offensive of 1917, a Study in Inevitability* (London: Cooper, 1977), 215, 343–47; idem, *The Smoke and the Fire: Myths and Anti-Myths of War, 1861–1945* (London: Sidgwick & Jackson, 1980), chaps. 3–5.

[42]Robin Prior, *Churchill's 'World Crisis' as History* (London: Croom Helm, 1983), 221–30; M. J. Williams, "Thirty Per Cent: A Study in Casualty Statistics," *Journal of the Royal United Services Institution* 109 (Feb. 1964): 51–55; idem, "The Treatment of the German Losses on the Somme in the British Official History: 'Military Operations France and Belgium, 1916' Volume II," ibid. 111 (Feb. 1966): 69–74.

[43]Prior, *Churchill's 'World Crisis' as History*, 228; the 3:2 is not a firm figure; a thorough analysis of British–German casualty ratios might well show a ratio more favorable to Britain. Churchill argued during the war that such offensives were unduly expensive and would not lead to victory (*World Crisis* 3:29, 42–44).

[44]See Spenser Wilkinson, "Killing No Murder: An Examination of Some New Theories of War," *Army Quarterly* 15 (Oct. 1927): esp. 14–19; also Paul M. Kennedy, *The Rise and Fall of British Naval Mastery* (London: Lane, 1976), chap. 9.

secured victory yet avoided the protracted conflict that developed on the Western Front. In 1930, F.M. Sir George Milne (the CIGS), who was well aware of Liddell Hart's criticism of the generals' conduct of the war, asked him if "it ever occurred to you to ask yourself 'How would you have conducted the Great War?'" Liddell Hart responded to the question without outlining an alternative policy:

> I have, in fact, tried to do what you suggest—although it is not really a test, as I know, from the enemy's account, what course [not described] would have paid. Further, it is really no part of an historian's job to argue what should have been done, in matters that are too late to mend. . . . It is not for me to say my own solution [not described] would have worked better. But what I can say is that I repeatedly find that the actual commander has chosen one of the solutions I considered first [not described] and rejected as too obvious or too fallible—and that in execution the solution fails as one had foreseen it would.[45]

The closest Liddell Hart ever came to explaining how Britain could have avoided participation in the war on the Western Front and still inflict a decisive defeat on the Second Reich was in his famous lecture on the British way in warfare delivered to the Royal United Services Institution in January 1931. In it he argued that Britain should have avoided raising a large army to fight on the Continent and have instead relied on a naval blockade and military operations in the Near East.[46] This proposal provided not a strategy for defeating Germany but rather one for ensuring that Russia and France, not Britain, would have the awful task of wearing down the Second Reich's powerful armies.

To defeat the Germans, Britain and her allies had no choice but to concentrate their forces in northeastern France and engage in a bloody war of attrition with frightening casualty levels. The leading British generals, to their credit, recognized this at the time and resisted all attempts to divert forces from the decisive arena in France.[47] The British generals—like their counterparts in France, Germany, and Russia—should be judged by how well they conducted the war of attrition they were consigned to fight. The British army not only did not crack

[45]Milne to LH, 2 Sept. 1930, and LH to Milne, 6 Sept. 1930, both in 1/512. See also Gen. William E. Ironside to LH, 19 Mar. 1937, and LH to Ironside, 23 Mar. 1937, both in 1/401.

[46]"Economic Pressure or Continental Victories," *Journal of the Royal United Services Institution* 76 (Aug. 1931): 486–510; rep. almost verbatim in LH, *The British Way in Warfare* (London: Faber, 1932), chap. 1.

[47]On the conflict over this issue, see David R. Woodward, "Britain in a Continental War: The Civil-Military Debate over the Strategical Direction of the Great War of 1914–1918," *Albion* 12 (Spring 1980): 37–65; also useful: Paul Guinn, *British Strategy and Politics, 1914–1918* (London: Clarendon, 1965); Lord Hankey, *The Supreme Command, 1914–1918*, 2 vols. (London: Allen & Unwin, 1961); Robertson, *Soldiers and Statesmen*.

but was the dominant army on the Western Front at the war's end. Her generals could not have been as incompetent as Liddell Hart and others claim.

It is easy to refute Liddell Hart's second charge, that he was an outsider during the interwar years who had difficulty finding an attentive audience among the army's leaders. During his postwar years in the army (1918–24), he worked closely with a handful of senior officers who exerted themselves to ensure that his views were given serious consideration (chap. 2). By his own admission, he was treated with genuine respect by high-ranking officers even though he was a mere junior officer. Remember, he wrote in 1923, "I am deeply grateful for the large measure of courtesy and encouragement I have received in regard to my own military theories; far more probably than any other profession would have shown to a comparatively junior officer."[48] In short, the evidence from his army years would suggest his ideas received serious consideration.

It is not true that his relationship with the generals was fine as long as he was wearing a uniform but that they refused to countenance his views when he left the service. He was in constant contact throughout the 1920s and 1930s with the army's most prominent generals and with many promising younger officers, as the vast correspondence from these years in his personal papers shows. He also met frequently and corresponded with the reigning CIGS. With the exception of Montgomery-Massingberd (CIGS, February 1933–April 1936), these officers were invariably cordial and willing to engage him in serious discussion. He remarked in his diary in July 1936, "I have received far more friendliness than hostility from Regulars."[49] Although Liddell Hart has left the impression that he was an outsider to the military establishment, one who was viewed with deep-seated suspicion and hostility, the following incidents do not bear out the description. They do, however, reflect the basic pattern of relations between Liddell Hart and the generals; they are not exceptions.

First, in late 1926, Liddell Hart was elected a member of the Army and Navy Club. He learned that his name had been proposed for membership by the CIGS, Field Marshal Milne, and that it was "seconded by . . . the Inspector of Artillery." Second, in April 1927, after he wrote that controversial article criticizing the army's handling of the experimental armored force, he was told he no longer had open access to the War Office but would need an escort to move about certain

[48]Letter, *Army Quarterly* 8 (Apr. 1924): 8.
[49]"Thoughts Jotted Down—To Be Expanded," memorandum for the record, 17 July 1936 entry, 11/1936/2-25c.

areas. His editor at the *Daily Telegraph* told him he was not surprised by this restriction because "other papers [had been] complaining about my *special privileges*." Third, when the editors at the *Times* were considering Liddell Hart for a position with the paper, inquiries were made about him at the War Office. As one of the editors notes in his diary, "My inquiries . . . show that his appointment would be welcome to many there, including the C.I.G.S." Fourth, in late 1935, Liddell Hart received a letter from Maj. Gen. Giffard Martel, who told him:

> I feel I must write you a line to tell you how very much all soldiers whom I have met, have appreciated your writings in *The Times* . . . you may think you can see no result from all this work of yours. Naturally results come slowly in the British Army, as in anything else that is British, but I have heard so many favourable comments on your work that I feel sure that it is having a far greater effect than you imagine.

Fifth, in June 1937 he received a letter from Lt. Gen. Sir John Evetts, who was stationed in Palestine: "When the C.I.G.S. was here last March, I asked him jokingly if one would still be black listed for corresponding with and talking to you. He was very amused and replied: 'On the contrary I shall encourage anyone who wants to develop new thoughts and ideas.'" In his response to Evetts, Liddell Hart noted, "Curiously, he said much the same thing to another Commander out in the Near East—in that case unprompted."[50] These incidents show that though relations between Liddell Hart and the generals were not always smooth and they did not always follow his advice, he was anything but an embattled outsider against a cohesive and hostile institution.

Key to understanding Liddell Hart's relationship with the army during the interwar period is recognition that his attitude toward individual officers was quite different from his attitude toward the army as an abstract institution.[51] There is little doubt that by the late 1920s he was hostile to the institution and held out little hope it would pay serious attention to his ideas. Despite this negative attitude toward *the* army, he had quite good relations with most of the wide-ranging body of officers with whom he was in constant contact. His correspondence

---

[50]"Diary Notes. 1926," 27 Nov. entry, 11/1926/1b; "Diary Notes—early 1927," 16 May entry, 11/1927/1b, emphasis added; Donald McLachlan, *In the Chair: Barrington-Ward of the Times, 1927–1948* (London: Weidenfeld & Nicolson, 1971), 155; Martel letter quoted in a joint talk by Anthony J. Trythall and Brian Bond, 12 Oct. 1978, at the Royal United Services Institution—see "The Fuller–Liddell Hart Lecture," *Journal of the Royal United Services Institution* 124 (Mar. 1979): 25; Evetts to LH, 18 June 1937, 1/272; LH to Evetts, 9 July 1937, 1/272.
[51]Reflected in LH, untitled note, 1 Dec. 1935, 11/1935/50.

implies he liked and respected the majority of officers he encountered. Thus he was not infrequently treated with respect because of genuine friendship and because the officers in question respected his views, even if he might not always agree with them.

There were other reasons, however, for officers to pay serious attention to Liddell Hart's views. He was a highly regarded journalist who wrote for a large audience. As military correspondent for the *Daily Telegraph* and later the *Times* he could help or hurt the army in important ways. Fuller told him as early as 1925, "When I make a criticism the Army Council is perturbed. When you make one it is shaken to its roots. . . . You have a much greater popular reputation."[52] That reputation, of course, grew substantially with the passage of time, as did the incentives to pay him serious attention.

An excellent example of Liddell Hart's ability to compel the army leadership to take him seriously involves an incident usually referred to as "the Tidworth affair." The secretary of state for war announced in March 1926 that an experimental armored force would soon be formed. The decision was made in December of that year to place Fuller in charge of the new unit, which was to be established in early 1927 at Tidworth on Salisbury Plain. Fuller eventually refused to take the position, for reasons not directly relevant here, and it appeared by the spring of 1927 that the army was reneging on its commitment to build the force. Liddell Hart then wrote his 22 April *Daily Telegraph* article accusing the army of backsliding. The article struck the War Office like a thunderbolt, forcing the army to move ahead promptly and moreover to reiterate publicly its commitment to the new mechanized force. It is difficult to disagree with Brian Bond's claim that this "was a striking example of Liddell Hart's successful use of the Press to affect Government policy."[53]

Army leaders came to recognize Liddell Hart could be a powerful ally in furthering service interests.[54] Some officers also recognized he could help them further their own careers, especially after Liddell Hart formed his partnership with Leslie Hore-Belisha in 1937 (chaps. 5,7).

[52]LH, "1929 Diary: Engagements and Notes," 2 Oct. entry, 11/1929/1b; see also F.M. Cyril Deverell to LH, 10, 15 Nov. 1937, 1/232; Milne to LH, 30 May 1927, 1/512.

[53]B. Bond, *British Military Policy*, 141. Trythall and Winton reach a similar conclusion; see Anthony J. Trythall, *'Boney' Fuller: The Intellectual General, 1878–1966* (New Brunswick, N.J.: Rutgers University Press, 1977), 143; Harold R. Winton, *To Change an Army: General Sir John Burnett-Stuart and British Armored Doctrine, 1927–1938* (Lawrence: University Press of Kansas, 1988), 86–87. On the Tidworth affair, see B. Bond, *British Military Policy*, 140–41; *Memoirs*, vol. 1, chap. 5; Luvaas, *Education of an Army*, 385–86; Trythall, *'Boney' Fuller*, chap. 6; Winton, *To Change an Army*, chap. 4.

[54]See, for example, LH, "Talk with Field Marshal Sir C. J. Deverell," memorandum for the record, 13 Nov. 1936, 11/1936/99; also Macksey, *Tank Pioneers*, 97, 100, 134–35.

Because he had the ear of the secretary of state for war, he was in an excellent position to push the careers of friendly officers and damage those of adversaries. He did in fact play a key role in convincing Hore-Belisha to remove the army's leaders in late 1937, then helped select the new leadership. Thus the officers who led Britain's army in the final two years of the interwar period were generally sympathetic to his views. This example alone should cast serious doubts on his claim that the army leadership invariably rejected his ideas. But Liddell Hart himself maintained after the war that his influence in personnel matters was not limited to Hore-Belisha's tenure. He wrote in 1965, for example:

> Hore-Belisha's practice was nothing new even in my own experience. His predecessor, Duff Cooper, had asked me to make an analysis of the Army List and compile a list of noteworthy officers from generals down to colonels; he evidently found this so helpful and so closely borne out by his own subsequent observation, that he showed this list to his successor in handing over office. Morever, for many years before that I had often been consulted on such matters by higher commanders who were members of the Selection Board, and realized that they themselves could not have had such an extensive knowledge of the candidates. . . . Presumably . . . they felt that I had no personal "axe to grind," since I was on the retired list and not in the race for promotion.[55]

One might argue that although the generals recognized Liddell Hart's importance and listened to his arguments, in the end, they disregarded his advice and remained firmly wedded to outdated and foolish ideas. This is the basis of his third charge against the generals: they were hostile to mechanization and the blitzkrieg strategy.[56] We already have reason to be skeptical of this argument: the British army's pioneering with armored forces in the 1920s and early 1930s is hardly likely to have obtained in an army led by officers adamantly opposed to mechanization. Although Britain eventually lost its leadership position in the mid-1930s, it was not because of military obscurantism but because of political decisions (chap. 7).

Liddell Hart's portrait of the generals' attitude toward mechanization is directly tied to his description of the fate of the horse cavalry in Britain. He goes to considerable lengths in his *Memoirs* and other post–World War II writings to describe the significant but negative influence of the horse cavalry lobby. He implies that in the 1920s and 1930s this

---

[55]Letter, *Army Quarterly* 91 (Oct. 1965): 5–6.
[56]LH was not a proponent of blitzkrieg from 1934 to 1940 (chap. 5), so the charge that the generals rejected his views about blitzkrieg—at least in that period—is baseless.

powerful lobby markedly hindered progress toward mechanization: "Cavalry circles loathed the idea of giving up the horse, and thus instinctively decried the tank. They found much support both in the War Office and in Parliament. Wellington's reputed saying that the Battle of Waterloo was won on the playing-fields of Eton is merely a legend, but it is painfully true that the early battles of World War II were lost in the Cavalry Club" (*Memoirs* 1:77). This assertion, too, must be treated skeptically. Although the British army was small and lacking in armor on the eve of World War II, it was the only army entirely equipped with track and motor transport. The army leadership had decided in the mid-1930s to mechanize all cavalry as well as infantry units, a considerable feat because the principle opponents of mechanization were often officers from these two branches. In his classic study of the role of horse cavalry in various industrialized nations, Edward Katzenbach points out that between the world wars, Britain and Germany were the most progressive countries. He acknowledges there were British officers who opposed reducing the horse cavalry's role but notes that such reactionaries were in the minority and consequently lost their battle to save the horse.[57]

Brian Bond's comprehensive study of the British army during the interwar period corroborates Katzenbach's argument.[58] Bond too recognizes there were reactionary officers in the army, but he also notes they were not dominant. Bond argues that within the officer corps there were "five categories of attitudes on mechanization" and only one of these contained "true reactionaries."[59] The officers in the other four categories all favored mechanization, although the members of one category, "the conservatives," were opposed to "the concept of independent armoured formations."[60] There is little doubt that officers from these four categories determined army policy during the interwar period.

Finally, there is little evidence from the period itself that Liddell Hart saw a powerful horse cavalry lobby as a serious obstacle to modernizing the army. There is ample evidence in his personal papers that he recognized at the time that the cavalry as well as the infantry were

[57]Edward L. Katzenbach, Jr., "The Horse Cavalry in the Twentieth Century," in Robert J. Art and Kenneth N. Waltz, eds., *The Use of Force* (Boston: Little, Brown, 1971), 277–97.

[58]B. Bond, *British Military Policy*, chap. 6; see also Robert H. Lawson, *The British Army and the Theory of Armored Warfare, 1918–1940* (Newark: University of Delaware Press, 1984), 16–32.

[59]B. Bond, *British Military Policy*, 130–32. Bond borrowed this useful categorization from Winton (see *To Change an Army*, 27–30).

[60]B. Bond, *British Military Policy*, 131.

being motorized and, in some cases, mechanized. For example, he complained in early 1937 to his editor at the *Times* that an article dealing with the important steps that had been taken to modernize the cavalry had been "tucked away in such an insignificant place" in the paper. "It seemed to show rather an inadequate appreciation of such a big step in the historical evolution of the British Army."[61]

It is also impossible to argue that despite this general receptivity to mechanization, the men at the helm were particularly conservative on this score. Field Marshal Milne (CIGS, February 1926–February 1933), Field Marshal Deverell (CIGS, April 1936–December 1937), and General Lord Gort (CIGS, December 1937–September 1939) were all committed to mechanizing the army, as Liddell Hart's files amply show. Only Montgomery-Massingberd (CIGS, February 1933–April 1936) was not keen about mechanization. He was not, however, overtly hostile, for he played a major role in the mechanization of the cavalry.[62]

Liddell Hart's account of the interwar period notwithstanding, whether to mechanize the British army was not much of an issue. The real issue, and not an easy one, was whether Britain should mechanize its traditional formations—cavalry and infantry—or create an independent armored force. The army had so little money that it had to choose between the options. If the army was to prepare to fight on the Continent, it made sense to create powerful armored divisions; for policing the Empire, it was preferable to mechanize existing cavalry and infantry units. Ultimately the army's leaders chose the latter course, but the decision-making process was lengthy and complicated. The evolution of the army's thinking has important implications for assessing its attitude toward the blitzkrieg.

The British army held its first large-scale maneuvers since the war in September 1925.[63] By then there was considerable interest in army circles in creating a brigade-sized armored force and experimenting with it in the annual maneuvers. There was certainly resistance to that idea, although it was eventually overcome when the Experimental

[61]LH to Robert Barrington-Ward, 2 Mar. 1937, 3/107. (Although his legal name was Robert, Barrington-Ward was usually called Robin. He is referred to as Robert throughout this book.) For other indications in his writing that he knew the cavalry was being modernized, see "Mechanisation of the Army," *Listener*, 1 Jan. 1936, 33; "The Army in 1935: Signs of Recovery," *English Review* 60 (Feb. 1935): 145–58; "Armament and Its Future Use," *Yale Review* 19 (June 1930): 658–59; "Cost of the Army," *Times*, 18 Mar. 1935, 19; "The Attack in Warfare: Changing Tactics," ibid., 10 Sept. 1937, 13–14.

[62]On Montgomery-Massingberd's impact on the mechanization of the British army, see Winton, *To Change an Army*, 188–189.

[63]The following discussion of army maneuvers and decision making about the fate of armored forces is based largely on B. Bond, *British Military Policy*, chaps. 5–6, and Winton, *To Change an Army*, chaps. 4–5, 7. Also useful are LH, *Tanks*, vol. 1, pt. 2; Macksey, *Tank Pioneers*, pts. 3, 5.

Mechanized Force was created in 1927. The army's exercising of this force in the 1927 and 1928 maneuvers attracted considerable attention at home and abroad and placed the British army in the forefront in the development of armored forces. Unfortunately, the renamed Armoured Force was disbanded after the 1928 maneuvers, and the army leadership decided to concentrate instead on mechanizing the traditional arms. Financial considerations played a key role, as did the fact that some influential senior officers wanted to mechanize existing infantry and cavalry units. Field Marshal Milne (the CIGS) maintained nevertheless that he would create a permanent armored brigade in 1930.

The period between 1929 and 1930 held little promise for proponents of an independent armored force. The annual maneuvers for those years were designed to forward the mechanization of the traditional arms. The only bright spot was the publication in 1929 of Col. Charles Broad's primer on armored warfare, *Mechanized and Armoured Formations*. Broad, a staunch proponent of the view that the tank was a revolutionary weapon that would dominate the battlefield in future wars, had actually been instructed by the CIGS to produce a manual describing the organization and employment of mechanized forces. This manual, often referred to as "the Purple Primer" because of the color of its cover, thus provided "official recognition to the concept of mechanized warfare."[64]

The British army, on a restricted budget throughout the 1920s, was further hurt by the financial crisis of 1931. Nevertheless, the 1931 exercises encouraged armor advocates. The army's three tank battalions and a light battalion were temporarily organized into an armored brigade under Broad's command. In the ensuing maneuvers, that force demonstrated for the first time that moving tanks could be commanded by radio, a development of seminal importance, for it meant it was possible to coordinate the rapid movement of large armored forces. The temporary armored brigade's impressive performance in the 1931 maneuvers was duplicated the next year. Shortly afterward Milne made known his intention to create a permanent armored brigade. The decision was not final, however, until the next year, by which time Montgomery-Massingberd had replaced Milne as CIGS.

The Tank Brigade was formed in the spring of 1934 and placed under the command of Col. Percy Hobart, one of Britain's most progressive thinkers about armored war.[65] At the same time, the decision was

---

[64]B. Bond, *British Military Policy*, 152.

[65]Kenneth J. Macksey, *Armoured Crusader: A Biography of Major-General Sir Percy Hobart* (London: Hutchinson, 1967).

made to foster close cooperation between the Tank Brigade and the semimechanized 7th Infantry Brigade. The aim was to begin thinking about creating an armored division, or what would come to be referred to as "the Mobile Division." The expectation was that the 1934 maneuvers would be a watershed demonstration of the potential of such a large armored force. At the time Hitler was assuming power in Germany, the British army was thus thinking seriously about developing an armored division that might fight on the Continent. This was a promising situation, because Germany did not form its first tank batallion until 1934.[66]

But the British effort to create an armored division faltered after 1933. The 1934 maneuvers, which held out so much promise, were at best a disappointment and at worst a setback for the advocates of armor. The Tank Brigade and the 7th Infantry Brigade were exercised together, with poor results. There appear to be three reasons for this important failure. First, Gen. Sir John Burnett-Stuart, who supervised the maneuvers, made a number of rulings about the conduct of the exercises that clearly hindered performance. Burnett-Stuart, who was *not* opposed to creating independent armored forces, but who could be mischievous, perceived a need to use the maneuvers to improve the infantry's morale and to highlight several of the tank brigade's weaknesses.[67] He designed the maneuvers accordingly. Second, the commander of the 7th Infantry Brigade (Brig. Gen. George Lindsay) and the Tank Brigade commander (Col. Hobart) had different ideas about the employment of armored forces, which led to trouble on the training field. Finally, personal relations among Burnett-Stuart, Hobart, and Lindsay left something to be desired. The disappointing results of the 1934 maneuvers were *not* a result of interference by officers opposed to independent armored forces. Hobart and Lindsay were forceful advocates of the need for large tank units, while Burnett-Stuart was sympathetic to this position.[68]

Despite the poor results, Montgomery-Massingberd, the CIGS, announced that a mobile division would be created; yet for the remainder of the 1930s the majority of the army's scarce resources went to mechanizing existing infantry and cavalry units. The Mobile Division foundered, in good part, because it had no clear-cut mission. Was it to fight on the Continent against the Wehrmacht or to prepare for a specific

---

[66]LH, *Tanks* 1:336.

[67]Winton, *To Change an Army*, 179.

[68]On Hobart's views, see Macksey, *Armoured Crusader;* on Burnett-Stuart's views, Winton, *To Change an Army;* on Lindsay's military thinking, Macksey, *Tank Pioneers,* 54–62, 129–34; see also B. Bond, *British Military Policy,* 130–31, where he categorizes attitudes on mechanization.

contingency in the Empire? The choice would determine its size and shape. The two alternatives are clearly laid out by Harold Winton, a scholar of the period:

> There were two polar positions. The first held that the division should be an armored formation, composed mostly of tanks, capable of conducting penetrations deep into the enemy's rear in a Continental war. The second advocated a motorized, or perhaps lightly armored, cavalry division, capable of performing reconnaissance and screening missions for motorized infantry just as the horse cavalry division had for foot-mobile infantry, but not designed specifically for a European war.[69]

British policy makers never directly resolved the issue, although the policy drifted toward creating a division to fight in the Empire. Britain did not accept a Continental commitment until 1939, although there was much wavering between 1934 and 1937. This policy drift made it virtually impossible to create an independent armored force that could engage the Germans in a war. Furthermore, emphasizing defending the Empire provided a sound basis for the decision to mechanize the cavalry and infantry units, with their historic role in protecting the Empire. This policy certainly looks foolish judged as a preparation for fighting a Continental war, but the British army was not told to prepare to fight the Wehrmacht until 1939, when it was too late to take the steps necessary to create a formidable deterrent.

It is difficult to judge what kind of force the British army would have developed had the other alternative been chosen. Almost certainly the force would have included many tanks, given the army's acceptance of mechanization. Even the French, who did not recognize their potential, had a significant number of tanks, in fact more than the Germans on 10 May 1940.[70] Whether British tanks would have been organized into armored divisions (like the Germans' tanks) or parceled out among infantry and cavalry divisions (the French approach, although they did have some armored divisions) cannot be answered conclusively. The army that was in the forefront of experimentation with armored forces before 1933 would have been likely, however, to create a body of powerful armored divisions.

The question still remains whether the British generals would have realized that those independent armored forces could be used to effect a blitzkrieg. There was no widespread support for such an idea in the

---

[69]Winton, *To Change an Army*, 174.
[70]Barry R. Posen, *Sources of Military Doctrine: France, Britain, and Germany between the World Wars* (Ithaca, N.Y.: Cornell University Press, 1984), 82–86; R. H. S. Stolfi, "Equipment for Victory in France in 1940," *History* 52 (Feb. 1970): 1–20.

army, where there were competing views on how to employ mechanized forces (Bond's "five categories of attitudes on mechanization"). It would be unrealistic, however, to expect the majority of senior officers in a tradition-bound institution like the British army to have become firmly committed to a radical strategy like blitzkrieg by 1939. The German experience is instructive in this regard.

The tendency has been to view the Wehrmacht as highly receptive to new ideas and new weapons. For example, Gen. Hans von Seeckt, the head of the German army in the 1920s, is often described as a progressive thinker of the first order. And it is commonly held that the leaders of the Wehrmacht, recognizing the tank's potential and the merit of Guderian's revolutionary ideas on armored warfare, developed the blitzkrieg in the 1930s. The record shows otherwise. Seeckt, his receptivity to ideas on restoring mobility to the battlefield notwithstanding, was advocating placing considerable reliance on horse cavalry as late as 1930.[71] Furthermore, he was hardly enthusiastic about the tank. Regarding the blitzkrieg, it was not until February 1940, when the high command was desperately searching for a strategy that would provide a decisive victory in France, that Guderian's ideas on armored warfare were finally accepted, and even then, resistance remained.[72] Throughout the 1930s, Germany's military leaders were mostly unreceptive to the claim that the tank offered a means to win a quick and decisive victory in a future world war.[73]

This does not mean the German army was dominated by reactionary officers, for it was not. It merely demonstrates some strong resistance to new ideas on armored warfare, which was only natural, given little empirical evidence on which to judge the capabilities of large panzer forces acting independently of the more traditional elements of an army. Failure to accept Guderian's ideas on armored warfare did not make an officer a hopeless reactionary; after all, F.M. Erich von Manstein was not attracted to Guderian's views during the 1930s, and Rommel was initially opposed to Guderian's claims about blitzkrieg. Of course the Germans finally accepted Guderian's ideas, although only after the war had started.

It is difficult to compare the British and German armies simply be-

[71]See, for example, the chapter "Modern Cavalry" in Gen. Hans von Seeckt, *Thoughts of a Soldier*, trans. Gilbert Waterhouse (London: Benn, 1930), 81–107.

[72]John J. Mearsheimer, *Conventional Deterrence* (Ithaca, N.Y.: Cornell University Press, 1983), chap. 4. On resistance, see, for example, Guderian's description of the problems he encountered during the French campaign in *Panzer Leader*, trans. Constantine Fitzgibbon (London: Joseph, 1952), chap. 5; also Hans-Adolf Jacobsen, "Dunkirk 1940," in Hans-Adolf Jacobsen and J. Rohwer, eds., Edward Fitzgerald, trans. *Decisive Battles of World War II: The German View* (New York: Putnam, 1965), 29–68.

[73]Matthew Cooper, *The German Army, 1933–1945* (New York: Stein & Day, 1978), pts. 1–2; Guderian, *Panzer Leader*, chaps. 2–3; Posen, *Sources of Military Doctrine*, 205–19.

cause it will never be known whether the British would have realized, before the war began, the potential inherent in large and independent armored forces. There is reason to believe they might have come to appreciate the revolutionary potential of the tank. There were, after all, a number of senior officers who either shared or were sympathetic to Fuller's and Liddell Hart's early ideas about armored warfare.[74] Then there is the interesting case of Lord Gort, who was the CIGS for the two years before the war started and who commanded the British army against the Germans in May 1940. He gained his position at the top of the army with Liddell Hart's assistance and was hardly a reactionary, although he was not identified with the position that the tank had the potential to revolutionize warfare.[75] Consider this comment about a possible German offensive against France, made to Liddell Hart in 1937: "May it not be possible for panzer divisions and concentrated air forces to effect a breach and this attack can take place with little previous warning. If by rapidity, deception and surprise it is possible to make a bridgehead then the war will pass into open country once more. I feel novelty lies in some such direction as this as Belgium is hackneyed."[76] Liddell Hart, who had by then become a staunch advocate of the superiority of the defense and denied the efficacy of blitzkrieg, told Gort that his prescient proposal was flawed because mechanization favored the defender.[77] Gort, however, hardly sounds like a commander who would have dismissed out of hand those officers who believed the tank had the potential to alter the conduct of war significantly.[78] One must be careful not to place too much emphasis on selected comments like Gort's because of the danger of painting too favorable a picture of Britain's military leaders; yet the British army was far more progressive than Liddell Hart allows.

WHY LIDDELL HART'S PERSPECTIVE CHANGED

Two points stand out when we look at the development of Liddell Hart's thinking about the generals and World War I. First, between

---

[74]B. Bond, *British Military Policy*, 130–31.

[75]See Gort's lengthy comments on LH's famous Oct. 1937 *Times* articles, "Defence or Attack?" (see chap. 5, n. 51). See Gort to LH, 20, 24, 31 Oct. 1937, 1/322; also B. Bond, *British Military Policy*, 131; J. R. Colville, *Man of Valour: The Life of Field-Marshal the Viscount Gort* (London: Collins, 1972).

[76]Quoted in B. Bond, *Liddell Hart*, 118, n. 41.

[77]"Defence or Attack—Notes on Gort's Notes," memorandum for the record, 6 Nov. 1937, 1/322/54.

[78]For two other examples of senior British officers, neither identified as an advocate of blitzkrieg, sounding like Gort, see Winton, *To Change an Army*, 186–87; Maj. Gen. H. Rowan-Robinson, "Defence or Attack? *The Times* Articles (A Review)," *Army Quarterly* 35 (Jan. 1938): 277–90.

1916 and 1932 he moved from a position of extreme adulation to one of deep-seated hostility. Second, his final assessment was simply wrong. The generals were certainly not the strategic geniuses he initially thought them to be, but they were by and large an able lot. Liddell Hart's flawed evaluation of them had serious consequences. It led him to alter his military thinking in significant ways, a development that is interesting not only intellectually but also because his ideas, which received so much attention, helped shape the way Britons thought about dealing with the Third Reich.

To a large extent the evolution of Liddell Hart's perspective on Britain's generals is a conventional story. After all, many other Britons reached similar conclusions. Even so, it is surprising that Liddell Hart arrived at such a categorically negative assessment. His good relations with many of the generals throughout the 1920s and early 1930s would at the very least have led one to expect a more tempered judgment. Why it turned out otherwise is a difficult question to answer. His personal papers and writings provide few clues. I can only speculate from studying Liddell Hart's life that one important experience served to fuel his hostility: his forced exit from the army in 1924.

He very much liked being an army officer and went to considerable lengths to avoid being separated from the army and remain on active duty.[79] This desire to remain a soldier was surely due in good part to his fascination with military issues, which he developed as a young boy and maintained all his life. It is neither an exaggeration nor a criticism to say his interest in military matters bordered on the fanatic. His commitment to remaining in the army was probably also driven by his belief he could develop a tactical theory or strategy to win the next war quickly and decisively. He probably felt it would be much more difficult to influence army thinking once he left the service.[80] Britain had no tradition of civilian experts significantly influencing army thinking about nitty-gritty tactical and strategic matters, and generals in all armies have disliked and distrusted outside experts.

Liddell Hart must have been deeply hurt by the army's decision to retire him. It meant separation from an institution and a way of life he had come to love. Moreover, the decision carried with it the message that the army either did not recognize or did not need his talents. They were *not* going to allow him to be the captain who teaches generals. Although there is no hard evidence, this hurt may eventually have translated into an all-consuming dislike of the army as an institution.

[79]*Memoirs* 1:34–36, 49–50, 62–65.
[80]Ibid., 65.

He wrote in 1936, "For I loved the Army all the years I was in it, and my perception of its faults has developed *subsequently* to leaving."[81]

Regardless of how much impact his separation from the service had on his growing disaffection from Britain's generals, there is no disputing that Liddell Hart had become fervently committed by 1933 to making sure that Britain never again fought a Continental war. His crusade would not only lead him to alter his military thinking but to advocate policies that worked to undermine whatever chance there was of deterring Hitler and avoiding British participation in another European land war.

---

[81] "Thoughts Jotted Down—To Be Expanded," memorandum for the record, entry for 17 July 1936, 11/1936/2–25c, emphasis added. He writes also in his *Memoirs* (1:65) about being forced to leave "the profession which I loved."

[4]

Grand Strategy and the Indirect Approach, 1925–1932

During the mid-1920s, a short time after he began to develop his ideas on blitzkrieg, Liddell Hart became interested in grand strategy, and there his attention remained the rest of the interwar period. He specifically focused on the issue of a Continental commitment. Although he continued to write about the blitzkrieg, his interest in it tapered off in the late 1920s. He wrote little about armored strategy between 1929 and 1932, and never provided a comprehensive discussion of his ideas on the blitzkrieg. He might well have produced a work along the lines of *Lectures on F. S. R. III*,[1] in which Fuller lays out in considerable detail his ideas on armored warfare. Liddell Hart did not, although he did radically alter his views on the blitzkrieg in the latter half of the 1930s. His change of views did not lead to a scholarly exposition because the change was not the result of a careful reevaluation of his theory but merely necessary to accommodate his changing views about British grand strategy.

Liddell Hart never lost sight of the fact Britain might again be faced with a military threat from a European power. He questioned, however, the assumption Britain had to meet that challenge by committing ground forces to fight on the Continent. Britain, he argued, should instead place greater emphasis on economic and diplomatic instruments and, if military force became necessary, find an alternative to raising a mass army to fight another land war in Europe. Britain should use other means, possibly airpower or its navy, to defeat an adversary seeking to establish a hegemony on the Continent. This policy prescription he eventually translated into a call for an indirect approach, which he maintained Britain had historically relied upon to defeat Continental foes. This was, after all, the British way in warfare.

[1](London: Sifton Praed, 1932).

There are several reasons for Liddell Hart's interest in grand strategy. His intellectual curiosity was simply too great for him not to move from the narrower realm of strategy and tactics to broader questions of grand strategy; serious students of war eventually discover that the study of strategy and tactics benefits from considering grand strategy.[2] After leaving the army in 1924 he depended almost solely on writing to earn his income, so it was to his advantage to appeal to a wide audience by writing about the broad contours of military policy as well as the more specialized subjects of strategy and tactics. Most important, there was Liddell Hart's changing assessment of Britain's military leaders and especially their conduct of World War I. He came to believe that in the event of another war on the Continent, Britain's generals would repeat the experience of the Western Front. Because he was determined that should never happen, he began to look for ways to defeat a Continental foe without sending a large British army to the Continent. The first reasons help account for his interest in grand strategy, while the last one explains, for the most part, the content of his evolving ideas about grand strategy. Britain, he concluded, needed to employ an indirect approach to defeat a Continental foe.[3] This position on grand strategy, in turn, directly influenced his thinking about strategy and tactics. In fact, because his views on grand strategy called for avoiding participation in any future European land war, his interest in strategy and tactics naturally began to wane. Nevertheless, he would eventually have to alter his thinking about armored strategy radically so as to accommodate his views on grand strategy.

Liddell Hart was beginning to doubt by the mid-1920s whether the blitzkrieg would provide a means to avoid another world war. These initial doubts, however, had nothing to do with the strategy per se, for he did not believe at this point that a defender who used his tanks intelligently could thwart a blitzkrieg, nor did he think there were antitank weapons being developed that would present a serious challenge to the tank. Rather, his initial doubts were directly linked to his estimate of the British generals. He believed they would not accept his ideas about the blitzkrieg and thus would fail to use armored forces to

---

[2] LH made this point in "Note," 1939, 11/1939/141.

[3] I refer throughout to the *"theory* of the indirect approach," although it is usually referred to as the *"strategy* of the indirect approach." The indirect approach was originally identified with *grand strategic* issues, not *strategic* issues (as I define these two terms), although it is such a vague concept it can be used interchangeably; that is why I refrain from calling it the strategy of the indirect approach. Because the concept is so vague, there is reason to doubt whether it makes sense to use my term *theory* to describe what is largely a tautological argument; I acknowledge the problem but nevertheless think it the least confusing terminology.

produce a quick and decisive victory in a future war. It was the generals' resistance to new ideas, in other words, that fueled his doubts.

Liddell Hart had these reservations as early as 1923, and they were strengthened by his changing view of World War I.[4] This important linkage is reflected in his first book dealing with grand strategy, *Paris, or The Future of War* (1925). He argues in the opening chapter that the war was an "empty triumph" and "we are justified, standing amid the *debris*, in questioning the strategic aim and direction of the war." Nevertheless, he maintains there is no use "crying over spilt milk. . . . What we are concerned with is the future." He does not, however, disguise his pessimism about that future:

> It is the worst of omens that the orthodox military school, still generally in power as the advisers of governments, cling obstinately to this dogma, blind apparently to the futility of the Great War, both in its strategy and its fruits. Of these military Bourbons, restored to the seats of authority in most capitals, the saying may be echoed: "They have learnt nothing and forgotten nothing. . . ."
>
> New weapons would seem to be regarded as an additional tap through which the bath of blood can be filled all the sooner.[5]

He believed the "widespread prejudice" of these officers biased them "against even examining the suggestions of an amateur, let alone admitting their value or accepting them."[6] This conclusion undermined his hope that his innovative ideas would influence the next war.

Liddell Hart, however, did not completely despair in these early years. In his more sanguine moments, which admittedly were few, he maintained that the powerful logic of his position would force the public and the country's political leaders to demand that the generals accept his ideas.[7] Moreover, he maintained a certain amount of faith in younger officers, who, he believed, might see the wisdom of his teachings. Liddell Hart also had good relations with Field Marshal Milne (the CIGS) and a number of other senior officers from 1925 until 1927, when he wrote the *Daily Telegraph* article critical of the army's handling of the experimental armored force. The bad feelings caused by that controversy notwithstanding, Liddell Hart's relationship with Milne, who was CIGS until 1933, was quite cordial and respectful.[8]

4"Study and Reflection v. Practical Experience," *Army Quarterly* 6 (July 1923): 318–31.

5(New York: Dutton), 6–7; see also 4–5.

6*The Remaking of Modern Armies* (London: Murray, 1927), 178; see also 12–13, 54, chap. 11; "Study and Reflection v. Practical Experience"; Brian Bond, *Liddell Hart: A Study of his Military Thought* (London: Cassell, 1977), 82–84.

7*Remaking of Modern Armies*, 29–31.

8On younger officers, see, for example, LH, "Diary Notes. 1926," 13 Nov. entry,

Disenchantment, however, eventually led to his famous theory of the indirect approach.[9] The key to understanding the indirect approach is to realize that it is a vague and therefore elastic theory. At a purely conceptual level, its real meaning is difficult, if not impossible, to discern. Virtually every military victory can be ascribed to the indirect approach. Liddell Hart once concluded that "the history of strategy is, fundamentally, a record of the application and evolution of the indirect approach." He maintained that "throughout the ages decisive results in war have only been reached when the approach has been indirect."[10] These comments point up the fact the theory of the indirect approach is a circular argument.[11] Every military victory is, by definition, the result of an indirect approach. This major problem with the general theory aside, Liddell Hart did have *some* specific ideas about the indirect approach when he wrote in the late 1920s and early 1930s; the aim here is to pin down as much as possible what he meant.

It has become commonplace for students of military affairs to link the indirect approach with the blitzkrieg, a connection that Liddell Hart stressed *after* World War II.[12] This is not a difficult link to make because the indirect approach is such an elastic concept. Nevertheless, when Liddell Hart spoke about the indirect approach during the interwar period, he was not talking about blitzkrieg but of finding a way to defeat a Continental foe without having to engage his armies. The indirect approach was to provide a means for avoiding the commitment of ground forces to Europe.[13] If he could not convince the British

---

11/1926/1b; LH to Brig. Gen. J. E. Edmonds, 10 Feb. 1934, 1/259. On relations with senior officers, recall chap. 3. The relationship with Milne is clearly reflected in their correspondence (see 1/512) and *Memoirs* 1: chap. 5; see also LH, "Seven Years: The Regime of Field-Marshal Lord Milne," *English Review* 56 (Apr. 1933): 376–86.

[9]LH's principal works on the indirect approach are *Paris; The Decisive Wars of History: A Study in Strategy* (Boston: Little, Brown, 1929)—later issued in revised form as *Strategy: The Indirect Approach* (London: Faber, 1954); *The British Way in Warfare* (London: Faber, 1932)—later issued in a revised and enlarged version as *When Britain Goes to War* (London: Faber, 1935). Chap. 7 of *Remaking of Modern Armies* is also important because it repeats many key ideas from *Paris*.

[10]*Strategy*, 18; *Decisive Wars of History*, 4; see also 5 and *Strategy*, chap. 10.

[11]Other authors have reached the same conclusion: B. Bond, *Liddell Hart*, 54–61; idem, "Further Reflections on the Indirect Approach," *Journal of the Royal United Services Institution* 116 (Dec. 1971): 70; Tuvia Ben-Moshe, "Liddell Hart and the Israel Defence Forces: A Reappraisal," *Journal of Contemporary History* 16 (Apr. 1981): 369–72; R. A. Mason, "Sir Basil Liddell Hart and the Strategy of the Indirect Approach," *Journal of the Royal United Services Institution* 115 (June 1970): 41.

[12]See, for example, *Memoirs* 1:161–68, 179–82. The discussion of the indirect approach in *Memoirs* does not reflect what he actually intended that theory to mean during the interwar years.

[13]A caveat: in *Decisive Wars of History* he did consider the possibility of using ground forces to implement an indirect approach, but he did not envision using them to engage the opponent's army in battle.

generals to fight a land war according to his innovative theories, he had to find a way to obviate the need to engage the opponent's army.

Liddell Hart's general theory of the indirect approach was based on an assumption that every nation-state has an Achilles' heel that could cause collapse in a war. That vulnerable point need not be some part of the nation-state's military forces, although he did not exclude that possibility. The principal goal in war is to discover the opponent's Achilles' heel and find a way to strike quickly at it to achieve a rapid and decisive victory. The attacking forces, Liddell Hart argued, should behave like "a boxer who . . . aims to strike a single decisive blow as early as possible against some vital point—the chin or the solar plexus—which will instantaneously paralyse his opponent's resistance." The ultimate objective of the approach was "to subdue the enemy's will to resist, with the least possible human and economic loss to itself," to gain victory with a minimum of bloodshed, which could only be achieved by reducing the actual fighting "to the slenderest possible proportions." Best of all would be finding a way to defeat an opponent without ever having to engage forces, as he wrote in 1929 in one of his principal works on the indirect approach: "The perfection of strategy would . . . be to produce a decision—the destruction of the enemy's armed forces through their unarming by surrender—without any fighting."[14]

This discussion of Liddell Hart's general theory notwithstanding, did he go on to be more specific about what he considered to be the Achilles' heel of a nation, and moreover, how did he propose to strike at that vulnerable point? In other words, how was his vague theory to be operationalized? He basically argued during this period that an opponent's Achilles' heel is his civilian population. The key to success in war is to break the morale of the enemy's civilian population, not to destroy his military forces, which of course is what the blitzkrieg is concerned with. Thus there is much talk in *Paris*, his first book dealing with the indirect approach, about the "means to the moral objective" (27) and "subjugation of the opposing will" (20). He believed that if the attacker could "demoralize one section of the nation, the collapse of its will to resist compels the surrender of the whole" (21). This argument was based on the assumption that the modern nation-state is a delicate mechanism that can easily be brought to the point of collapse: "With the growth of civilization the dislocation or control of an enemy's industrial centres and communications becomes both more effective and more easy as the means by which to subdue his will to resist" (35).[15] It

---

[14]*Remaking of Modern Armies*, 104–5; *Paris*, 19; *Decisive Wars of History*, 153; ibid., 153–54.

[15]World War II obviously proved this hypothesis wrong.

would be relatively easy, he argued, to so disrupt "an enemy people . . . that they will sue for peace rather than face a continuation of the struggle" (28). Surrender would be the "lesser evil" (29). This focus on the "moral dislocation" of the enemy's civilian population is manifestly apparent in his other books dealing with the indirect approach.[16]

Liddell Hart advocated a variety of means to achieve this broad objective: "defeat in the field, propaganda, blockade, diplomacy, or attack on the centres of government and population." He also emphasized striking the opponent's economy from the air.[17] The indirect approach properly understood, he maintained, did not emphasize any single instrument; the means depended on the case at hand. He desired a situation in which, "instead of being tied to one fixed means, we are free to weigh the respective merits of each."[18] This catholicism regarding instruments, coupled with the notion that each nation has a loosely defined Achilles' heel, is, of course, what makes the indirect approach so elastic. Still, Liddell Hart did focus his attention on different military instruments, and moreover, he usually placed particular emphasis on one of them.

Liddell Hart was very enthusiastic about airpower in his initial work on the indirect approach. He saw strategic bombing as an excellent means of destroying enemy morale. He seems to have believed that a rapid and massive air strike against an adversary's cities would so disrupt and so demoralize his population that he would sue for peace. His arguments in favor of airpower in *Paris* and *The Remaking of Modern Armies* are similar to the ideas of early airpower advocates like Giulio Douhet, Billy Mitchell, and Hugh Trenchard.[19] Consider this quotation from *Paris:*

> Imagine for a moment that, of two centralized nations at war, one possesses a superior air force, the other a superior army. Provided that the blow be sufficiently swift and powerful, there is no reason why within a

[16]*Decisive Wars of History*, 146.
[17]*Paris*, 20. See 14–15, 27–53; *Remaking of Modern Armies*, chap. 7.
[18]*Paris*, 20.
[19]For LH's views on airpower, see n. 17 above; also the sections in *Paris* where he downplays the importance of armies and navies (32–37, 53–62). On the views of those early airpower advocates, see Edward Warner, "Douhet, Mitchell, Seversky: Theories of Air Warfare," in Edward Mead Earle, ed., *Makers of Modern Strategy: Military Thought from Machiavelli to Hitler* (Princeton, N.J.: Princeton University Press, 1943), 485–503; David MacIsaac, "Voices from the Central Blue: The Air Power Theorists," in Peter Paret, ed., *Makers of Modern Strategy: From Machiavelli to the Nuclear Age* (Princeton, N.J.: Princeton University Press, 1986), 624–47. Of course the Royal Air Force was very impressed with LH's writings about airpower; see B. Bond, *Liddell Hart*, 43; Jay Luvaas, *The Education of an Army: British Military Thought, 1815–1940* (Chicago: University of Chicago Press, 1964), 387.

few hours, or at most days from the commencement of hostilities, the nerve system of the country inferior in air power should not be paralysed.

A modern state is such a complex and interdependent fabric that it offers a target highly sensitive to a sudden and overwhelming blow from the air. (40–41)

Liddell Hart was aware of the obvious moral problems associated with terror bombing. He countered with a utilitarian argument: an air attack like the one described above would certainly kill and injure many civilians, but with its short duration it would ultimately result in many fewer casualties than a protracted land war. He also thought the attacking aircraft might well substitute gas for standard explosive bombs to reduce the horror of strategic bombing. He saw gas as a relatively humane but effective weapon: "Gas may well prove the salvation of civilization from the otherwise inevitable collapse in case of another world war."[20]

Liddell Hart had largely abandoned his arguments about airpower by the time he published *The Decisive Wars of History*, his second major work on the indirect approach. He never directly explained why he lost interest, although there were probably several reasons. He eventually became convinced that measures could be taken to protect a civilian population from a gas attack. "The danger," he argued, would then "be reduced to proportions that make such attack scarcely worth the effort in comparison with other uses of airpower." Furthermore, he surely must have recognized that if using gas against enemy cities made war less horrible, the victim population would be less likely to press for peace. It could then be necessary to use explosive bombs or accept a protracted war—hardly attractive options.[21] He apparently also came to doubt whether even an air war conducted with explosive bombs could be quickly won. He wrote in 1935, for example, "It seems a fairly safe calculation that the tonnage of high-explosive bombs required to destroy any large city far exceeds the capacity of any country's existing bombers." Thus he did not argue in the 1930s that airpower provided the means to deliver a knock-out blow against an adversary; to do so certainly would have undermined his utilitarian moral argument.[22] Furthermore, it was possible the Germans would

[20]*Paris*, 45; on the moral problems of terror bombing, see 43–53.

[21]*When Britain Goes To War*, 50. Although he lost faith in his early claims about the efficacy of air attacks with gas, LH did remain a strong supporter of gas warfare throughout his life; see Brian H. Reid, "Gas Warfare: The Perils of Prediction," in David Carlton and Carlo Schaerf, eds., *Reassessing Arms Control* (London: Macmillan, 1985), 143–58.

[22]*When Britain Goes to War*, 49–50. There was much concern in Britain during the late 1930s that Germany would quickly knock Britain out of a future war with a strategic

see the wisdom of airpower and bomb England from the air at the war's outset. The question would then become Which side is more vulnerable to strategic bombing and therefore likely to quit first? Liddell Hart concluded that Germany, *not* Britain, held the advantage.[23]

The Decisive Wars of History is a history of land warfare with the central message that an army is capable of executing the indirect approach, by which Liddell Hart did *not* mean using an army to defeat another army with a blitzkrieg. He was deeply concerned about avoiding direct engagement between the opposing armies: "The perfection of strategy would . . . be . . . the destruction of the enemy's armed forces through their unarming by surrender—without any fighting" (153–54). His hope was that the attacking forces would either go around the enemy army's flanks or come in from behind that army and strike directly at the opponent's civilian population. When Liddell Hart discusses the need for "a move directed towards the enemy's rear" (155) in *The Decisive Wars of History,* he is not talking about a strike against the vulnerable command and control network that is the essential target of a blitzkrieg but about attacks against the opponent's home front. Specifically, he hoped to use the army to inflict massive punishment on the enemy's civilian population and thus destroy its morale.

The model he had in mind was surely Gen. William Sherman, the American Civil War commander famous for his devastating march through the deep South in the last year of that conflict.[24] Liddell Hart was, after all, doing a major biography of Sherman at the same time he was working on *The Decisive Wars of History*. Both books were published in 1929. His discussion of Sherman in *The Decisive Wars of History* is laudatory, and his assessment of Sherman's impact on the outcome of the Civil War is clear:[25] "The collapse of the Confederate resistance was due to the emptiness of its stomach reacting on its morale. The indirect approach to the enemy's economic and moral rear had proved as decisive in the ultimate phase as it had been in the successive steps by which that decision was prepared in the west. The truth comes

---

bombing offensive; LH did not accept this argument, as is clearly reflected in *Europe in Arms* (London: Faber, 1937) and *The Defence of Britain* (London: Faber, 1939). LH did not treat the moral issues surrounding bombing lightly. He was a staunch opponent of strategic bombing in World War II, and his position was predicated largely on moral grounds; see his correspondence with George Bell, the bishop of Chichester, 1/58; B. Bond, *Liddell Hart*, 144–48.

[23]*When Britain Goes to War,* 55–57.

[24]On Sherman's campaign, see Joseph T. Glatthaar, *The March to the Sea and Beyond: Sherman's Troops in the Savannah and Carolinas Campaign* (New York: New York University Press, 1985).

[25]*Decisive Wars of History,* 123–34.

home to anyone who undertakes a careful and comprehensive study of the war" (133).

Liddell Hart maintained after World War II that it was when studying the campaigns of Sherman that he came to appreciate the central importance of the deep strategic penetration for the blitzkrieg (chap. 2). He also clearly intimated that some of his early thinking about blitzkrieg is laid out in *Sherman* and *The Decisive Wars of History*.[26] This is not the case. There is hardly any discussion of tank warfare in these books, and moreover, there is little evidence from these years that he appreciated the importance of the deep strategic penetration. Furthermore, his notion that an army should be used *not* to strike at the opponent's army but to strike instead directly at his civilian population—what I call "the Sherman model"—is fundamentally different from the blitzkrieg.

Liddell Hart's interest in the Sherman model was short lived.[27] He never explained why he moved away from this variant of the indirect approach, although he probably recognized it was unlikely Britain would be able to use Sherman's methods in the early stages of a Continental war; there certainly had been no such opportunity in World War I. Moreover, he probably realized that Sherman could not have executed his march in the early years of the war but only after a lengthy war of attrition created the opportunity.[28] There was also a serious moral problem associated with this policy. As Brian Reid notes, the Sherman model "would transfer the horrors of great battles of attrition away from armies and unleash them upon the civil population."[29] Finally, and perhaps most important, this version of the indirect approach would mean raising a large army and accepting a Continental commitment.

Liddell Hart outlined a third and final version of the indirect ap-

[26]See, for example, *Memoirs* 1:162–172; LH, Foreword, *Memoirs of General William T. Sherman* (Bloomington: Indiana University Press, 1957), xi–xvi.

[27]There is one qualification: LH published two short chapters (5, 16) in *When Britain Goes to War* that draw on his central arguments in *Decisive Wars of History*.

[28]Fuller wrote a biography of Ulysses S. Grant—*The Generalship of Ulysses S. Grant* (London: Murray, 1929)—at the same time LH was writing *Sherman: Soldier, Realist, American* (New York: Dodd, Mead, 1929). The two British strategists quarreled seriously at the time over Civil War strategy, with Fuller making the argument that Grant's victories provided the key to Sherman's success. See B. Bond, *Liddell Hart*, 49; Brian H. Reid, "British Military Intellectuals and the American Civil War: F. B. Maurice, J. F. C. Fuller and B. H. Liddell Hart," in Chris Wrigley, ed., *Warfare, Diplomacy and Politics: Essays in Honour of A. J. P. Taylor* (London: Hamilton, 1986), 42–57; idem, *J. F. C. Fuller: Military Thinker* (London: Macmillan, 1987), chap. 5.

[29]Reid, "British Military Intellectuals," 50.

proach in *The British Way in Warfare* (1932).[30] His central thesis is that British military strategy traditionally had been to avoid committing large-scale ground forces to fight on the Continent and instead to use naval forces to place tremendous economic pressure on adversaries. The British way in warfare was essentially "economic pressure exercised through sea-power" (37). Britain's acceptance of a Continental commitment in World War I, Liddell Hart argued, was a historical aberration Britain should avoid in future. The ultimate aim of his maritime strategy was to place severe economic hardships on the adversary's civilian population, thus weakening morale and collapsing the will to fight.

The faith in the navy that Liddell Hart expresses in *The British Way in Warfare* stands in contrast to his serious reservations about naval power expressed elsewhere. He maintained throughout the interwar period that the Allies' naval blockade had been the decisive weapon in World War I;[31] yet he argued as early as 1925 in *Paris* that developments in naval technology, especially the submarine, seriously undermined "the naval weapon."[32] This surely helps explain why he was so interested in airpower in the mid-1920s. Furthermore, when faced with the question after 1933 of how to deal with the Third Reich, he moved away from the position staked out in *The British Way in Warfare* and reverted to the earlier one in *Paris*.[33] Although he wrote in 1938 about how the loss of Czechoslovakia would affect a prospective British blockade of Germany (a perplexing argument itself), he exhibited little interest in naval power during the latter half of the 1930s. Thus the British way in warfare was a short-lived idea, lasting from about 1931 to 1933.

STRATEGY AND TACTICS

Liddell Hart's ideas on strategy and tactics, in contrast to his changed views on the war and grand strategy, remained largely unchanged dur-

[30]The first chapter in this book is actually a slightly different version of a talk before the Royal United Services Institution in January 1931; see "Economic Pressure or Continental Victories," *Journal of the Royal United Services Institution* 76 (Aug. 1931): 486–510. For an excellent critique of Liddell Hart's argument, see Michael Howard, *The British Way in Warfare: A Reappraisal*, The 1974 Neale Lecture in English History (London: Cape, 1975).
[31]See, for example, *The Real War, 1914–1918* (London: Faber, 1930), 470–76; see also *Decisive Wars of History*, 231.
[32]*Paris*, 56–62.
[33]On his views on the navy after Hitler came to power, see chaps. 5 and 6.

ing this period. He wrote little about infantry tactics after the early 1920s, the principal exception being a lecture to the army's Southern Command during the winter of 1931–32. Basically a restatement of his early ideas about infantry tactics, the talk was published as a short book (*The Future of Infantry*) in 1933.[34] By 1925–32 his thinking about winning wars on the battlefield revolved around armored strategy, not infantry tactics. Furthermore, his hostility toward a Continental commitment removed much of the incentive to think about how to fight a ground war in Europe.

Many of Liddell Hart's principal writings about the blitzkrieg appeared in the mid-1920s, although he had begun developing his ideas on that subject in the early 1920s.[35] Both *Paris* and *The Remaking of Modern Armies*, which contain his first thoughts on the indirect approach, also include sections on the blitzkrieg. Paradoxically, these two books contain some of his principal writings on both the blitzkrieg and strategic bombing. It is apparent, nevertheless, from his writings that he was rapidly losing interest in the subject of armored war during the years between 1925 and 1932. He seldom discussed his ideas on blitzkrieg in the *Daily Telegraph* after 1929 and not at all in *The Decisive Wars of History* (1929). He barely touched on the subject in two 1930 magazine articles on what a future war would look like. The only clear-cut exceptions were the two articles about armored war in the *Army Quarterly* in the first part of 1933.[36]

Liddell Hart produced no work during the interwar years in which he systematically laid out his thinking on the blitzkrieg. Jay Luvaas maintains he did not do so because he "had become deeply involved with other and more pressing problems, and time did not permit a final synthesis of his views on armored warfare."[37] This argument is difficult to accept, for Liddell Hart had the last half of the 1920s and all of the 1930s—considerable time for such a prolific writer—to produce at least an article on the subject. It is difficult as well to imagine a "more pressing problem" for Liddell Hart than armored strategy, so closely linked with avoiding another World War I stalemate.

---

[34](London: Faber, 1933).
[35]See chap. 2, n. 58.
[36]Copies of the *Daily Telegraph* articles are in sec. 10 of his personal papers. The absence of writings about blitzkrieg in the *Daily Telegraph* pieces after 1929 is reflected in "Suggestions and Forecasts: Salient Points from Captain Liddell Hart's Articles in the Daily Telegraph, 1925–1934," undated memorandum for the record, 13/3. On the nature of a future war: "Armament and Its Future Use," *Yale Review* (June 1930): 649–77; "The Next War," *Fortnightly Review*, 1 May 1930, 585–98; on armored war: "Mind and Machine: Part I. Tactical Training in 1932," *Army Quarterly* 25 (Jan. 1933): 237–50; "Mind and Machine: Part II. Tank Brigade Training, 1932," ibid. 26 (Apr. 1933): 51–58.
[37]Luvaas, *Education of an Army*, 406.

Perhaps his dwindling interest in blitzkrieg was due to a reassessment of his views on the offense–defense balance on an armored battlefield. Perhaps he concluded the tank is fundamentally a defensive weapon or, more modestly, that it could be used by an able defender to thwart a blitzkrieg. He did make these arguments in the second half of the 1930s, but well after he had stopped discussing the blitzkrieg. There is no contemporary evidence he considered them. I suggest he moved away from the blitzkrieg not because he had "more pressing problems" to deal with or because he had changed his views about the essentials of armored warfare, but because he was losing faith in the generals who would have to employ his ideas in the next European war.

BIOGRAPHICAL WORKS

Between 1926 and 1934 Liddell Hart produced four biographies and two collections of biographical sketches. With the possible exception of his biography of T. E. Lawrence, these books, as one would expect with works turned out at such a rapid pace, are not carefully researched scholarly tracts; their purpose is largely didactic. Liddell Hart uses history to provide evidence for and to illuminate his military theories; he describes the past almost exclusively in terms of the present. As Jay Luvaas aptly notes, he "encouraged his subjects to speak out on questions of tactics, strategy, and organization for the benefit of contemporaries."[38] Readers recognized at the time that he used his historical writings as a vehicle for promoting his ideas on contemporary military strategy. After reading an essay on Jenghiz Khan that Liddell Hart wrote in the early 1920s, General Maxse, who helped promote Liddell Hart's military career, wrote him, "I enjoyed Jenghiz Khan and especially the masterly infiltration into it of our platoon training effort!"[39] Commenting on *Great Captains Unveiled* (1927), his good friend J. M. Scammel wrote, "These sketches are more than biographies—they are propaganda . . . a good word is said on behalf of tanks on every appropriate occasion."[40] Because Liddell Hart's historical writings are so infused with his ideas on contemporary military strategy, they are worth examining.

These biographies by their very nature show the great importance

---

[38]Ibid., 388.
[39]Quoted in B. Bond, *Liddell Hart*, 46. The article, first published in 1924 in *Blackwood's*, is reprinted in LH, *Great Captains Unveiled* (London: Blackwood, 1927), chap. 1.
[40]Quoted in B. Bond, *Liddell Hart*, 46.

Liddell Hart attached to individual commanders, or what he termed "great captains." William T. Sherman, for example, is "the last . . . Great Captain,"[41] while one collection of biographical sketches is aptly titled *Great Captains Unveiled*. Of course the importance of ideas—the wisdoms offered by these great captains—is stressed throughout these works. The exploits of these great men, he implies, can provide insights that will help Britain to avoid another conflict like World War I: He writes, for example, in the preface to *A Greater Than Napoleon: Scipio Africanus* (1926):

> The excuse for this book is that no recent biography of Scipio exists. . . . The reason for this book is that . . . his military work has a greater value to modern students of war than that of any other great captain of the past . . . it is because Scipio's battles are richer in stratagems and ruses— many still feasible to-day—than those of any other commander in history that they are an unfailing object-lesson to soldiers.[42]

Two of the six biographical works focus on commanders from the Great War. *Reputations* (1928) is an assessment of some of the war's principal commanders written ten years after the armistice. The sketches, while not a damning indictment of the generals, clearly reflect how disenchanted with them Liddell Hart had by then become.[43] *Foch* (1931) is an unflattering portrait of the French field marshal who led the Allied armies to victory in 1918. The book was apparently not published in France because of official dissatisfaction.[44]

Liddell Hart's dislike of Foch was not simply based on his critical assessment of the field marshal's performance during the war. He also considered Foch one of the principal proponents in the years before World War I of Clausewitz's military theories, which Liddell Hart believed principally responsible for the course that war followed.[45] Foch,

---

[41]Liddell Hart, *Sherman*, 403.

[42]*A Greater Than Napoleon: Scipio Africanus* (London: Blackwood, 1926), vii. See also *Sherman*, vii–viii.

[43]LH (as I explained in chap. 3, n. 22) tempered his criticisms of the generals in his published works.

[44]The book's reviewers, not surprisingly, emphasized the derogatory picture of Foch; see 9/9/9. LH, "Note on the French 'Banning' of My Book on *Foch*," 1933, 11/1933/34; Luvaas, *Education of an Army*, 391; articles in 9/9/10.

[45]See *Foch: The Man of Orleans* (London: Eyre & Spottiswoode, 1931), 23–26; LH, *The Ghost of Napoleon* (London: Faber, 1933), 132–39; LH, "French Military Ideas before the First World War," in Martin Gilbert, ed., *A Century of Conflict, 1850–1950: Essays for A. J. P. Taylor* (London: Hamilton, 1966), 135–48. For LH's views on Clausewitz and World War I, recall chap. 2. For more on Foch's pre-World War I military writings, see Stefan T. Possony and Etienne Mantoux, "DuPicq and Foch: The French School," in Earle, *Makers of Modern Strategy*, 206–33.

that ardent advocate of the *offense à outrance*, "acted as an amplifier for Clausewitz's more extreme notes," he asserted. Furthermore, he held Foch responsible for convincing British policy makers to accept a Continental commitment in the decade before World War I, an agreement he considered a great mistake by the time he wrote *Foch*.[46]

Reputations and *Foch* say little about Liddell Hart's thinking on armored warfare and grand strategy. This is not the case, however, with the other four biographical works; we can quite easily trace in them the development of his military thinking. *A Greater Than Napoleon* and *Great Captains Unveiled* (1927) are sprinkled with thinly veiled references to blitzkrieg. Scipio's greatness, he argues, is due in large part to his understanding that "the tactical key to victory lay in the possession of a superior mobile arm of decision—cavalry." He had the foresight "to break loose from the fetters of a great tradition . . . built on the power of . . . infantry."[47] *Great Captains Unveiled* contains many favorable references to cavalry, which is identified as the precursor of modern armored forces. "Only cavalry," he writes in the chapter on Gustavus Adolphus, "can *shatter* . . . [an enemy force] and break up its organization irretrievably—in other words, cavalry is essentially the decisive arm" (120). After lamenting the devastating effect of modern firearms on horse cavalry, he notes, "Fortunately science has come to our rescue and provided us with an armoured and mechanical charger—the tank; when it is realised that the latter is but the modern form of cavalry, in the swift tank assault of to-morrow we shall see the rebirth of the cavalry charge—and with it the decisive warfare of the Great Captains" (120).

There is no reference in these two books to employing an indirect approach as an alternative to engaging the opponent's army directly.[48] This is surprising given that *Paris*, which contains his incipient writings on the theory of the indirect approach, appeared in 1925, before both of these books. A possible explanation is that because both *A Greater Than Napoleon* and *Great Captains Unveiled* deal with land warfare and because Liddell Hart still held out some hope in these years that his ideas about blitzkrieg would be adopted by the military establishment, he chose to inform his historical discussion with his ideas about armored warfare and not the indirect approach.

There is, naturally, hardly any mention of tanks and their revolutionary potential in either of his next two biographies: *Sherman* (1929)

[46]*Foch*, 24, chap. 6; *Memoirs* 1:280–83.
[47]*A Greater Than Napoleon*, 96, 97.
[48]I am assuming *here* that the indirect approach and the blitzkrieg are competing military policies.

and '*T. E. Lawrence'* in *Arabia and After* (1934). As I have said, Liddell Hart maintained in later years that he developed his appreciation of the importance of the deep strategic penetration for the blitzkrieg when doing the research for *Sherman*. There is in that book no discussion of blitzkrieg with emphasis on the importance of the deep strategic penetration, not even veiled references to those subjects. Although *Sherman* is a book that deals with land warfare, it is in fact mainly a paean to the indirect approach (understood as an *alternative* to blitzkrieg), or what I earlier called the "Sherman model." Specifically, Liddell Hart lauds Sherman not because he directly engaged and defeated the Confederate armies but because he avoided them and concentrated instead on striking at the civilian population in the rear of those armies. He praises Sherman for recognizing "that the strength of an armed nation depends on the morale of its citizens—that if this crumbles the resistance of their armies will also crumble, as an inevitable sequel" (330). He elaborates on this point in the epilogue, revealing in the process how his focus had shifted away from the battlefield, where a blitzkrieg would be executed: "To interrupt the ordinary life of the people and quench hope of its resumption is more effective than any military result short of the complete destruction of the armies. The last is an ideal rarely attained in the past, and increasingly difficult since the appearance of nations in arms" (429).[49]

'*T. E. Lawrence'* in *Arabia and After* is about a man Liddell Hart greatly admired. It is probably not an exaggeration to say that he worshipped Lawrence, whom he describes in the book's final sentence as "the Spirit of Freedom, come incarnate to a world in fetters."[50] Lawrence, in Liddell Hart's opinion, was a brilliant military leader, probably the only commander in World War I who exhibited an understanding of the indirect approach. But there is no discussion of the indirect approach or how it would apply in a future war in this book either, which points up the difficulty Liddell Hart faced in operationalizing his vaguely defined concept so it could be employed to Britain's advantage against a Continental foe. There is as well no significant discussion in this 1934 book of the promise of tanks, although Liddell Hart could easily have used Lawrence's military experiences to highlight his theory of armored war. Liddell Hart could offer no satisfactory military theory for fighting another European war. Despite his efforts of the 1920s and early 1930s, it appeared that should there be a second world war, it would resemble World War I. This undoubtedly became a matter of great concern for him when Hitler came to power in 1933.

---

[49]More generally, see *Sherman*, 428–31.

[50]'*T. E. Lawrence'* in *Arabia and After* (London: Cape, 1934), 448. On LH's relationship with Lawrence, see Brian H. Reid, "T. E. Lawrence and Liddell Hart," *History* 70 (June 1985): 218–31.

[5]

Liddell Hart and Nazi Germany: Military Policy, 1933–1940

Germany was an abstract threat during the 1920s and early 1930s when Liddell Hart propounded his military theories. German military strength had been greatly reduced by the Versailles Treaty, and the Weimar political leadership showed little interest in turning its military into a powerful instrument for aggression. Then Hitler assumed power in January 1933, and Europe faced the real possibility of serious trouble. Liddell Hart naturally paid close attention to the question of how Britain should deal with Nazi Germany. This chapter and the next examine the policies he advocated during the 1930s, especially how his policy prescriptions compared with the theories he developed during the 1920s. This chapter is on his military thinking, on strategy and grand strategy. How Britain should deal with Nazi Germany encompassed more than just military measures, however, so he also addressed economic sanctions and diplomacy. His specific foreign policy recommendations are the subject of the next chapter.

Before turning to the specifics of Liddell Hart's military thinking in the years after 1933, there are two important issues to consider: the grand strategic situation that Britain faced in the 1930s as well as the broad contours of official British *military* policy; and the position Liddell Hart held in Britain during the 1930s and his relationship with individuals and the army. An assessment of his role in the policy-making process is left for chapter 7.

For British military policy, complacency had been the postwar order of the day. Although national security planners had been concerned about a possible Soviet threat to India in the 1920s, the period was relatively peaceful. It was not the Germans but the Japanese who first shook this sense of complacency when they invaded Manchuria in 1931. Britain was therefore already thinking about the sorry state of her greatly weakened military forces when Hitler became chancellor. Britain's limited resources for building a military, together with the evidence of a possible Japanese threat in the Pacific as well as a renewed German threat in Europe (and later an Italian threat in the Mediterranean) prompted serious questions about grand strategy[1]—specifically, which threat was the most serious, and what kinds of military forces were necessary to deal with these different opponents? The government established the Defence Requirements Committee (DRC) in the fall of 1933 to study these questions. The DRC's first report, issued in February 1934, called for seeking friendly relations with Japan and called Germany "the ultimate potential enemy against whom all our 'long range' defence policy must be directed."[2] Thus it appeared at this early date that Britain would probably accept a Continental commitment—the very policy Liddell Hart was so anxious to avoid.

The British, however, could not reach agreement about the seriousness of the German threat, and furthermore they were not sure how to deal with it. Lengthy debate between 1934 and the spring of 1937 produced no firm conclusions, and consequently the army languished. Then, in May 1937, Neville Chamberlain replaced Stanley Baldwin as prime minister. The forceful and dynamic Chamberlain was determined to resolve these issues.[3] His cabinet debated until 22 December, when a historic cabinet meeting decided that Britain would *not* prepare an army for a war on the Continent. She would instead concentrate on protecting the homeland, guarding sea lanes, and policing the Empire. The majority of defense money would go to the air force and the navy. The army, whose fate was linked with the Continental commitment, would be starved of funds. Liddell Hart succinctly summarized the situation in the *Times* for 17 June 1938: "Last year was marked by a notable change in, and clarification of, our military policy. . . . It is clear that in last winter's review of military policy the dispatch of a field force to the Continent was relegated to the background, while the idea of repeating the mass effort of 1914–1918 was excluded altogether."[4]

---

[1]On British grand strategy during the 1930s, see Norman H. Gibbs, *Grand Strategy*, vol. 1 (London: Her Majesty's Stationery Office, 1976); Michael Howard, *The Continental Commitment: The Dilemma of British Defence Policy in the Era of the Two World Wars* (Harmondsworth: Penguin, 1974), chaps. 4–6; Paul M. Kennedy, *The Realities behind Diplomacy: Background Influences on British External Policy, 1865–1980* (London: Fontana, 1981), pt. 3.

[2]Brian Bond, *British Military Policy between the Two World Wars* (New York: Oxford University Press, 1980), 195.

[3]On Chamberlain, see David Dilks, *Neville Chamberlain*, vol. 1: *Pioneering and Reform, 1869–1929* (London: Cambridge University Press, 1984); Keith Feiling, *The Life of Neville Chamberlain* (London: Macmillan, 1946); Larry W. Fuchser, *Neville Chamberlain and Appeasement: A Study in the Politics of History* (New York: Norton, 1982); Iain Macleod, *Neville Chamberlain* (London: Muller, 1961).

[4]"The Field Force Question," 17. On the cabinet decision, see Gibbs, *Grand Strategy*, 282–89, 467–72. Although this decision was very important, Britain had been drifting toward it since the early 1930s; it was in no way a sharp break with past policy.

The decision to abandon the Continental commitment was directly tied to the Chamberlain government's thinking about the broader foreign policy issues addressed in the next chapter. Suffice it to say here that although Chamberlain and his chief lieutenants recognized that Germany was a potential threat to world peace, they believed diplomatic means—specifically, diplomatic concessions—could stop Hitler from precipitating a general war. This was the policy of appeasement—in essence, a decision to deal with the German problem by diplomacy instead of the threat of military force.

By rejecting a Continental commitment—which meant the British army would remain small and weak—Britain of course forfeited the only real military lever she could bring to bear against the Third Reich. A powerful British army acting with the French army could threaten to attack Germany if Hitler showed aggressive intentions in the East; that same British army could help defend France, should Hitler strike first in the West. The air force and the navy, although important for defending Britain herself and for protecting certain British interests outside Europe, could not be used to put significant pressure on the Third Reich in a crisis.[5] Only the army could do that.

Serious doubts about the 22 December decision and the more general policy of appeasement surfaced during the Munich crisis in September 1938. Many policymakers began to recognize that Nazi Germany was a much more aggressive foe than appeasement allowed for and that if a major land war broke out on the Continent, Britain would have to join forces with France and her allies to fight against Germany. Britain would again have to raise a mass army for the Continent. The Munich crisis, however, did not lead directly to a change in the priorities established at the 22 December cabinet meeting. At the start of 1939, less than one year before the start of World War II, official British policy continued to reject a Continental commitment. This policy began to unravel in the early months of 1939 and was largely abandoned in late March 1939, after Hitler took the rest of Czechoslovakia. Chamberlain then took the controversial step of committing Britain to the defense of Poland and, later, Roumania and Greece. It was, as one general exclaimed at the time, "a continental commitment with a vengeance."[6] Britain immediately began to raise a large army that could fight along with France.

[5]Considerable money was spent on an air force aimed at the German threat but it was designed to deter Germany from using its air force to attack Britain. On British air policy, see Malcolm Smith, *British Air Strategy between the Wars* (Oxford: Clarendon, 1984); also Gibbs, *Grand Strategy*, chaps. 14–15; George H. Quester, *Deterrence before Hiroshima: The Airpower Background of Modern Strategy* (New York: Wiley, 1966); H. Montgomery Hyde, *British Air Policy between the Wars 1918–1939* (London: Heinemann, 1976).

[6]Brian Bond, ed., *Chief of Staff: The Diaries of Lieutenant-General Sir Henry Pownall* (London: Cooper, 1972), 1:197.

Thus, as the war drew near, Liddell Hart's worst fears were being realized. He did not hold an official government position during the 1930s. His principal occupation was writing. He had left his position as military correspondent for the *Daily Telegraph* in early 1935 to accept a similar one with the more prestigious and influential *Times*, where he remained through November 1939. He also wrote numerous journal articles and published three important books: *When Britain Goes to War* (1935), *Europe in Arms* (1937), and *The Defence of Britain* (1939), each widely reviewed and almost entirely favorably.[7] In fact, if the reviews are an accurate indicator, each succeeding book received more attention and lavish praise than its predecessor. The reviews of *The Defence of Britain*, his last book from the interwar period, certainly give the impression that many Britons viewed its publication as a landmark event. A friend's note to Liddell Hart, written shortly after the book's publication in July 1939, is typical: "Congratulations on the reception of your book! I have never seen anything quite like it. The book may easily affect the course of history."[8]

Liddell Hart also met frequently with policy makers and corresponded with important people in the British establishment. His *Memoirs*, not to mention his papers, provide abundant evidence of his extensive personal contacts during these years. Liddell Hart (as chap. 3 emphasizes) was simply not an outsider who had trouble getting important people to listen. As Michael Howard notes, he "never lacked an influential and sympathetic audience for his views."[9] There was a single relationship, however, that stands above the others. When Chamberlain assumed the prime ministership in May 1937, Leslie Hore-Belisha was appointed secretary of state for war. Hore-Belisha, who knew little about military affairs, met Liddell Hart soon after taking office and was very impressed with him.[10] As his *Memoirs* show—and there is no reason to doubt his account—Liddell Hart wielded considerable influence with Hore-Belisha. The secretary of state for war himself remarked at one point to Liddell Hart, "I owe

[7]*When Britain Goes to War* (London: Faber, 1935); *Europe in Arms* (London: Faber, 1937); *The Defence of Britain* (London: Faber, 1939), essentially a compilation of previously published articles. *When Britain Goes to War* was a rev. and enlarged ed. of *The British Way in Warfare* (London: Faber, 1932). For reviews of *When Britain Goes to War*, see 9/10/18; for *Europe in Arms*, 9/15/8; for *Defence of Britain*, 9/17/9.

[8]Bernard Newman to LH, 19 July 1939, 9/17/9.

[9]Michael Howard, "Englishmen at Arms," rev. of *Memoirs*, vol. 1, *Sunday Times*, 30 May 1965, 24; see also Brian Bond, *Liddell Hart: A Study of His Military Thought* (London: Cassell, 1977), chap. 4, esp. 105–15.

[10]See Brian Bond, "Leslie Hore-Belisha at the War Office," in Ian Beckett and John Gooch, eds., *Politicians and Defence: Studies in the Formulation of British Defence Policy, 1845–1970* (Manchester: Manchester University Press, 1981), 110–31.

everything to your advice, which I have followed at every step."[11] Liddell Hart not only influenced Hore-Belisha's thinking about a Continental commitment and the role of the army but (as I have already said) was also directly involved in selecting senior officers for the military hierarchy, among other matters. This close working relationship lasted approximately one year and covered the crucial period from May to December 1937 when the decision against the Continental commitment was made.

What sort of relationship did Liddell Hart—already very hostile to the British military by late 1932—have with the British high command during these years? He saw little prospect that the army leadership would adopt his progressive ideas on armored war, thus guaranteeing that the next war would differ little from the Great War. "The progress of weapons," he wrote in April 1932, "has outstripped the progress of the mind—especially in the class who wield weapons. Each successive war of modern times has revealed the increasing lag due to the slow pace of mental adaptation. . . . Whatever virtues may be momentarily evoked will eventually be forfeited in futility and fatuity."[12]

Some developments immediately after Hitler assumed power undoubtedly worked to confirm Liddell Hart's worst suspicions about the generals. Most important, General Montgomery-Massingberd became CIGS just after Hitler assumed the chancellorship. Liddell Hart intensely disliked the new CIGS, whom he called "the high priest of humbug," who is "only positive in stamping out originality." Although Liddell Hart held no CIGS of the interwar period in high regard, Montgomery-Massingberd was the only chief he seemed to loath.[13] In light of the importance Liddell Hart ascribed to senior officers listening to and following his advice, the simultaneous rise to power of Hitler and Montgomery-Massingberd could only reinforce his commitment to keeping the British army off the Continent.

---

[11]Quoted in Jay Luvaas, *The Education of an Army: British Military Thought, 1815–1940* (Chicago: University of Chicago Press, 1964), 408. See *Memoirs* 2: chaps. 1–3; also *Defence of Britain*, where LH details his close relationship with Hore-Belisha; chap. 7 in this book.

[12]"War and Peace," *English Review* 54 (Apr. 1932): 440. See also LH, "Seven Years: The Regime of Field-Marshal Lord Milne," ibid. 56 (Apr. 1933): 376–86; LH, "The Grave Deficiencies of the Army," ibid. 56 (Feb. 1933): 147–51.

[13]"1930 Diary. Engagements and Notes," 13 Sept. entry, 11/1930/1b. For other examples of LH's dislike of Montgomery-Massingberd, see "Some Odd Notes for History (1933)," memorandum for the record, 11/1933/35; "Note on the C.I.G.S., Sir A. A. Montgomery-Massingberd," 1934, 11/1934/64; "Self-Revelation, Lieut.-General—Sir A. A. Montgomery-Massingberd on the Subject of Colonel Fuller and His Writings," memorandum for the record, n.d., 11/1934/70; LH to Maurice Hankey, 2 Dec. 1932, 1/352; see also the correspondence between them in 1/520 and LH's comments about Montgomery-Massingberd in his *Memoirs*.

Other developments involving the British Army in the first year or two after Hitler came to power also seem to have disturbed Liddell Hart very much. The army announced in June 1933 that the American Civil War would be the subject of the military history portion of the officers' promotion examination.[14] Two of the three books prescribed for study were Fuller's *Grant and Lee* and Liddell Hart's *Sherman*. One month later the subject of study was changed, apparently on the orders of Montgomery-Massingberd. "The objection," according to Liddell Hart's information, was that the CIGS felt that he and Fuller "were subversive writers, whose books should not be encouraged."

From Liddell Hart's perspective, the situation did not improve in 1934. He had his first heated exchange with Brig. Gen. Edmonds (see chap. 3) that year—over the official historian's unwillingness to state the unvarnished truth in the histories. Edmonds willingly provided Liddell Hart with damning evidence and judgments about the generals but was unwilling to provide that information directly to a wider audience. A deeply bothered Liddell Hart concluded, "Soldiership cannot be divorced from loyalties and loyalty to anything but the truth makes scientific enquiry farcical. So the succession of errors must go on and the lessons remain unlearnt."[15] Undoubtedly he was also disturbed by the dismal results of the 1934 maneuvers. Because these exercises were to test the concept of an armored division for the first time, the outcome could only have confirmed Liddell Hart's worst suspicions about British military leaders. In late 1934, Liddell Hart began to move away from the position that the tank offered a means to restore the offense to its dominant position on the battlefield and toward the opposite position that the defense reigned supreme, even on a tank-dominated battlefield. This move was undoubtedly the result of his belief that there was no longer any hope of convincing the generals of the wisdom of his armored warfare theories.

Montgomery-Massingberd retired in April 1936 and was replaced by F. M. Sir Cyril Deverell. Liddell Hart considered him an improvement, although he generally held him in low regard. In fact he encouraged Hore-Belisha to remove Deverell from his post as CIGS, which happened in December 1937. Liddell Hart then played an important role in selecting Deverell's successor as well as in making a number of other senior army appointments.[16] Naturally he was on friendly terms with

---

[14]The account of this episode is from "Some Odd Notes for History (1933)" and *Memoirs* 1:172.

[15]LH to Brig. Gen. J. E. Edmonds, 13 Nov. 1934, 1/259.

[16]*Memoirs* 2: chap. 2.

the new CIGS, Lord Gort, and some of his chief lieutenants. Liddell Hart actually had long-standing friendships with some of those new leaders.[17]

It did not take long, however, for relations to sour. The generals resented Liddell Hart's close relationship with Hore-Belisha. They considered it improper for the secretary of state for war to rely on an unofficial civilian adviser for military counsel when he had official military advisers for that purpose.[18] They came to see Liddell Hart as a direct threat to their authority. Liddell Hart's distrust of the military had meanwhile become so deepseated that, almost inevitably, initial differences of opinion would spiral and Liddell Hart would end up as an adversary of the military chiefs he had helped to select.[19] This, of course, is just what happened.[20] Thus with hardly any abatement in Liddell Hart's suspicion of the military in the years after Hitler assumed power, he remained overtly hostile to the Continental commitment throughout the decade.

THE EMERGENCE OF A NEW MILITARY THEORY: THE PROBLEMS

This discussion of Liddell Hart's firm opposition to a Continental commitment in the face of the growing threat from the Third Reich brings us to a central question: What military policies did Liddell Hart advocate for meeting the German threat? Did he rely on the military theories he developed before 1933, the indirect approach and the blitzkrieg, or did he develop new ideas? He abandoned his early theories and developed completely new military arguments in the 1930s. He hardly mentioned the indirect approach in the years between 1933 and 1940; he simply did not argue that Germany could be defeated by such an approach. Brian Bond shows he actually opposed those British military operations in the early stages of World War II that might be considered examples of it. Liddell Hart was, for example, opposed to

[17]See, for example, his correspondence files with generals Ronald Adam (1/4), Lord Gort (1/322), and William E. Ironside (1/401).

[18]See, for example, Maj. Gen. Sir John Kennedy, *The Business of War* (London: Hutchinson, 1957), 14. Those same generals were not above consulting with LH and using him for their own purposes *before* they were elevated to their new positions in December 1937.

[19]Although LH applauded the coming of the army's new regime, he did have some reservations; see LH to Edmonds, 4 Dec. 1937, 1/259; Luvaas, *Education of an Army*, 410.

[20]*Memoirs*, vol. 2, esp. chap. 3. See also correspondence between LH and Geoffrey Dawson over a piece LH wrote for the *Times*, "New Forms and Old Habits," which Dawson did not want to publish; copies of relevant papers and correspondence in 3/108.

Britain's launching an offensive against Norway in the spring of 1940 because Britain should avoid "getting strategically frozen in trying to get a flanking grip on some remote part of the enemy's territory."[21] It was not until after World War II that he resurrected the indirect approach and gave it new life by identifying it with the blitzkrieg.[22]

Although Liddell Hart did not speak about the general theory of the indirect approach in those troubled years after Hitler came to power, he might have been expected to emphasize that Britain could use its navy effectively against Nazi Germany. After all, his final variant of the indirect approach was the British way in warfare, which focused on the navy's purported ability to put significant economic pressure on an adversary. Instead he argued in the first article he wrote for the *Times* that naval power held little promise for Britain in a war against a Continental power: "To regain our old naval strength, relative to other fleets, would involve an immense outlay; and this would, almost for certain, have to be increased on account of the armament race that would thereby be stimulated. But even supposing we could stand the financial strain, we could not regain our old degree of real sea-power, for conditions have changed." He saw Britain's position as a great naval power undermined by the development of "shore-based aircraft . . . high-speed light craft," and especially submarines. These three weapons, he argued, made it virtually impossible to effect a close blockade against a Continental power and very difficult to place significant economic pressure on Germany. At the same time, the submarine provided a Continental power with the means to wreak havoc on Britain's sea lines of communications, as demonstrated in World War I.[23]

His first article elicited a letter to the *Times* from a "Sailor," who challenged Liddell Hart's views about naval power.[24] Liddell Hart responded with a letter of his own, in which he again expressed his doubts about the utility of naval power. He emphasized in the letter's final paragraph that although he still believed naval power had been decisive in Germany's defeat in World War I, it would have little relevance in a future war against Germany: "My own view of the importance of sea power is expressed in the conclusion which I have recorded elsewhere, that the issue of the War was decided by the pressure of the British Navy rather than by the defeat of the German

---

[21]Quoted in B. Bond, *Liddell Hart*, 130; see 130–31.
[22]See chap. 2, n. 64.
[23]"The Defence of Britain: Arms and Policy," *Times*, 14 Mar. 1935, 16. See *Defence of Britain*, 135–46; LH, "Reflections on *Naval Strategy*," memorandum for the record, 1 June 1939, 11/1939/57b. LH had actually first made these arguments in *Paris, or The Future of War* (New York: Dutton, 1925).
[24]Sailor, "Capital Ships and Defence," letter, *Times*, 19 Mar. 1935, 12.

Army. *But one must be ready to recognize qualifying facts as well as changing conditions.*"[25] Liddell Hart remained skeptical about the utility of sea power throughout the 1930s,[26] although he did hint during the Munich crisis (chap. 6) that a blockade might be an effective weapon.

Liddell Hart also abandoned his theory of the blitzkrieg and adopted instead the opposite argument: that regardless of whether an attacker employed tanks, the defender would almost always stop the offender on the battlefield. He was by the late 1930s an extreme advocate of the view that the defender would have the advantage in another European war.

The development of Liddell Hart's military thinking during the 1930s is best understood in historical perspective. During the early 1920s he was mainly concerned with discovering a way to restore the supremacy of the offense and win a quick and decisive victory on the battlefield, assuming all the time that Britain's military leaders would adopt his solution. This was the ultimate goal behind his study of infantry tactics and, later, armored strategy. His growing interest in grand strategy during the mid-1920s was directly tied to a second deep concern, avoiding a Continental commitment, a concern that remained strong in the early 1930s. Thus from about 1925 to the time of Hitler's rise to power, Liddell Hart had two goals: at the strategic level, to ensure battlefield success for the British army in a future European war; at the grand strategic level, to ensure that Britain did not send an army to fight in just such a land war. There were two fundamental problems with his thinking, and both revolved around his theory of blitzkrieg, which he eventually had to abandon.

First, there was a deep-seated tension between his ideas on armored strategy and those on grand strategy. His theory of blitzkrieg, with its emphasis on winning rapid victories, was hardly likely to discourage British policy makers from raising a large army and sending it to the Continent. The blitzkrieg, he argued, restored the offense to its dominant position on the battlefield and provided the means of avoiding a protracted and bloody conflict. Moreover, because he had not addressed the question of how a defender might thwart a blitzkrieg, he had helped create the impression that an army using that strategy would be nearly unbeatable. This argument was likely to encourage wavering British decision makers to accept a Continental commitment; after all, Liddell Hart had provided them with hope that the next war would be quick.

[25]"Sea-power and New Conditions," letter, *Times*, 20 Mar. 1935, 10; emphasis added. See also Sailor, letter, ibid., 23 Mar. 1935, 8.
[26]See, for example, *Defence of Britain*, 135–64; "Reflections on *Naval Strategy*."

This problem was compounded for Liddell Hart by his strongly held belief that military leaders are instinctively attracted to offensive strategies, a common theme in his writings during the 1930s. "Attack is so deeply rooted in the military tradition," he wrote in the *Times* in September 1937, "that its power to succeed, as a natural result of the offensive spirit properly directed, is the first article of the soldier's creed."[27] Thus there was the danger the British generals, with their offensive proclivities, might latch onto the general claim that the tank had great offensive potential without really understanding the essentials of the blitzkrieg.[28] Here was the root of the problem: the blitzkrieg did provide the means to quick victories on the battlefield, but the British generals, ignoring Liddell Hart's ideas, were hardly likely to understand how to employ the tank properly. Thus, Britain would end up in a world war with no formula for avoiding a war of attrition. Instead, their thinking would be informed by false illusions.

Liddell Hart probably perceived the danger in buttressing these illusions by talking openly about the offensive potential inherent in armored forces. Although there is no direct evidence this was the case, the fact he did not write much about the blitzkrieg after 1929 strongly suggests he was aware of the problem. The significant change in his military thinking after 1933 is further evidence he recognized that expounding the virtues of the blitzkrieg hindered his efforts to avoid a Continental commitment.

There was a second major problem with Liddell Hart's advocacy of blitzkrieg. Deterrence was undermined by emphasizing that offense would succeed on the battlefield. It made no sense to tell the Germans, or any potential aggressor, that proper employment of tanks would allow them quickly to overrun a neighboring country. If anything, deterrence would best be served by convincing an adversary that defense had a significant advantage and therefore aggression would probably lead to a war of attrition.

Liddell Hart had paid scarce attention to deterrence during the 1920s. Fighting wars was his principal concern, not preventing them.[29]

---

[27]"The Attack in Warfare: Changing Tactics," *Times*, 10 Sept. 1937, 13; see also *Defence of Britain*, 101, 374. Substantial evidence shows militaries prefer offensive strategies. This was certainly true before World War 1; two important books which deal with this subject are Barry R. Posen, *The Sources of Military Doctrine: France, Britain, and Germany between the World Wars* (Ithaca, N.Y.: Cornell University Press, 1984); Jack L. Snyder, *The Ideology of the Offensive: Military Decision Making and the Disasters of 1914* (Ithaca, N.Y.: Cornell University Press, 1984).

[28]LH's concern was undoubtedly heightened further by his belief that "the military mind" is characterized by its "irrepressible optimism"; see "Would Another War End Civilization?" *Harpers Magazine*, February 1935, 321.

[29]*Memoirs* 1: 183.

He first started thinking about deterrence in the spring of 1931, when he was asked to advise the British government on the position it should take at the upcoming Disarmament Conference in Geneva. He immersed himself in the subject and soon came to the conclusion that the "root" of the deterrence problem was "weapons which inherently favoured the offensive."[30] Specifically, it was the tank employed according to the dictates of the blitzkrieg that made aggression easy and war therefore more likely.[31] This conclusion pointed up to him that his efforts "to revive the offensive power of armies" would actually work to increase the prospects of war in some future crisis,[32] a point he makes clearly in his *Memoirs* when describing his efforts to provide the government with guidance for the Disarmament Conference:

> It was the hardest test that ever confronted me in striving to take a completely objective view. . . . For I soon realised that the obvious solution would entail annulling not only the development of tanks as a military tool but the whole concept of reviving the power of the offensive and the art of war, by "lightning" strokes with highly mobile mechanised forces—thus cancelling out all I had done during the past ten years to develop and preach this new military concept [the blitzkrieg]. If I propounded the "disarmament" antidote to it, and helped to obtain its adoption at the coming conference, it would mean strangling my own "baby." (1:186)

Despite those initial misgivings, Liddell Hart became a forceful advocate of qualitative arms control and argued eloquently for abolishing tanks from the world's major armies. His overarching goal was to "help the defender far more than the invader" or in other words to "place a definite handicap on the offensive, and so on aggression." This could best be accomplished, he argued, by stifling the development of tanks: "So long . . . as armies retain their 'tin-openers,' the possibility of aggression remains. . . . Professional military advisers may still be found to hold out hopes of success to war-minded statesmen, militarily ignorant. Only by making the impotence of the offensive obvious beyond concealment can we remove this potential encouragement."[33]

---

[30]Ibid., 186; see also n. 42 below. See *Memoirs* 1: chap. 8, for a lengthy discussion of LH's experience advising on Geneva.

[31]He also viewed heavy artillery as an offensive weapon; see his "Aggression and the Problem of Weapons," *English Review* 55 (July 1932): 74–78.

[32]Ibid., LH wrote this article in response to an earlier piece in the same journal by Fuller, "What Is an Aggressive Weapon?" 54 (June 1932): 601–5.

[33]"Aggression and the Problem of Weapons," 73, 75, 76.

It was apparent by the time Hitler came to power in early 1933 that any attempt "to seal the supremacy of the defensive on land" through arms control was not going to succeed.[34] Nevertheless, for the remainder of the decade, Liddell Hart poured his energies into finding a way to deter a future aggressor instead of addressing the question of how Britain could best fight a war against that aggressor. He must have concluded that Britain could not win a war and deterrence was imperative.

In short, Liddell Hart was preoccupied after 1932 with two broad goals. He wanted to ensure that Britain did not accept a Continental commitment and build a large peacetime army that could be used in another world war; and he sought to devise an acceptable policy for deterring Germany from starting a new world war. These two goals were, of course, closely linked, for a successful deterrence policy would largely moot the issue of Britain's being dragged into another Continental war.

There was, however, an important tension between these goals because the threat to commit the British army to fight against Hitler was an effective instrument of deterrence. One could argue that a Continental commitment was the only realistic way Britain might deter Hitler—a matter discussed at some length in chapter 7. Suffice it to say here, there was considerable pressure on British policy makers to embrace a Continental commitment. Liddell Hart therefore needed to develop a set of military ideas that would guarantee deterrence without that commitment.

THE EMERGENCE OF A NEW MILITARY THEORY: THE SOLUTION

Liddell Hart adopted basically the same three-pronged solution to both problems. The best way to avoid going back onto the Continent was to argue first, that the defense has a great advantage over the offense on the battlefield and, second, that as a consequence, World War II would be a mere replay of World War I. The thing to do was not to speak about the tank as a revolutionary weapon but instead to emphasize that, even with tanks, an attacker is very unlikely to succeed. The next war, in other words, would closely resemble the Great War. Given this picture of a future war, British policy makers would not be tempted to repeat the "mistake" of sending an army to the

---

[34]Ibid. On the 1932 Disarmament Conference, see Marion W. Boggs, *Attempts to Define and Limit "Aggressive" Armament in Diplomacy and Strategy* (Columbia: University of Missouri, 1941).

Continent. In essence, Liddell Hart had to bring his views on strategy into line with his proposed grand strategy. To do this, however, he would have to abandon his views on blitzkrieg and adopt instead the opposite position, that defense almost always enjoys a *great* advantage over offense.

Believing, as he did, that military leaders are attracted to offensive strategies, Liddell Hart naturally was concerned about German proclivities for offense. He believed, however, that this penchant for offense was also found among British and French officers, and he was especially concerned about the French. He recognized, quite correctly, that they had adopted a defensive strategy for meeting the German threat, but he strongly believed "the French temperament was offensive, and in the Army that tempermental trend was deepened by its doctrine and training, which were still mainly concentrated on offensive action." Thus he worried that in a crisis the French would abandon their defensive posture and launch an attack against Germany, dragging Britain into the war in the process.[35] It is important to emphasize that his message about the virtual impossibility of offense succeeding on the modern battlefield was directed at the British and especially the French as well as the Germans. Perhaps his thinking about deterrence is best captured by a statement he made in the spring of 1939: "The only hope for our civilisation lies in nobody winning the next war, or, better still, in everybody being brought to realise beforehand the futility of trying to win it."[36] This argument could not coexist with his early views about the revolutionary potential of the tank; his thinking about armored strategy had to change.

There was a third dimension to Liddell Hart's approach to keeping Britain from a Continental commitment. He had to concern himself with the widely accepted view that France alone was no match for Germany, with her larger population and more powerful industrial base, an imbalance that provided a compelling reason for committing British ground forces to the Continent. A convincing argument that the

[35]*Memoirs* 2:244. For an example of LH's thinking about the French army and offense, see *Defence of Britain*, chap. 11; also *Europe in Arms*, chap. 4. On French doctrine during the interwar years, see Posen, *Sources of Military Doctrine*, 82–94, 105–40. For examples of LH's fear that France would pursue an offensive, see "Field Force Question," 18; "The Defence of the Empire," *Fortnightly* 143 (Jan. 1938): 28–29; "Talk with Anthony Eden," memorandum for the record, 12 Sept. 1938, 15/5/36; memorandum for the record, 11/1936/64; LH to F. H. France, 19 Nov. 1936, 3/111; *Defence of Britain*, 209. In addition to discouraging the French from pursuing an offensive strategy by emphasizing the supremacy of the defense, LH thought it virtually impossible for France to strike against Germany without a British field force on the Continent; see France letter.

[36]"Reflection," memorandum for the record, 19 Apr. 1939, 11/1939/43b; see also *Defence of Britain*, 26.

French army was more powerful and the German army less formidable would weaken the case for coming to the aid of France. Liddell Hart, however, had argued (presciently) throughout the 1920s that the French army was a feeble force, the German army a potent fighting machine.[37] He would also have to change that assessment.

The changes were not sudden. Liddell Hart could not credibly embrace the ascendancy of the defense; he was, after all, clearly identified by the early 1930s with the view that the tank is an offensive weapon. Fortunately for him, the changing international environment accommodated a gradual shift in his pronouncements about the offense–defense equation. Specifically, the true nature of the German threat was hard to discern immediately after Hitler assumed power. The Third Reich was not perceived in 1934 as the menace it appeared to be in 1939. The pressure for a Continental commitment to deal with this threat built slowly, allowing Liddell Hart to shift his views on armored strategy gradually.

The first evidence Liddell Hart was altering his views about the blitzkrieg is found in two articles he wrote in late 1934 on what a future war would look like.[38] He concluded that World War II would pick up where World War I left off. He emphasized that "the advantage of the defensive is even greater than before."[39] He was not unaware of the shift beginning to take place in his views: "Inasmuch as I have been a prophet of mechanization for years and have so often proclaimed the power of tanks to resurrect mobility, it may seem strange that I should demur to some extent when the highest official authorities come to accept these ideas." He went on to explain, however, that his doubts were based on the belief that military leaders were hostile to mechanization, which he distinguished from motorization. They favored motorization, or providing armies with wheeled vehicles; they were antagonistic toward mechanization, which meant employing tracked vehicles like the tank:

> So far as recent developments in equipment have gone, the armies are becoming motorized but not bullet-proof. They have far more mobility—

[37]For his principal writings from the 1920s about these two armies, see *The Remaking of Modern Armies* (London: Murray, 1927), esp. chaps. 13, 15, 18, originally written in 1926 for the *Daily Telegraph*.

[38]"Speed!—and More Speed!—in War," *New York Times Magazine*, 2 Dec. 1934, 3–18 (rptd. in *When Britain Goes to War*, chap. 3); "Would Another War End Civilization?" 312–22 (written Nov. 1934—see 10/1934/138). The last major articles that contain some of his early ideas on blitzkrieg without mentioning the impact of the defender's capabilities are "Mind and Machine: Part I. Tactical Training in 1932," *Army Quarterly* 25 (Jan. 1933): 237–50; "New Armies for Old," *Current History* 37 (Mar. 1933): 641–48; "Mind and Machine: Part II. Tank Brigade Training, 1932," *Army Quarterly* 26 (Apr. 1933): 51–58.

[39]"Would Another War End Civilization?" 319.

until they meet opposition. To retain mobility when one comes under fire one needs armored mobility [i.e., tanks].

Contrary to the prevailing military belief, I think that the motorization of armies is more likely to strengthen the defensive than to revive the power of the offensive.[40]

Liddell Hart still maintained at this point that mechanization provided the means—the tank—to avoid another World War I, but he doubted Britain's military leaders would come to agree.

Liddell Hart moved to the *Times* early in 1935; that November he published a three-part series in the *Times*, "The Army To-day."[41] He again extolled the power of the defense, but without referring to the distinction between motorization and mechanization. In fact he clearly implied, contrary to what he had written in the two 1934 articles, that even *with* mechanization, the power of the defense had increased significantly:

My own view is that these potential developments in offensive power are far exceeded by the actual growth, largely unrecognized, of defensive power, and that the progress of mechanisation hitherto has already reinforced the capacity for resistance more than it has any good prospect of strengthening the capacity for attack. Not only fire, but the means of obstruction and of demolition, may now be moved more swiftly to any threatened spot to thwart a hostile concentration of force.[42]

Although he believed the offense was at a marked disadvantage in a mechanized world, he did note that "radically different . . . methods" from those used in the Great War—presumably the blitzkrieg—might restore the primacy of the offense.[43] Even this argument, however, would eventually disappear from his writings.

[40]"Speed in War," 18.
[41]"The Army To-day: Conditions of Efficiency," *Times*, 25 Nov. 1935, 13–14; "A New Technique Needed," ibid., 26 Nov. 1935, 15–16; "Getting There First," ibid., 27 Nov. 1935, 15–16.
[42]"New Technique Needed," 15. I agree with the thrust of LH's argument. The claim that the tank is essentially an offensive weapon is wrong; a skilled defender who employs his tanks properly can thwart a blitzkrieg. Two points are in order, however, on LH's evolving position on the superiority of the defense. First, his early discussion of the blitzkrieg (chap. 2) did not raise the issue of whether the defender could employ tanks to his advantage. His writings implied that a blitzkrieg executed as he prescribed would succeed axiomatically; this argument about defense was a shift in his thinking. Second, in *subsequent* pieces on the strength of the defense, especially those written in the late 1930s, he failed to discuss the significant offensive potential of the tank when a defender does not understand how to employ tanks on the battlefield (i.e., he failed to emphasize that a blitzkrieg was possible under certain circumstances). In effect, he exchanged one extreme position for another.
[43]"Army To-day," 14; see also "Getting There First," 16.

One year later (October–November 1936), Liddell Hart had a two-part series in the *Times*, in which he again addressed the issue of the offense–defense equation.[44] His conclusions were similar to those in the "Army To-day" series except that he omitted his claim that the tank, properly employed, might produce a quick and decisive victory. He discussed instead the difficulties the tank would have on the modern battlefield, emphasizing for the first time that "the development of anti-tank weapons is an increasing threat to the tank."[45]

One month later the *Atlantic Monthly* published an article of Liddell Hart's on future warfare, in which he again directly challenged his earlier position that "mechanization has given the General Staffs a new ground for belief in mobile warfare."[46] He emphasized instead that mechanization provided the defender with the wherewithal to move his forces rapidly to threatened points along the front. He argued that "despite the apparent advantage that mechanization has brought to the offensive, its reenforcement of the defensive may prove greater still." He again emphasized that the tank was threatened by "the great and widespread development of armor-piercing weapons." He concluded that "there is reason to doubt whether this mechanized spearhead [the key element in the blitzkrieg] will produce the decisive advantage which is sought."[47]

By 1937, Liddell Hart had gone a long way toward embracing the argument that defense was far superior to offense and that World War II was therefore likely to replay World War I. It was to be a crucial year: Neville Chamberlain, who assumed the prime ministership in May, was determined to make a concrete decision on the Continental commitment; his government decided in December to eschew it. Liddell Hart's *Europe in Arms* was published in March. The book was basically a compilation of newspaper and journal articles written over the previous three years. The chapters on strategy contained, for the most part, the previously cited articles that elaborated his evolving position on the primacy of the defense. Virtually all the reviewers latched onto the theme of the supremacy of defense on the modern battlefield.[48]

The other major theme in *Europe in Arms*, also grasped by reviewers and also explicit in the earlier articles, was the need to avoid a Continental commitment.[49] Chamberlain became prime minister shortly

---

[44]"The Army under Change: A Realistic View," *Times*, 30 Oct. 1936, 17–18; "The Army under Change: 'Reckless Caution,'" ibid., 2 Nov. 1936, 15–16.
[45]"Army under Change: 'Reckless Caution,'" 16.
[46]158 (Dec. 1936): 687–95, quotation 692.
[47]Ibid., 693.
[48]See reviews in 9/15/8.
[49]LH told Will Spens, his former master at Corpus Christi College, Cambridge, that avoiding a Continental commitment was "the main theme" of *Europe in Arms*; see Spens to LH, 15 Feb. 1937, and LH to Spens, 16 Feb. 1937, both in 1/650.

after publication. When he had read the book, he wrote Liddell Hart, "I found your articles in the *Times* on the role of the Army extremely useful and suggestive. I am quite sure we shall never again send to the Continent an Army on the scale of that which we put into the field in the Great War."[50]

A few months later, in October, when there was much public discussion about foreign policy commitments, not to mention a full-fledged debate in the government, Liddell Hart wrote three important articles for the *Times* on defense versus attack.[51] After briefly mentioning in the first article that "there were still possibilities for the strategic offensive," he went on to argue, "The defensive has a great and growing superiority." The second and third articles painted a stark picture of modern warfare in which the defender held almost all the cards:

> But the assumption—that war inevitably means a fight to a finish—has an illusory foundation. It is maintained only by the failure to recognize the improbability of any decisive issue by arms against an equal opponent, and the difficulties of attaining it even against a much inferior foe. So great is the power of the defensive nowadays that a small reinforcement may suffice to establish a deadlock.[52]

Liddell Hart believed there was evidence in that crucial year of 1937 that the British army was moving to adopt an offensive doctrine. The head of the British army, for example, had noted in an important address that caught Liddell Hart's attention that "attack will always get the better of defence."[53] Moreover, the army's 1937 maneuvers were offensively oriented.[54] The "Defence or Attack?" series was clearly aimed in part at the generals he believed were enamored of offensive strategies.

In these key articles in the *Times*, Liddell Hart linked his arguments about the supremacy of the defense to his views on the Continental commitment and to his theory of deterrence. He maintained there was little to be gained by taking the offensive because the defender has

[50]Neville Chamberlain to LH, 8 Mar. 1937, 1/519/1. Also in LH's papers is a copy of Chamberlain to Leslie Hore-Belisha, 29 Oct. 1937, 1/519/2, advising him to read the chapter on the role of the army in *Europe in Arms*.

[51]"Defence or Attack? The Aim of Army Training," *Times*, 25 Oct. 1937, 15–16; "Defence or Attack? The British Role in War," ibid., 26 Oct. 1937, 15–16; "Defence or Attack? The Futility of Aggression," ibid., 27 Oct. 1937, 15–16.

[52]"Defence or Attack? The Aim of Army Training," 15–16; "Defence or Attack? The Futility of Aggression," 16.

[53]"Defence or Attack? The Aim of Army Training," 16. The chief of the Imperial General Staff (Field Marshal Deverell) and LH subsequently engaged in a heated debate over this matter; see their correspondence in 1/232.

[54]See LH, "Attack in Warfare: Changing Tactics," 13; LH, "Field Force Question," 17; LH, "New Military Problems: Value of Skeleton Exercise," *Times*, 24 Sept. 1937, 7.

such an advantage on the modern battlefield. If Germany's leaders recognized this, they would probably not challenge the status quo, thus allowing Britain to return to her "traditional policy and strategy." It was therefore imperative to "confine our military aim to what is possible—to convincing any opponent [Germany] that he cannot defeat us." It was necessary in other words to promote the "spreading recognition of [war's] indecisive trend." The message was aimed not only at Germany but also at those French generals who might think the Allies could launch a successful offensive against Germany: "It becomes our responsibility to dissuade any allies from endangering their defensive prospects by embarking on the offensive." In short, Liddell Hart believed that once all sides came "to see the strength of the defensive in modern war, the potentialities of carrying on a war defensively . . . the world might be brought nearer than by any ideals to making collective security a reality."[55] If all parties recognized the tremendous power of the defense, deterrence would obtain and there would be no need for a Continental commitment.[56] And Liddell Hart's views on strategy were now consistent with his views on grand strategy.

During the final two years of peace, Liddell Hart continued to hammer away at the probable success of the defender. He published, for example, an important article during the Munich Crisis (September 1938) in which he emphasized that one of "the fundamental military conditions of the present time . . . [is] the increasing power of the defence over attack," which, he argued, "is already very marked." His supporting argument is worth quoting at length because it shows clearly how little faith he had in the tank in the final year before the war:

> It was the machine-gun above all which held up the attack in 1914–1918. There is now a much higher proportion of machine-guns, light and heavy, in all armies. And *no counter-weapon has been proportionately developed.* It is true that tanks have been improved and increased, but anti-tank weapons have made still more rapid progress—and, being cheaper, can be multiplied faster. Mechanization and motorisation quicken the advance, but help the defence even more—by enabling it to rush machine-guns and anti-tank guns to any threatened spot.[57]

[55]"Defence or Attack? The Futility of Aggression."

[56]This close linkage of LH's thinking about the supremacy of the defense, deterrence, and a Continental commitment is found throughout his writings of the period, for example, "The Role of the Army," letter, *Times*, 11 Nov. 1936, 17; "Can Warfare Be Limited?" ibid., 10 June 1938, 15–16; *Defence of Britain*, pt. 1.

[57]"Military and Strategic Advantages of Collective Security in Europe," *New Commonwealth Quarterly* 4 (Sept. 1938): 144, emphasis added. See also 149 on Germany's bleak prospects for military success in a war against France and her allies.

He wrote a Belgian journalist friend during the following summer (July 1939), "The main reality of modern war [is] . . . the superiority of defence. . . . On the main fronts, deadlock is likely to develop very early."[58] Liddell Hart actually believed it likely the next war would see the return of trench warfare. A reviewer of *Through the Fog of War*, his book about World War I published in late 1938, argued, "He gives several valuable lessons on how not to wage trench warfare. But for all anybody knows we may never again have to do so." Liddell Hart responded, "While nothing can be certain, it would appear from the experience of the present war in Spain that trench warfare is likely to recur in any larger European war of the near future. For the ratio of space to force is likely to be higher than it is in Spain, thus allowing still less scope for manoeuvre—this is the condition which produces trench warfare."[59] This argument supported Liddell Hart's premise that World War II would resemble the Great War. With Europe seemingly on the brink of another war, the publication of this book about World War I recounting many of Liddell Hart's by-then-familiar horror stories about the British military profession left the general impression that little had changed in the twenty years since World War I, and many reviewers addressed this implication.[60]

An episode from February 1938 involving the *Times*'s coverage of the Spanish Civil War reveals how deeply committed Liddell Hart had become to making the case for the supremacy of the defense. He was very upset about the *Times*'s descriptions of General Franco's offensives, which he thought had "a wider bearing—on the general line we have taken in the Times about British military policy under modern conditions." He outlined his dissatisfaction in a letter to the paper's editor: "We have constantly reported the recent offensives in the Teruel region from the Nationalist side only, and by our headlines have accentuated the impression of *their* claims to success. We are therefore encouraging our own public and military opinion to persist in the old delusion—that attack is good policy for its own sake."[61] He was still complaining the following year about various stories in the *Times* that he thought "lent their support to the out-of-date argument that 'attack is the best defence' in disregard of the numerous articles in

---

[58]LH to Robert Leurquin, 17 July 1939, 1/441.
[59]George Martelli, "The Stalemate," rev. of *Through the Fog of War*, by LH, *World Review* (Feb. 1939): 62; LH, letter, ibid. (Mar. 1939): 65.
[60]Reviews in 9/16/7. That World War II would differ little from World War I is also predicted in *Europe in Arms*, esp. pt. 4.
[61]LH to Robert Barrington-Ward, 25 Feb. 1938, 3/108. See also LH to Barrington-Ward, 2 Apr. 1937, 3/107.

which I have pointed out its underlying fallacy in modern conditions of war." He went on to argue that "the effect" of such reporting would be "a fresh plunge into Passchendaele-like follies."[62]

Naturally, when Liddell Hart himself wrote about conflicts like the Spanish Civil War and the Abyssinian war, he went to considerable lengths to bolster his own views. Consider his widely circulated analysis of the Spanish Civil War, where he commented:

> On land, the experience of the war has strongly supported the evidence of the World War that the defence is paramount at present. This has added significance because relatively small forces in vast areas offered the attack more scope, and a better chance, than it had on the closely packed Western Front. There have been a few successes gained merely by manoeuvre. But offensives by either side have in general had small effect in proportion to their cost of life. And, even when a local moral breakdown has momentarily cleared the attackers' path, experience has again confirmed that of the World War in showing that conditions set a term to their powers of exploiting it.[63]

Given Liddell Hart's aim of convincing European leaders that offense does not pay, the lessons being drawn from the conflicts in Abyssinia, Spain, and later Poland had to be matters of concern. After all, the aggressor was successful in each case, which could only undermine deterrence. Still, Liddell Hart staunchly maintained right up to the German attack on France that these conflicts supported his claims about the superiority of the defense.[64]

Liddell Hart's last important statement before the war on the subject of defense versus offense came in *The Defence of Britain*, published in July 1939. This book, like *Europe in Arms*, is mainly a compilation of articles from previous years. The message was therefore familiar, and the reviewers had no trouble discerning it. One reviewer nicely captured his thinking about the supremacy of the defense by noting that he "worships the *defense à outrance*." A review in *Punch*, which appeared two weeks before the outbreak of war, reflects the message that the overwhelming majority of reviewers took from the book: "He agrees with other competent writers—English and German—in believing that defence is gaining on attack, so that frontier war under mod-

---

[62]LH to Geoffrey Dawson, 9 May 1939, 3/109. See also LH to Barrington-Ward, 17 Mar. 1939, 3/109.

[63]"Lessons of the Spanish War," *National Review* 109 (Nov. 1937): 613 (also pub. as chap. 24 of *Europe in Arms* and as "Military Lessons from Spain," *New Republic*, 4 Aug. 1937, 357–59. For his views on Abyssinia, see *Europe in Arms*, chap. 23. See also "Role of the Army," 17, on both conflicts.

[64]See, for example, "Power of Defence," *Evening Standard*, 17 Feb. 1940, 7.

ern conditions must soon become nearly static, with immense masses of machinery futilely clanging one against the other under a minimum of human control."[65] John Buchan did point out to Liddell Hart that "perhaps you put your views on the Defensive a little too absolutely," but he went on to say that that was "right [because] a little exaggeration is necessary to switch the public away from the opposite and most dangerous heresy."[66]

One final development in Liddell Hart's thinking about the offense–defense balance bears mentioning. It concerns the complex issue of how numbers of forces affect the prospects for military success. He had argued in the 1920s that with the advent of small but powerful armored forces, mobility, not any advantage in numbers, would provide the key to victory in war (chap. 2). In fact he maintained that a smaller armored force would almost surely defeat a much larger mass army. It was feasible with tanks, he believed, to fight outnumbered and win. In the 1930s, as he sought to describe a future war in terms of two mass armies clashing in World War I fashion, he argued that numbers *would* matter greatly in determining the outcome. Specifically, he maintained that to achieve success the attacker would need an *overall* advantage in forces of at least 3:1, an advantage neither Germany nor the Allies could hope to achieve.[67] It followed that neither side could gain a victory.

There is no doubt that *ceteris paribus* an attacker is more likely to succeed if he has an overall advantage of 3:1 rather than 2:1 or 1.5:1. This is especially true in a war of attrition, where there is little prospect of either side finding a strategy to win quickly and decisively.[68] There is always a very real possibility, however, that an attacker will find a strategy that will allow him to succeed even without an overall advantage in numbers, or with a small advantage, over the defender. The Germans in 1940 did not have a force advantage over the Allies, and yet they managed to score a stunning military victory.[69]

The key to the Germans' success was that they achieved overwhelming superiority at their main point of attack; they were able to overwhelm the French forces in the crucial breakthrough battle opposite the Ardennes. This victory then led to the deep strategic penetration

[65]Britain versus Germany," rev. of *Defence of Britain*, by LH, *National Review* 113 (Oct. 1939): 523; "Form Threes!" rev. of *Defence of Britain*, LH, *Punch*, 16 Aug. 1939, 194.

[66]John Buchan to LH, 1 Aug. 1939, 9/17/9.

[67]See, for example, *Defence of Britain*, 25, 53, 104, 117, 122.

[68]See John J. Mearsheimer, *Conventional Deterrence* (Ithaca, N.Y.: Cornell University Press, 1983), 58–60.

[69]Posen, *Sources of Military Doctrine*, 82–86; R. H. S. Stolfi, "Equipment for Victory in France in 1940," *History* 52 (Feb. 1970): 1–20.

that sealed the Allies' fate. The important point here is that the 3 : 1 figure is a useful rule of thumb when applied to specific breakthrough battles the winning of which might lead to a decisive victory in the war.[70] An attacker, generally speaking, needs a *local* superiority of 3 : 1 or greater to win a breakthrough battle. It is very misleading if not simply wrong to argue that an attacker requires an *overall* superiority of 3 : 1 to gain victory.

Liddell Hart was actually challenged twice on this point in the late winter of 1940. General Edmonds disputed his claim in the *Spectator*, and an army major challenged him on the pages of the *Evening Standard*.[71] Liddell Hart, who was concerned at the time with making sure the Phoney War did not turn real, challenged Edmonds's claim that although a 3 : 1 local superiority was usually necessary to win specific battles, success in war does not require "a general superiority of 3 to 1."[72] Liddell Hart's position supported his claim that neither side could hope for victory along the Western Front, as neither the Allies nor the Germans could hope to achieve an overall advantage of 3 : 1 or more.[73] Also, because he had abandoned his belief in the blitzkrieg, with its emphasis on winning breakthrough battles, and adopted instead the position that the next war would be like the Great War, where there were few breakthroughs, there was little reason for him to focus on what was necessary to effect a breakthrough on a narrow front. This was an important mistake.[74]

Although Liddell Hart's claims about force ratios were flawed, he briefly sketched a second argument about numbers and war that has proved most useful for understanding battlefield outcomes. To assess an attacker's prospects for success, he pointed out, it is necessary to

[70]Nevertheless, this rule of thumb must be applied carefully; see chap. 3, n. 39.

[71]See Brig. Gen. J. E. Edmonds, letter, *Spectator*, 1 Mar. 1940, 287; LH, letter, ibid., 8 Mar. 1940, 330–31; Edmonds, letter, ibid., 15 Mar. 1940, 364; LH, letter, ibid., 22 Mar. 1940, 415; R. Pope-Hennessy, letter, ibid., 29 Mar. 1940, 449. On the other controversy, see LH, "The Way to Win the War," *Evening Standard*, 3 Feb. 1940, 8; Maj. J. R. Kennedy, letter, ibid., 17 Feb. 1940, 7; LH, "Power of Defence."

[72]Edmonds, letter, Spectator, 15 Mar. 1940, 364.

[73]LH wrote, for example, in September 1938, "Even if the bulk of the German army could be concentrated in the West, it would be far too short of a three-to-one superiority unless a great part of the French strength could be drawn away" ("Military and Strategic Advantages," 149).

[74]It is not surprising that immediately after the Fall of France, LH blamed the Allies' defeat in part on the Germans' "immense superiority of force" (letter, *New York Times*, 1 Dec. 1940, sec. 4, 63). See also LH, letter, *New Statesman and Nation*, 5 Oct. 1940, 332, where he makes the same argument about Germany's superiority in numbers but also states, "I emphasized [before the war] that Germany was likely to be able to mobilise twice as many divisions as the French and that the addition of the Italians could make the hostile total more than 3 to 1." Compare this claim with the quotation in the previous note. He eventually abandoned this argument about German numerical superiority when it became clear there was rough parity on the Western Front in the spring of 1940.

consider the defender's force-to-space ratio.[75] Specifically, there is an optimal number of forces a defender needs to cover a fixed length of front. Once the defender achieves that force level and also has robust operational reserves, it becomes extremely difficult for the offender to pierce the defender's forward positions regardless of the relative balance of forces. Liddell Hart, as best I can ascertain, was the first military analyst to point out this matter and discuss it in any detail.

Liddell Hart's writings about force-to-space ratios were designed to foster the impression that neither side could gain a victory in the West and, moreover, that France by herself had adequate forces to cover its front with Germany, thus making it unnecessary for Britain to send a large army to the Continent. He wrote, for example, in an important 1938 article dealing with the question of sending the British army to help France:

> When account is taken of the power of modern defence, the limited length of the Franco-German frontier in relation to the size of the French Army, and the strength of the fortifications there, it is not easy to imagine that any assault upon it could have much chance of success. . . . The same reasons which cast doubt on the practicability of a German attack against the French frontier apply at least equally to a French move in the opposite direction.[76]

Britain, of course, sent a field force to the Continent, but because the Allies left the area opposite the Ardennes thinly defended, the Germans had little difficulty effecting a breakthrough.

Liddell Hart's writings about force-to-space ratios were designed to foster the impression that neither side could gain a victory in the West and, moreover, that France by herself had adequate forces to cover its French security, he had argued, was threatened "unless France entirely remodels her army and its conditions." The German army, on the other hand, he had described glowingly, emphasizing the great attention "paid by the German doctrine to surprise, mobility, and manoeuvre." It was, he had noted, "on the subject of manoeuvre that the German doctrine stands out in the most striking contrast to the French." The Germans also paid careful attention to how best to exploit a breakthrough.[77] Liddell Hart had even raised the ultimate ques-

---

[75]See, for example, "Field Force Question," 17–18; LH, "An Army across Channel?" *Times*, 8 Feb. 1939, 15. LH actually did not write comprehensively about force-to-space ratios until after World War II; see "The Ratio of Troops to Space," *Armor* 69 (May–June 1960): 24–30 (copy in LH, *Deterrent or Defence* [London: Stevens & Sons, 1960], chap. 10). See also Mearsheimer, *Conventional Deterrence*, 44–48, 181–83.

[76]"Field Force Question," 17–18; see also "Army across Channel?" 15.

[77]*Remaking Modern Armies*, 274, 217 (see also 250), 220, 230–31.

tion: "How will the French steam-roller fare if its enemy declines to roll ponderously against it, and instead, barring large areas with gas, concentrates its highly trained forces for mobile thrusts aimed to dislocate the complex French war-machine?"[78] He did not directly answer it, but his views are easy to discern.

Liddell Hart first presented a significantly altered view of these two armies in two articles for the *Spectator* in December 1936.[79] Concerning the German army, which was then expanding under Hitler, he argued, "With increase of size the German Army seems to have rather lost sight of the need for subtlety and surprise on which Seeckt insisted in the post-War era." There is "cause for doubt whether the German Army has yet developed either the equipment or the tactics to solve the problems created by a strong and thoroughly modern defence."[80] He often repeated this assessment in the remaining years of peace, always painting a picture of a less than formidable German threat.[81] He recognized by mid-1939 that "German military literature is lit up with the theme of the *blitzkrieg*—the 'lightning war' "; yet he ascribed no importance to this fact and instead argued that "the soldier's dream of the 'lightning war' has a decreasing prospect of fulfilment."[82]

In contrast to his negative view of the German army, Liddell Hart had new-found respect for the French army. He wrote in the *Spectator*, "In the last year or two there has been a rapid evolution—towards a more flexible and mobile type of force and action." The French Army was developing "a new picture of warfare," leaving behind the outdated ideas of the 1920s.[83] He became convinced that the French army, although not a superb fighting force, was well-suited for defending France against a German offensive:

> Contrary to traditional notions of the French Army, it is nowadays pedestrian rather than athletic in nature, solid rather than brilliant in perfor-

[78]Ibid., 250; see also 248–49.

[79]"The Armies of Europe: II. Germany," *Spectator*, 11 Dec. 1936, 1330–31; "The Armies of Europe: III. France," ibid., 18 Dec. 1936, 1074–75. Between these and *Remaking of Modern Armies* (1927), he wrote little on the capabilities of the Continental armies. Two exceptions are "Are the Generals Ready? The True State of the Armed Forces of Europe," *Scribner's Magazine*, September 1934, 129–37; and "The New German Army," *Times*, 18 Mar. 1935, 14, in which the seeds of the views presented in the *Spectator* are evident.

[80]"Armies of Europe: Germany," 1031.

[81]See, for example, "The Armies of Europe," *Foreign Affairs* 15 (Jan. 1937): 235–53; *Europe in Arms*, pt. 1; *Defence of Britain*, chaps. 3–5, 11.

[82]*Defence of Britain*, 101, 42. This was probably one of the first times the term *blitzkrieg* was used (the chapter was written on 12 July 1939; see 10/1939/68), and apparently the only time LH used it in the interwar period. See chap. 2, n. 56.

[83]"Armies of Europe: France," 1074.

mance; but its training has a thoroughness which that of the newly expanded German army can hardly expect to attain as yet—and its step are very sure.[84]

In quality it [the French army] should prove equal, at the present time, to any that it might meet. And the quantity should suffice for adequate insurance against the success of any hostile attack, helped by the inherent advantages that defence enjoys in modern war.[85]

Liddell Hart maintained throughout the late 1930s that France alone was capable of meeting a German attack. A British contribution was not "needed to maintain the integrity of the French frontiers." So describing the French and German armies would of course help ensure that Britain did not commit ground forces to help France in a war with Germany.[86]

LIDDELL HART, THE PHONEY WAR AND THE FALL OF FRANCE

War broke out on 1 September 1939 when Germany attacked Poland. The Wehrmacht quickly defeated the Poles, and by early October, Hitler was making plans to launch an offensive in the West. The Allies, meanwhile, remained on the defensive. They had no intention of attacking Germany but instead planned to wait for the Germans to strike first. This attack did not come until 10 May 1940, giving rise to talk about a "Phoney War," or "Sitzkrieg." Liddell Hart actually hoped this state of affairs would lead to a settlement or, at worst, some limited skirmishes, but not a major war. He wrote in his diary in mid-September: "The papers are asking for a new war song—for our Army. . . . The most appropriate would be a revival—'All dressed up and nowhere to go.' This war may be decided by boredom rather than blood."[87] His writings were of course designed to discourage all sides from taking the offensive, as Alfred Vagts pointed out during the Phoney War in an essay in the *New Republic*. He remarked that anyone

[84]*Defence of Britain*, 198.
[85]"The French Army: Old Traditions and New Formations," *Times*, spec. suppl. on "French Number," 19 July 1938, x.
[86]*Defence of Britain*, 59, also 209–211. The French quickly picked up this point; see, for example, "A French View of the *Times* Articles: Defence or Attack?" *Army Quarterly* 36 (Apr. 1938): 123–26. Also, LH believed the French would have no choice but to remain on the defensive if forced to fight alone; he feared they might pursue an offensive strategy should Britain send over a field force (n. 35 above).
[87]"Diary Notes," 19 Sept. 1939 entry, 11/1939/110b. On Allied and German decision making during this period, see Mearsheimer, *Conventional Deterrence*, chaps. 3–4.

who wanted to understand the stalemate behind the Phoney War should read *The Defence of Britain*.[88]

Liddell Hart was quite confident that there would not be a "real war." He made a study of Hitler's options before Christmas 1939 and concluded that "the Germans were unlikely to attack in the West because the probable costs and the difficulties were out of proportion to the prospects." He then boasted in his diary in February 1940: "There is no offence more unforgivable to small minds than that of having achieved something—in this case a programme of army reform—which they failed to initiate; or that of being proved right when they are wrong—about the present paralysis of the offensive on the Western Front."[89]

Liddell Hart continued to write newspaper articles after the war began, although he had effectively stopped writing for the *Times* by September 1939. His most important article on the military situation on the Western Front appeared in the *Sunday Express* on 18 February 1940.[90] His basic thesis was a familiar one: "No stretch of the imagination can find on either side now the potential means of victory in a total war." He stressed that the "frontiers of the west are inviolate—owing to the increased power of modern defence." His comments about Gen. Sir William Ironside (the British CIGS) and Gen. Maurice Gamelin (the commander of Allied forces on the Western Front) are worth quoting, especially because Liddell Hart was one of the many who heaped scorn upon Gamelin after the war for his hidebound ideas and his failure to recognize the impact of the tank on warfare.

> Fortunately, soldiers who have had practical experience in command of men are apt to develop a rugged common sense which shakes off the dead hand of time-honoured military custom. In England, Sir Edmund Ironside has long been an example of nonconformity with such ritual. In France, General Gamelin has a natural logic of mind which has tended to work in a similar way. . . . The urge for reckless action, for action's sake, would seem to come rather from impatient civilians or retired generals who are out of touch with the facts of the situation.[91]

He dealt directly in this article with the possibility of a German victory: "So far as can be gauged, only the introduction of some radically new

---

[88]"Liberalism Goes to War," *New Republic*, 25 Oct. 1939, 347–48.

[89]"Talk Notes," 6 Mar. 1940 entry, 11/1940/14; "Diary Notes," 5 Feb. 1940 entry, 11/1940/6.

[90]This and other significant pieces he wrote during the Phoney War are reprinted in *The Current of War* (London: Hutchinson, 1941), pts. 3–5. This article (from which the subsequent quotations in this paragraph are taken) is on 202–8.

[91]LH also wrote other laudatory articles about Gamelin in the months before the attack in the West; see, for example, "Gamelin," *Life*, 20 Feb. 1939, 56–63; "'Good Luck Gamelin,'" *Sunday Express*, 29 Oct. 1939, 7.

weapon, or extraordinarily bad generalship on the Allies' side, could give them any chance of real success." Notice that Liddell Hart, who had been so closely identified with the blitzkrieg throughout the 1920s and early 1930s, does *not* mention the possibility of the Germans employing that strategy.

Liddell Hart's efforts to deter a German offensive and perpetuate the Phoney War were of course unsuccessful. The Germans struck in the West on 10 May 1940. During the German offensive, his claims about the supremacy of the defense, his argument that World War II would look much like World War I, and his estimates of the fighting capabilities of the French and German armies were proven completely wrong.

Liddell Hart actually wrote a series of articles *during* the first days of the German offensive that show very well that he had no inkling of what was going to happen when the Germans finally struck.[92] The articles also show how deeply committed he was to the military ideas he had developed in the years after Hitler came to power. The first article was written on 11 May 1940, one day after the attack began. He was sanguine about the Allies' prospects: "In regard to Belgium, it can safely be said that both her [Britain's] defences and her forces are much stronger than they were in 1914. The thrusting power of the German Army lies largely in its mechanized forces, and to these the Low Countries offer far less suitable going than they found in Poland."[93] He wrote two more articles on 13 and 15 May.[94] His most revealing piece, however, was written on 19 May, by which time the government had alerted the British public to the fact the Germans had crossed the Meuse River and the Allies were in grave danger of suffering a decisive defeat.[95] Liddell Hart's response to this development is worth quoting at some length:

> But the actual, as distinct from the potential, progress achieved by the Germans in France has hardly gone far enough to justify the tone and terms in which its effect was semi-officially described on Friday night. 'Serious' would seem to be a more precise term than 'grave,' for the situation up to the moment. . . .
>
> Moreover, even with a steel-shod thrust, the point may have lost its original sharpness when it has to be used for a second thrust. It will

[92]Nevertheless, I deal further in chap. 7 with whether LH anticipated the Fall of France. These articles are reprinted in *Current of War* pt. 6; copies of the originals in 10/1940.

[93]*Current of War*, 299–301.

[94]Ibid., 302–11.

[95]See LH's description of the picture presented to the public during this critical period in ibid., 312–14; see also *Times* for this period.

certainly be contrary to all experience hitherto if a renewal of the push attains the same proportionate measure of success as the first effort did.

The law of diminishing returns has prevailed with remarkable consistency in the operations of modern warfare between armies of more or less similar quality and equipment. . . .

The German break-through . . . does not compare with the serious strategic effect of the three great bulges which the Germans made in the Allied front in 1918, still less with the desperately ominous situation of the Allied armies on the eve of the Battle of the Marne in 1914.[96]

The next day, 20 May, he wrote an article that reveals he finally understood what was happening:

There is a fundamental difference between the method on which the present German offensive has been carried out and that of 1914 . . . the Germans have realized, and exploited, the decisive importance of machine-power compared with man-power . . . they have pinned their faith to the penetrative power of a highly mechanized force.[97]

Liddell Hart now recognized that the Germans were employing their forces in accordance with those ideas about armored strategy he had championed so fervently in the 1920s but discarded in the 1930s.

Some may say it is unfair to criticize Liddell Hart for not understanding what was occurring on the battlefield, for he was not privy to the flow of official battlefield intelligence, and moreover, he was forced to make snap judgments from afar about a constantly changing situation. I am not trying to make Liddell Hart look foolish but to show that, despite what he wanted people to believe, he did not foresee what would happen when the Germans struck in the West. Moreover, if there was anyone who should have suspected what was going to happen and therefore recognized the gravity of the situation in those early days, it was Liddell Hart. Is it unfair to hold the man who claimed to be the intellectual father of the blitzkrieg to higher standards on this matter?

In sum, Liddell Hart's widely accepted claim that he foresaw not only defeat in the West but the Germans' choice of methods cannot stand against the available evidence. Instead, his mass of writings from the late 1930s and early 1940 make him look like the proverbial general caught preparing for the last war. His reputation could not survive the events of May 1940.

[96]Ibid., 314–19.
[97]Ibid., 320–22.

[6]

Liddell Hart and Nazi Germany: Foreign Policy, 1933–1940

British policy makers were not only concerned with the question of how to use their military to deal with Hitler but also with using the political and economic means at their disposal. Their aim was to determine how best to integrate these three instruments—the diplomatic, the economic, and the military—so as to maximize the prospects of maintaining peace in Europe. Liddell Hart's keen interest in military matters notwithstanding, he had definite views about British foreign policy. His military ideas were, in effect, the core of a broader policy perspective. His effort to convince Europeans they were operating in a defense-dominant world was a central ingredient in his formula for dealing with the Third Reich. This chapter examines his foreign policy prescriptions with special attention to how his views compared with those of the Chamberlain government.

To analyze how Liddell Hart and the Chamberlain government thought about dealing with Hitler, it is best to think in terms of four broad policy options. The first is *appeasement,* which emphasized finding a diplomatic resolution to any problems that might arise. The fundamental assumption was that Hitler had legitimate and limited territorial and economic objectives in Central Europe that could be accommodated by political compromise, leaving him with no reason to threaten war. Appeasement placed little emphasis on threatening Hitler with military force or, for that matter, with diplomatic or economic sanctions. This policy was certainly well-suited for Britain as long as she had a grand strategy that eschewed a Continental commitment.

The other three options rejected the assumption that Hitler could be appeased and focused instead on deterring with direct threats. *Direct military force* was predicated on the assumption it was necessary to threaten Hitler with military action if he pursued aggressive policies.

Specifically, significant military pressure, mainly in the form of powerful land forces, would be necessary to keep the Third Reich in line. This policy meant Britain would have to first accept a Continental commitment and raise a large army that could be used in conjunction with French ground forces, then find allies in Eastern Europe so as to present Germany with the threat of a two-front war. In effect, the threat of another world war would be used to deter Hitler. This option paid little attention to economic and diplomatic sanctions.

The *collective security* option was also based on the premise that Britain had to work in close conjunction with her allies to put pressure on Germany or any other nation bent on upsetting the status quo. Collective security, however, did not emphasize the threat of military force but instead stressed economic and political sanctions. Regarding the possible use of military force, a division of labor different from the one needed to support the preceding option was envisioned. Britain would concentrate on building a powerful navy and air force but not build a formidable army to fight on the Continent. She would instead rely on the French army to place direct pressure on Hitler. Should another world war break out, Britain would thus avoid being dragged into the ensuing land battles on the Western Front. It was widely recognized, however, that as long as Britain refused to build an army for the Continent, as long as she pursued what was referred to as a policy of "limited liability," there was little hope of having an effective military lever to use against the Third Reich. Collective security was thus based mainly on economic and diplomatic sanctions.

The remaining option, *advocacy of the defense à outrance* (discussed in chapter 5), was principally a rhetorical one. Similar to the direct military force option, its ultimate success depended on convincing Germany that military aggression does not pay and is in fact likely to lead to a conflict as horrible as World War I. There was a crucial difference, however: the direct military force option actually called for creating a defensive advantage by promising to move British ground forces to the Continent in the event of war, whereas this option simply sought to persuade the adversary that this defensive advantage *already* existed. There was therefore no need to commit British forces to a Continental war.

The Chamberlain government, coming to power in the spring of 1937, opted to appease.[1] Chamberlain and his close advisers were well

---

[1] On the Chamberlain government's foreign policy, see Paul M. Kennedy, *The Realities behind Diplomacy: Background Influences on British External Policy, 1865–1980* (London: Fontana, 1981), pt. 3; Keith Middlemas, *The Strategy of Appeasement: The British Government and Germany, 1937–1939* (Chicago: Quadrangle, 1972); Wolfgang Mommsen and Lothar Kettenacker, eds., *The Fascist Challenge and the Policy of Appeasement* (Boston: Allen & Unwin, 1983); Gustav Schmidt, *The Politics and Economics of Appeasement: British Foreign Policy in the 1930s*, trans. Jackie Bennett-Ruete (New York: St. Martin's, 1986).

aware the Third Reich was a threat to the status quo and that they had to deal directly with that threat because Britain's security was so obviously linked to developments on the Continent. But they did not believe Hitler was so bent on aggression that Britain's defense posture had to be tailored to put significant military pressure on Germany; they were convinced he could be placated. Chamberlain and his lieutenants also believed the British economy too weak to provide the military wherewithal to deal simultaneously with the Japanese threat in the Pacific, the Italian threat in the Mediterranean, and the German threat in the heart of Europe.[2] Any significant increase in defense spending, they reasoned, would seriously damage the British economy. The resulting policy of appeasement, with its emphasis on diplomatic concessions and no Continental commitment, made a neat fit between their grand strategy and foreign policy.

The British policy of appeasement was embodied in the September 1938 Munich agreement.[3] Chamberlain conceded a substantial portion of Czechoslovakia to Germany in return for what he believed would be the Third Reich's acceptance of the new status quo. Hitler was not satisfied, however, and appeasement began to unravel in the months after Munich. Britain quickly began moving toward reliance on the threat to use military force. When Germany captured the rest of Czechoslovakia in mid-March 1939, Britain moved sharply away from appeasement and adopted instead the direct military force option. But British policy makers had not completely abandoned hope of reaching an accommodation with Germany.[4] Instead they had accepted the widespread belief that Hitler could only be made to behave in accordance with British interests by threatening him with military force.

This switch in basic foreign policy required Britain to jettison the grand strategy adopted in December 1937 and accept a Continental commitment. She moved rapidly toward that commitment in the early months of 1939, with final acceptance coming on 31 March 1939, when, in the aftermath of the German takeover of Czechoslovakia, she provided Poland with a guarantee to come to her defense. Similar guarantees were given to Roumania and Greece one week later. Conscription was instituted at the end of April, and defense spending, which the

[2]Recent scholarship on British foreign policy in the 1930s shows it was motivated at least as much by economics as by judgments about the nature of the German threat. The policy of appeasement grew largely out of the widespread belief that Britain could not confront Germany at reasonable cost.

[3]Roy Douglas, *In the Year of Munich* (London: Macmillan, 1977); Keith Robbins, *Munich 1938* (London: Cassell, 1968); Telford Taylor, *Munich: The Price of Peace* (New York: Doubleday, 1979).

[4]See, for example, Peter W. Ludlow, "The Unwinding of Appeasement," in Lothar Kettenacker, ed., *The "Other Germany" in the Second World War* (Stuttgart: Klett, 1977), 9–48.

government had worked hard to control in its first two years, began to increase rapidly. The story of the Chamberlain government's foreign policy is, in short, one of moving from the first to the second option, with an attendant change in grand strategy, and with little attention to the other options (collective security and advocacy of the supremacy of the defense).

Liddell Hart's foreign policy prescriptions emphasized those other options, but before outlining his views, it is necessary to deal with a possible misconception about his thinking in the 1930s. He was not an isolationist, a point he made clearly in a memorandum to his editor at the *Times* in March 1938: "Before I took over my post on *The Times* I had made a prolonged examination of the world situation in relation to the defence of Britain. Although my historical studies had given me a strategic predisposition towards isolation, this examination of current problems in the light of modern technical conditions led me to see the necessity, for us, of collective security."[5] He was especially cognizant that British and French security were linked.[6] He did not pretend, despite the undoubtedly great temptation to do so, that Britain could simply ignore France's problem with Nazi Germany.

Liddell Hart was well aware after 1933 that there was serious danger of another world war. It would be wrong, however, to assume that this concern meant he fully comprehended the danger posed by the Third Reich. He did not. He was certainly suspicious of German intentions from the mid-1930s until the outbreak of war, but there is no evidence he fully understood at any point the malign nature of Hitler's foreign policy. He was *not* deeply concerned about the German threat per se before 1938, and amazingly, in the months before the war, he took the position made famous many years later by A. J. P. Taylor, that Hitler was basically a reasonable statesman whom the Allies were leading to aggression. It was only during the course of 1938—the year of the first Czechoslovakian crisis—that his writings showed serious concern about German intentions, and even then his assessment of the threat was ambivalent.

For meeting the German threat, Liddell Hart advocated a two-

---

[5]LH to Robert Barrington-Ward, 29 Mar. 1938, 3/108. See also LH, "Collective Security or Increasing Isolation," memorandum for the record, 31 Jan. 1938, 11/1938/17; LH, "The Defence of Britain: Arms and Policy," *Times*, 14 Mar. 1935, 15–16, the first article he wrote after joining the *Times*.

[6]A common theme in LH's writings from the late 1930s; see, for example, "The Neutrality Issue in 1914," memorandum for the record, 21 Mar. 1938, 11/1938/36b; LH to Barrington-Ward, 29 Mar. 1938, 3/108; "The Field Force Question," *Times*, 17 June 1938, 17–18; "Military and Strategic Advantages of Collective Security in Europe," *New Commonwealth Quarterly*, 4 (Sept. 1938): 147; "Strategy and Commitments," *Fortnightly* 143 (June 1938): 648.

pronged foreign policy focused on the third and fourth options: collective security and advocacy of the defense à outrance. At the grand strategic level he remained opposed to a Continental commitment throughout these years. Liddell Hart actually adopted this two-pronged foreign policy before Chamberlain became prime minister, although his advocacy of collective security was somewhat muted until 1938. He stuck with this two-track approach through the period of the Phoney War. Thus, unlike the Chamberlain government, which switched both its foreign policy and its grand strategy in the final year of peace, Liddell Hart stood by his earlier policy prescriptions. There is an important qualification to this point, however, and it concerns appeasement.

Liddell Hart did not embrace appeasement, although he was hardly an archfoe of that controversial policy. He had doubts about whether it would work with an adversary like Hitler. Thus, although he fully accepted the Chamberlain government's initial grand strategy—which of course he helped shape—he merely tolerated its foreign policy. He was deeply upset, however, when that government decided to threaten Hitler with direct military force and to accept a Continental commitment. Although there were indications in the late 1930s that he might accept a limited Continental commitment, that proved not to be the case. Liddell Hart simply could not bring himself to support a policy that relied on military force to confront the Third Reich. In those final months before the war, as the Chamberlain government moved toward increased reliance on its military and as it became evident Liddell Hart's two-pronged foreign policy might not provide a sufficient basis for deterring Hitler, he actually began to move toward appeasement. Nevertheless, he continued making his case for the supremacy of the defense and the wisdom of collective security. In short, from early April 1939 to the outbreak of war five months later, he stood in firm opposition to the government's grand strategy as well as its foreign policy.

LIDDELL HART AND THE MAJOR CRISES OF THE 1930S

The 1930s was a period of increasing turmoil for British policy makers. There was unrelenting pressure on the status quo from the Japanese, the Italians, and the Germans. Britain faced ten foreign policy crises during these years, and Liddell Hart's thinking about them provides an excellent vehicle for exploring his foreign policy views.

1. *First Far Eastern crisis* (1931). Japan invaded Manchuria and established the puppet state of Manchukuo. China unsuccessfully appealed to the League of Nations for help.

2. *First Austrian crisis* (1934). Hitler threatened to intervene in Austria after Austrian Nazis staged a putsch. He was deterred by the threat of Italian intervention.

3. *Abyssinian crisis* (1935–36). Italy invaded Abyssinia (Ethiopia) despite an appeal for protection from Emperor Haile Selassie to the League of Nations.

4. *Rhineland crisis* (1936). Hitler violated the Versailles and Locarno Treaties by sending German troops into the demilitarized Rhineland.

5. *Spanish Civil War* (1936–39). Gen. Francisco Franco's fascist forces fought and won a protracted civil war against the republican government. The fascists were supported by Italy and Germany.

6. *Second Far Eastern crisis* (1937). Japan launched a full-scale invasion of China.

7. *Second Austrian crisis* (1938). The Third Reich, which had shown keen interest since 1934 in controlling Austria, finally occupied the country.

8. *First Czechoslovakian crisis* (1938). Hitler threatened to start a general war if Germany was not given the Sudetenland, a part of Czechoslovakia with a large German population. The crisis was settled at Munich in late September 1938 when that demand was met in return for a German promise not to threaten what remained of Czechoslovakia.

9. *Second Czechoslovakian crisis* (1939). The Wehrmacht occupied the rest of Czechoslovakia on 15 March 1939.

10. *Polish crisis* (1939). Hitler made territorial demands on Poland, but before there was a resolution of the ensuing crisis, Germany attacked Poland, precipitating World War II.

Six crises directly involved Germany; the two Far Eastern crises, the Spanish Civil War, and the Abyssinian war did not.

There are two sets of questions about Liddell Hart's reaction to these crises: First, did he think the crisis at hand seriously threatened Britain's international position? and Did he think the crisis might have important strategic consequences? Second, what actions did he recommend? Did he invariably and forcefully argue for collective security? Did he at any point recommend taking military action? and Was he willing to pursue policies that carried a serious risk of war?

Liddell Hart showed little interest in the two Far Eastern crises. There is not much evidence of concern in his personal papers from the period, and he does not claim in his *Memoirs* to have been alarmed by these distant crises. The Abyssinian crisis was of considerable interest to him, although he does not appear to have been unduly concerned about it. He feared Italian control of that African country because he believed an Italian empire around the Mediterranean would threaten Britain's position in the Middle East.[7] Nevertheless, it appears Liddell

[7]For evidence of slight concern over the 1931 crisis, see LH, "Notes on the Chino-Japanese Affair," Mar. 1932, 11/1932/12b; LH, "Notes on the Chino-Japanese Affair,"

Hart said little privately and less publicly about how Britain should respond to Italian aggression. There is no doubt he supported the *Times*'s condemnation of Italian aggression as well as its harsh disapproval of the Hoare-Laval agreement, a bungled attempt by the French and British to allow Mussolini to keep most of Abyssinia in the hope he would stand with them against Hitler.[8] He never, however, explicitly condemned Italy in his own writings.

He claims in his *Memoirs* that he called at the time for "full economic sanctions" as well as "shut[ting] off oil supplies to Italy," and he also maintains he had problems with his editors at the *Times*, Robert Barrington-Ward and Geoffrey Dawson, because they refused to support these measures.[9] Calling for sanctions is certainly what one would expect from a proponent of collective security, and Liddell Hart was never shy about expressing his views on policy issues. There is, however, no evidence in his personal papers, including the correspondence with his editors, or in any of his published writings from the period that he advocated sanctions against Italy. Nor does he provide evidence in his *Memoirs* to support this claim. Furthermore, there are no signs of disagreement between him and his editors over the Abyssinian crisis; relations appear to have been remarkably harmonious throughout 1935 and 1936.[10] Consider, for example, Geoffrey Dawson's response to a note from Liddell Hart congratulating Dawson "on the line that 'The Times' had taken in condemning Italy's aggression in Abyssinia and denouncing the Hoare-Laval agreement." Dawson wrote, "Thank you so much for your note, which I value—you made a very notable contribution yourself to the series of leaders which, I am glad to say, were written by several hands, so that they really were a demonstration of team-work."[11]

At the height of the Munich crisis, in 1938, Liddell Hart wrote a

Mar. 1932, 11/1932/13b. The relevant pages in *Memoirs* are 1: 285, 291–92, 337–38, 363, and 2:132, 137, 142, 248. His principal writings from the 1930s on the Abyssinian crisis include a host of short pieces published in the *Times* (copies in sec. 10 of his personal papers and key sections rptd. in *Europe in Arms* [London: Faber, 1937], chap. 23) and a journal article, "The Strategic Future of the Mediterranean," *Yale Review* 26 (Dec. 1936): 232–45 (also pub. in *Fortnightly* 141 [Jan. 1937]: 14–24, and in *Europe in Arms*, chap. 9). In *Memoirs* he deals with this crisis in 1:275–77, 286–91, 327–31 and 2:125–26; there is good reason to be suspicious of the account. On fear of Italian control, see "The Strategic Future of the Mediterranean," 232–45.

[8]See correspondence with his editors for 1935 and 1936, 3/105 and 3/106.

[9]1:287; see also 2:126.

[10]I have carefully checked his memoranda for 1935 and 1936 (sec. 11 of his papers), his correspondence with individuals (sec. 1), and his private correspondence with his editors (3/105, 3/106).

[11]LH's original note to Dawson is not in his personal papers, although LH typed out a summary of his note on the top of Dawson's response; see Dawson to LH, 23 Dec. 1935, 3/105.

lengthy memorandum for the record tracing the development of his views on British foreign policy up to that point. It is one of the few times during the 1930s that he discussed the steps Britain should have pursued in the Far Eastern and Abyssinian crises:

> Over Manchuria military action was difficult but economic and moral pressure was practicable—yet we hesitated to apply them. It was argued that no direct British interests were involved. . . .
> Over Abyssinia, the strategic cards were in our hands. By oil sanctions coupled with munition help to the Abyssinians we could have crippled Italy's campaign. The risk of Italy making war on us in retaliation would not have been large. For although she could have inflicted considerable damage on us . . . we could have strangled her. As it was, our half-hearted attitude led to the breaking-up of the system of collective security that was the best guarantee of our own [security].[12]

Several points are in order. Liddell Hart does not claim here (or anywhere else during the 1930s) that he advocated these measures *at the time* of the respective crises. In neither case does his retrospective recommendation call for Britain to have taken direct military action. In the Abyssinian case, where there was a possibility of Britain becoming involved in a war, he candidly admits the risk was small (as will become increasingly evident, Liddell Hart did not favor using the threat of force to deter aggression and did not advocate policies that contained a serious risk of war). And he believed—at least by 1938—that the Abyssinian crisis had dealt a fatal blow to collective security, a policy he nevertheless continued to champion throughout 1938 and 1939.

The Spanish Civil War, unlike the Abyssinian crisis, deeply worried Liddell Hart because of the possibility of a fascist victory. The depth of his concern is reflected in his February 1938 comment: "Those who in this country desire the victory of Franco are traitors to England and all that England stands for." He extended himself, privately and publicly, to make his views about the war known.[13] No crisis save the 1938

[12]"Britain's Foreign Policy: A Reflection," memorandum for the record, 20 Sept. 1938, 11/1938/98b. A portion of this memorandum is reprinted in *The Defence of Britain* (London: Faber, 1939), 21–22.

[13]"Reflections—7.2.38," memorandum for the record, 11/1938/22b. For his published writings about the Spanish Civil War, see *Defence of Britain*, 66–73; "Strategic Future of the Mediterranean," 239–45; "Britain's Military Situation," *Yale Review* 28 (Dec. 1938): 240–41; "Strategy and Commitments," 641–45; "Military and Strategic Advantages," 147–49. See also *Memoirs* 2: chap. 4, esp. 127–30, 135–44. Relevant private papers: correspondence with his editors at the *Times* 1936–38 (3/106, 3/107, 3/108); memoranda 1936–38 (sec. 11 of his papers).

Czechoslovakian one seems to have concerned him so much. He believed a fascist victory over the republican forces would almost certainly result in close cooperation between Germany and Spain. Not only was there a natural ideological affinity between them, but Germany and Italy were providing Franco's rebel forces with substantial assistance. He thought, "it would seem stretching hope to the verge of credulity to expect that . . . [the Spanish fascists] will ungratefully reverse their attitude."[14] Furthermore, Spain would be "filled with the desire to renew its imperial role," which it could do best through cooperation with the other fascist states. Thus, he expected Franco's Spain to be an enemy of Britain and an ally of Nazi Germany.[15]

Liddell Hart found this prospect particularly disturbing, not because of its likely impact on the situation in Central Europe per se, but because Spain was well positioned to interdict Britain's sea lines of communication. Spain had the potential, he believed, to control access to the western Mediterranean as well as to make it extremely difficult for Britain to use the trade routes around the Cape of Good Hope. He was especially cognizant of how airpower enhanced Spain's ability to project power in the seas around her.[16] Spain was therefore in an excellent position to block or seriously hinder British access to the Middle East and the Far East. Liddell Hart had of course argued forcefully throughout 1937 that Britain should concentrate on protecting her sea lines of communication and maintaining the security of her Empire, a position the Chamberlain government eventually adopted. The Spanish Civil War threatened to undermine this policy.

Another reason Liddell Hart may have been concerned about a fascist victory in Spain, although there is no direct evidence for it, is that military experts at the time looked to the battlefields of Spain to determine what a future world war might look like, making Spain an important testing ground for Liddell Hart's claims about the superiority of defense and the consequent futility of offense. This would explain why he was so upset about the *Times*'s description of that war's key battles, which he thought gave the false impression that offense pays. A victory for Franco's armies, the main offenders in this conflict, on top of the offender's success in Abyssinia, would certainly have appeared to contradict Liddell Hart's claims about the near-invincibility of the defense.

[14]"Strategy and Commitments," 644; see 643–45.
[15]"Strategic Future of the Mediterranean," 240. LH's fears, of course, proved unfounded. This issue caused serious friction between LH and his editors at the *Times*, who did not believe that Spain under Franco was likely to be hostile to Britain; see LH to Barrington-Ward, 29 Mar. 1938, and Barrington-Ward to LH, 30 Mar. and 1 Apr. 1938, all in 3/108.
[16]"Strategic Future of the Mediterreanean," 239–43; *Memoirs* 1: chap. 14.

Despite his concern Liddell Hart was reluctant for Britain to take concrete measures to deal with the crisis. He argued at the end of April 1937, almost one year after the civil war began and long after he recognized that Italy and Germany were providing aid, that for Britain, "non-intervention is the wisest policy in the Spanish War."[17] He changed his mind about intervention in March 1938, after Franco's forces scored a major victory in the Battle of Teruel. This successful offensive provided the first solid evidence that the fascists were likely to win.[18] Liddell Hart's response was to argue in a memorandum that Britain should allow the Spanish government "to purchase on nominal terms enough material resources to restore the balance." He went on:

> If Germany and Italy were to reply by a large increase in the quantities of material they have already sent, France and Britain are in a better strategic position than they are for such competition. . . . If they dared to press their objections to the point of war, we should fight with all the advantages of the defensive and under more favorable circumstances of strategic geography than we could hope for once Spain has been conquered. For these reasons the risk seems less than that presented by any other contingency that can be foreseen.[19]

Two points stand out: Liddell Hart's interest in avoiding risk-laden policies (he did not advocate pursuing a strategy that carried a serious risk of war) and the modest scope of his proposed intervention (his aim was not a government victory but only a balance of power between the two sides). His ultimate goal, as he said in September 1938, was to produce "a condition of stalemate favorable to mediation."[20]

This memorandum notwithstanding, it is still not clear Liddell Hart was seriously committed to aiding the forces fighting Franco's armies. Consider that Hore-Belisha, after reading the above memorandum, asked him "to write a memorandum on the strategic problem of the western Mediterranean, with particular regard to the Spanish political situation." He wanted the memorandum "as a guide for a paper he

---

[17]*Memoirs*, 2:132. See also his 30 Apr. 1937 letter to Barrington-Ward, where after stating that "non-intervention is the wisest policy in the Spanish War," he calls for the *Times* to take "a firm line in insisting on genuine non-intervention" (3/107). Nor did he recommend any measures in "Strategic Future of the Mediterranean."

[18]On the Spanish Civil War, see Anthony Beevor, *The Spanish Civil War* (New York: Bedrick, 1983); Pierre Broue and Emile Temime, *The Revolution and the Civil War in Spain* (Cambridge, Mass.: MIT Press, 1972); George Hills, *The Battle for Madrid* (London: Vantage, 1976); Hugh Thomas, *The Spanish Civil War*, rev. ed. (New York: Harper & Row, 1977).

[19]*Memoirs* 2:142; original memorandum in 11/1938/30b. See also 11/1938/30c.

[20]"Military and Strategic Advantages," 148.

wished to write for the Cabinet."[21] Liddell Hart's response does not call for any form of British intervention in Spain. Most of the memorandum outlines the strategic importance of Spain. It concludes with the argument that "the hope that a Francoist Spain will not become a strategic lever in the hands of his present helpers rests on a rather slender possibility, while the graveness of the danger if it does is a certainty."[22] Liddell Hart was definitely worried about a fascist victory in Spain, but he seems to have been unwilling to advocate substantial measures to prevent it.

Liddell Hart was not deeply concerned by Germany's reoccupation of the Rhineland (1936) or by Germany's annexation of Austria (1938). He gives the impression in his *Memoirs* (2:126) that he viewed the takeover of the Rhineland as a development with ominous strategic overtones, but the evidence from the period does not support this claim. He disliked the surreptitious way the Germans moved, but no evidence available shows he was concerned at the time about the strategic implications.[23] He paid little attention to the two Austrian crises, although the day after the Germans occupied Austria he did write a short note for Hore-Belisha in which he argued, "It was the definite interest of France, Britain, and Czechoslovakia to maintain the integrity of Austria," but concluded, "Militarily it was impossible for any of them to help Austria without Italy's cooperation."[24] Liddell Hart certainly did not believe England and her allies should make a stand over these initial crises with Germany.

The 1938 Czechoslovakian crisis was the first confrontation directly involving Germany that Liddell Hart considered of major strategic significance for Britain.[25] He believed German control of Czechoslovakia would be calamitous. It would significantly lessen the possibility of confronting Germany with a two-front war, and a two-front war (rather than a single-front war) significantly lessened the prospects of a German victory, thus contributing to deterrence.[26] Furthermore, with

---

[21]*Memoirs* 2:143.

[22]Memorandum rptd. in *Defence of Britain*, 66–70; quotation on 70.

[23]See LH, "Note on the Reoccupation of the Rhineland Demilitarized Zone, and Hitler's Accompanying Offer—7/3/36," 11/1936/45; Brian Bond, *Liddell Hart: A Study of His Military Thought* (London: Cassell, 1977), 101.

[24]Memorandum rptd. in *Defence of Britain*, 63–64, and *Memoirs* 2:141–42.

[25]For his published writings about the first Czechoslovakian crisis, see *Defence of Britain*, pt. 1; "Strategy and Commitments," 645–49; "Britain's Military Situation," 230–45; "Military and Strategic Advantages," 150–55; also *Memoirs* 2: chap. 4. Important memoranda on this crisis in LH's personal papers (see 11/1938) have virtually all been incorporated, in some form, into the publications cited. See also his 1938 correspondence with his editors at the *Times* (3/108).

[26]See "Britain's Military Situation," 239, and chap. 7 in this book.

allies in the East capable of tying down German units, France was less likely to need British ground forces to help defend the Western Front, a point not lost on Liddell Hart, who wrote in early 1939: "In my judgement such reinforcement on land was not a necessity so long as France could rely on a distraction in the East to Germany's power to concentrate in the West, but may become necessary now in view of the altered balance of forces." Liddell Hart was hoping the Czechs would serve as France's main partner on Germany's eastern flank. This alliance was especially important because France and the Soviet Union were not close to reaching an agreement to come to each other's aid in the event of a German attack against one of them, and "even if France and Russia still contemplated mutual support, in case of threat to either, . . . the disappearance of Czechoslovakia's forces [would] remove a considerable weight from their side of the scales."[27]

German suzerainty over Czechoslovakia would also make it extremely difficult for Britain to place effective economic pressure on Germany, which would have control of the Czechoslovakian economy and would be well positioned to conquer other Eastern European countries. Such an eventuality would strike a deadly blow at collective security, which was heavily dependent on the threat of economic pressure to maintain the status quo. And Liddell Hart's concern about losing economic leverage had another dimension. He mentioned on a few occasions during and after the crisis that German control of Czechoslovakia would mean that in a war, Britain's "master-weapon, blockade, will lose much of its power."[28] This is a puzzling claim because he had expressed serious doubts about the efficacy of blockade in early 1935 and, moreover, frequently restated that position throughout the late 1930s (chap. 5). There is no indication from Liddell Hart's writings in the late 1930s that he seriously believed there were any prospects of hurting Germany with naval power. In 1938 did he fear that German control of Czechoslovakia would remove any lingering public hope of using naval power to punish Germany and thereby undermine his favored division of labor—France handling war on land, Britain at sea? In short, Liddell Hart believed the loss of Czechoslovakia would have several grave strategic consequences.[29]

Liddell Hart pictured himself in his *Memoirs* as an archopponent of appeasement who was willing to confront Germany over Czechoslovakia, a stance consistent with his assessment of the strategic situation.

[27]LH to Barrington-Ward, 21 Feb. 1939, 3/109; "Strategy and Commitments," 648–49.
[28]*Defence of Britain*, 24; also his "Britain's Foreign Policy: A Reflection," memorandum for the record, 20 Sept. 1938, 11/1938/98b; and "The Strategic Problems of Europe," speech to Liberal Party, 14 Feb. 1939, 12/1939/3.
[29]See *Defence of Britain*, chap. 4.

He claims in his *Memoirs* that he argued in late September 1938 "that although the strategic ground for a stand was much less favourable than over Abyssinia in 1935, over the Rhineland in 1936, and over Spain in the last two years, it was better to make a stand now than to postpone it" (2:170). There is no evidence available to support this claim. A careful reading of his *Memoirs* reveals no references to letters, memoranda, or articles in which he proposed taking action over Czechoslovakia. There is also no evidence in his personal papers. In fact the historical record shows quite clearly that he had no solution to the Czechoslovakian problem just as he had none to the Spanish problem. At no point in 1938 did he recommend that Britain take concrete steps to deal with the crisis.[30]

He certainly did not advocate that the democracies threaten to take military action against Germany if the Wehrmacht moved against Czechoslovakia. He in fact feared the Allies *would* adopt that course of action. Specifically, he worried that France might launch an offensive against Germany and drag Britain along. There was actually some talk during the crisis about attacking the Siegfried Line, should the Germans move against Czechoslovakia. Anthony Eden told him Gamelin believed those fortifications "could easily be forced." Liddell Hart, in his own words, "was somewhat horrified to hear of this fresh evidence of excessive confidence in the offensive."[31] Of course Liddell Hart's views on the supremacy of the defense naturally led him to conclude that a French offensive against Germany would almost certainly fail and to oppose giving Czechoslovakia a guarantee to come to her defense in the case of a German attack just as he would oppose the Polish guarantee in the spring of 1939.[32]

[30]See LH to Geoffrey Dawson of the *Times*, outlining his disagreements over time with the editors, 9 May 1939, 3/109. His comments on the Czechoslovakian crisis show he recommended no action during the crisis and that his disagreement with the *Times* was mainly over his belief the editors would not allow him to alert the public to the strategic consequences of German control of Czechoslovakia. See also LH to Barrington-Ward, 20 Sept. 1938, and LH to Dawson, 5 Oct. 1938, both in 3/108, which indicate LH thought there was nothing Britain could do to save Czechoslovakia. During the 1930s the European countries that feared Hitler attempted to shift the burden of dealing with him onto each other; on this buck-passing, see Barry R. Posen, *The Sources of Military Doctrine: France, Britain, and Germany between the World Wars* (Ithaca, N.Y.: Cornell University Press, 1984). LH's policy prescriptions in these years are fully consistent with this pattern of behavior.

[31]"Talk with Anthony Eden," memorandum for the record, 12 Sept. 1938, 11/1938/95. LH, "Talk with Brigadier G. Le Q. Martel," memorandum for the record, 28 Nov. 1938, 11/1938/122 and chap. 5, n. 35.

[32]Chamberlain made an important speech before the House of Commons on 24 Mar. 1938, in which he said that Britain would not make a commitment to defend Czechoslovakia; see "British Attitude in Europe: Mr. Chamberlain's Statement," *Times*, 25 Mar.

Did Liddell Hart consider his arguments about the supremacy of the defense in the context of a German attack on Czechoslovakia? In fact he was impressed by the Czech defenses and concluded, "It is doubtful whether the Germans are capable of conquering Czechoslovakia as a whole unless they were free to concentrate the bulk of their forces against her—which would hardly be practicable unless the French were 'neutralized.'" He then argued, "The French Army could help Czechoslovakia by detaining large German forces in the West—by the threat of attack emphasized by limited operations in the nature of an offensive 'demonstration.'"[33] Liddell Hart clearly believed that France, with an offensive posture, could seriously threaten Germany with a two-front war, a most desirable circumstance. He should therefore have sanctioned if not advocated a French offensive option.

He did *not* do so, arguing that it was "not likely that the Germans could be ejected from any lodgement they gained in the frontier belt of Czechoslovakia." Being on the defensive would work in Germany's favor, and in light of the manifest advantages accruing to the defense, "the war might go on for years without showing an adequate result for the effort expended."[34] The logic of Liddell Hart's position is baffling. The very purpose of creating a two-front war problem for Germany was, after all, to increase the prospects that the Wehrmacht would not score a quick victory and would find itself in a long war with little prospect of victory. France had the capability, according to Liddell Hart, but he would not support developing an offensive option, which was necessary to turn that capability into a meaningful threat. It certainly would have been preferable for France to be able to inflict a quick defeat on Germany, but absent that capability, being able to thwart a Wehrmacht offensive against Czechoslovakia and force Germany into a lengthy war of attrition was a capability that had significant deterrent value. What makes Liddell Hart's position even more puzzling is that he believed "Germany lacked the resources for a prolonged war, so that the ultimate prospect would have been adverse to her."[35]

1938, 14. LH wrote the day after the speech: "I thought the Prime Minister's speech met the French-German situation pretty well on the whole, but was depressed by the superficial way it treated the Spanish-Italian situation" (LH to Barrington-Ward, 25 Mar. 1938, 3/108).

[33]"Britain's Military Situation," 231; relevant portions rptd. in *Defence of Britain,* 74–77. See also LH, "Appreciation of the War Which Now Threatens," memorandum for the record, 28 Sept. 1938, 11/1938/103.

[34]"Britain's Military Situation," 232.

[35]*Defence of Britain,* 22. See also "Military and Strategic Advantages," 152, where he writes, "While the increased danger of Czechoslovakia's position is obvious . . . we should not lose sight of the present inadequacy of Germany's resources—and the natural superiority of those which might be opposed to her—*for a prolonged struggle.*"

Another perplexing aspect of Liddell Hart's thinking about the two-front war problem is that France had a vested interest in convincing the Czechs, as well as any other allies on Germany's eastern flank, that France would come to their assistance if Germany struck them first. Otherwise, how could the French expect the Czechs to help them, should the Germans strike first in the West? France therefore needed a credible offensive option. Liddell Hart apparently did not consider this important issue, which further suggests his thinking about the two-front problem was muddled.

Liddell Hart's preferred policy for dealing with the Czechoslovakian crisis was to emphasize the rhetoric of collective security, whose key elements were economic and moral pressure. This was actually the first crisis in which he argued for collective security in a serious way. He stated, for example, in a 9 September 1938 memorandum that if Hitler moved against Czechoslovakia, "the best hope of compelling Germany to relinquish her lodgment would be the development of general economic pressure, which would be reinforced by the evidence of moral isolation."[36] This was hardly a realistic policy given his belief that German control of Czechoslovakia would make it almost impossible to bring meaningful economic pressure to bear on Germany. (In fact, as noted earlier, he seems to have believed as early as the Abyssinian crisis, 1935–36, that collective security was no longer a viable policy option.) There is ample evidence he did not view economic pressure as a serious option in 1938, a point reflected in one of his final memoranda on the crisis, where he briefly prescribed a course of action for Britain: "We must realise that we cannot win a war against Germany except by economic pressure—and it is becoming doubtful whether this weapon will remain effective enough to produce victory. Our best chance of salvation seems to lie in making ourselves a tough morsel to chew."[37] These are hardly the words of a proponent of confrontation with Nazi Germany.

What about Liddell Hart and appeasement? He portrayed himself in later years as an archfoe of that policy. He writes in his *Memoirs*, for example, that during the Munich crisis, he was "nauseated by the tone of *The Times* leaders, and shocked at the illusions they showed."[38] This

[36]"Note on the Military Aspect of the Situation," 9 Sept. 1938, 11/1938/92b. See also *Memoirs* 2: 162; *Defence of Britain*, 76.

[37]"Reflections on the Situation, Its Future and Our Policy," memorandum for the record, 12 Oct. 1938, 11/1938/114. See also "Britain's Military Situation," 243–44; "Strategy and Commitments," 649.

[38]*Memoirs*, 2:172. See also LH, *The German Generals Talk* (New York: Morrow, 1948), x. The reader should also note how LH tries in *Memoirs* 2:170–71 to link himself with Winston Churchill, who eventually came to be seen as the symbol of the antiappease-

is almost certainly an overstatement, for he does not adduce any evidence from the interwar period that shows him to have been an archfoe of appeasement. Had such evidence existed, would he not have quoted it in his *Memoirs*?[39] In fact, he had ambivalent feelings about appeasement. He was not an advocate at this point, largely because he did not think it would work. He sensed—quite correctly as it turned out—that Hitler was bent on radically altering the map of Europe. His problem was that he could not prescribe an effective policy for thwarting Hitler. His rhetorical support for collective security notwithstanding, by 1938 he surely recognized this toothless policy was not a serious option. His refusal to countenance using military force against the Third Reich, or any other adversary for that matter, made it difficult, if not impossible, to deter adversaries or achieve favorable outcomes. Without meaningful policy prescriptions for dealing with Hitler, Liddell Hart had no choice but to tolerate appeasement, despite the well-founded misgivings he had by 1938. Of course Britain's strategic position became increasingly precarious with each new crisis. A letter he wrote to his editor at the *Times* in late March 1938 lays out his thinking:

> In the years that have passed since then [when he came to the *Times* in March 1935], each time a crisis has arisen anywhere *The Times* as well as the Government have found reasons for avoiding the issue and refraining from the action necessary to uphold collective security. On each occasion you and I have discussed the reasons, and I have been ready to admit their validity. But the difference between us has been that while you have seemed to embrace them confidently I have regarded them doubtfully—admitting the risks of action but expressing concern lest the risks of inaction should prove the worse. And in the sequel the situation for an ultimate stand has seemed to me to have become worse. Thus my doubts tend to grow stronger by the time the next issue arises.[40]

The 1938 Czechoslovakian crisis, which culminated in the Munich accords, was and still is the most controversial case of appeasement. Liddell Hart's thinking at the time is recorded in a letter he wrote to

---

ment movement. LH was neither an archopponent of appeasement nor an ally or confidant of Churchill during the late 1930s. Furthermore, he was very critical of Churchill during World War II, mainly because of Churchill's advocacy of unconditional surrender for Germany. LH favored a negotiated settlement with the Third Reich. For a more accurate indication of how LH viewed Churchill, see LH, "Churchill in War," *Encounter* 26 (Apr. 1966): 14–22.

[39]See *Memoirs* 2: chap. 4. I could find no evidence in his personal papers he might have quoted to support his position.

[40]LH to Barrington-Ward, 29 Mar. 1938, 3/108. See also ibid., 8 Nov. 1939.

Barrington-Ward shortly after the crisis had been settled. They were arguing at the time about the wording of a piece Liddell Hart had written for the newspaper.

> I did not say that foreign policy should "be firmer" (i.e. in attitude) but that a truer recognition of the military conditions would provide it with "a firmer foundation" (i.e. of knowledge). If you prefer it you might alter this expression to "a clearer basis for foreign policy."
>
>   As a historically minded onlooker I am not prepared to attempt a judgement (historical, as distinct from moral) on the wisdom of our policy at the present time. That it has been a series of retreats is clear to anyone who has regularly kept, and looks back through, a file of ministerial speeches and also of *Times* leaders as I have. But it may ultimately appear as a strategic retreat—reculer pour mieux sauter—with a beneficial end, for us if not for the luckless outpost states who have served as shock-absorbers. On the other hand, it may appear the successive stages of a British "decline and fall". The judgement must be left to the future historian.[41]

These are hardly the words of an archfoe of appeasement. Rather, they portray a mind pulled in two directions.

The next crisis came on 15 March 1939 when Germany took the rest of Czechoslovakia. This move galvanized British policy makers, who had been moving since Munich toward a Continental commitment and a foreign policy that emphasized confronting the Third Reich with the threat of direct military force. They now adopted those policies. Britain had finally decided to take a stand. Contrary to accepted opinion, Liddell Hart did not support the new policy but adamantly opposed it.

There were signs throughout 1938 and in the early months of 1939 that Liddell Hart might be willing to support sending a small armored force to France in the event of a German attack. He was unwilling to countenance a full-scale Continental commitment but mentioned the possibility of two or three armored divisions that could be used as part of a strategic reserve. He had a strong preference for a small mechanized force because he thought its features would preclude Britain from repeating its experience in the Great War. He believed a mechanized force, unlike a traditional infantry force, could not be used to occupy a sector of the front but only as part of the strategic reserve and therefore would not be available for the bloody slugging matches along the front lines. Also, a mechanized force, because of the high cost of its equipment, "would be . . . less quickly replacable and expandable" than an infantry-dominated force, thus working to check any tendency to raise another mass army. Finally, Liddell Hart saw this token force

[41]Ibid., 23 Oct. 1937, 3/107. See also "Strategy and Commitments," 649.

as a means of checking French proclivities for taking "unprofitable offensive action." Not surprisingly, he insisted that Britain "make it a condition"[42] with the French that British armored divisions "should not be employed in an offensive campaign."[43]

Liddell Hart first raised the issue of sending a small mechanized force to the Continent in an article published in January 1938, only a short time after the Chamberlain government formally jettisoned the Continental commitment.[44] He repeated the argument on a handful of occasions over the following year.[45] At the same time, however, he argued elsewhere against *any* form of Continental commitment. For example, in an April 1938 article on the role of the army he argued, "While the maintenance of land forces adequate for home and Empire defence is a necessity, the maintenance of anything beyond this, specifically for use on the Continent, cannot be rated as more than desirable—and is, even so, a potentially dangerous desire." He noted in the article's final sentence, "The scale of the Army should not exceed the necessities of Imperial Defence."[46] Six months later, shortly after the Munich crisis was settled, he again argued against sending any forces to the Continent "to relieve the strain on the French in defending their frontiers."[47]

What are we to make of these contradictory positions? It appears that between January 1938 and February 1939, Liddell Hart seriously considered a limited Continental commitment but could not make up his mind because of strong fears that a small commitment would grow into a large one, that Britain would use its small mechanized force as a base for building a mass army. It is hard to disagree with Brian Bond's conclusion: "although the arguments for a small, high-quality mechanized force—which Britain did not possess before 1939—sound plausible, there is a strong impression that Liddell Hart was fundamentally opposed to the idea of sending even a single soldier to the Continent lest the dreadful experience of 1914–1918 should be repeated."[48]

The Polish guarantee in the spring of 1939 eliminated this tension in Liddell Hart's thinking. He interpreted this decision to mean Britain

---

[42]This discussion is based on "Field Force Question," 17–18.

[43]"The Defence of the Empire," *Fortnightly* 143 (Jan. 1938): 29.

[44]Ibid., 20–30.

[45]See, for example "Diary Notes," 30 Jan. 1939 entry, 11/1939/6; letter, *World Review* 6 (Mar. 1939): 65–66; "Field Force Question"; "An Army across Channel?" *Times*, Feb. 7–8, 1939, 15–16 for both pieces.

[46]"Does the Organization of the Army Fit Its Functions?" *Fighting Forces* (Apr. 1938): 32, 33; rptd. in *Defence of Britain*, chap. 15.

[47]"Reflections on the Situation, Its Future and Our Policy," memorandum for the record, 12 Oct. 1938, 11/1938/114. See also LH to Barrington-Ward, 21 Feb. 1939, 3/109.

[48]B. Bond, *Liddell Hart*, 104–5.

had "now been dragged into the course of building a great land force," thus obviating the option of a small mechanized force.[49] Consequently he adamantly criticized the Polish guarantee and in the remaining months of peace argued forcefully against a Continental commitment.[50] Liddell Hart was not merely opposed to the decision; he was distraught over it.[51] He believed that "an insanity wave" was "spreading" in Britain. "The most ominous aspect of Germany's invasion of Czecho-Slovakia," he argued, was "the wave of hysteria it has produced here."[52] Liddell Hart, in the end, simply could not bring himself to support the use of military force against Hitler—which of course was what the Continental commitment was all about.[53]

The Polish guarantee led to what appeared to be an important development in Liddell Hart's evaluation of the Nazi threat. He argued not simply that Chamberlain's new policy would not work but that it would actually provoke Hitler: "It is wise to realise that this pledge is far more provocative than would have been an earlier declaration that we were resolved to fulfill our obligations under the League Covenant . . . our sudden reversal of policy makes it far more difficult for Hitler to save face."[54] Here we see the seeds of the controversial but not serious claim, made famous years later by A. J. P. Taylor, that the Allies actually led Hitler into war.[55] This argument says, in effect, that Hitler was looking for a way to avoid future conflicts, but Britain made it impossible for him to do so. The fundamental assumption is that Hitler was not bent on aggression, which of course was the assumption underpinning appeasement. Liddell Hart was soon to adopt a position,

[49]*Defence of Britain*, 45–46.

[50]There is abundant evidence of LH's deep-seated opposition to the Polish guarantee and to a Continental commitment in his memoranda and diary notes of March–September 1939 (see sec. 11 of his personal papers); also *Defence of Britain*, pts. 1, 4. He remained convinced for life that the Polish guarantee was a grave blunder; see LH, *History of the Second World War* (London: Cassell, 1970), chap. 1.

[51]See his correspondence with Brig. Gen. J. E. Edmonds, which led Edmonds to conclude, "I think that we had better not meet at the present" (Edmonds to LH, 24 May 1939); see also LH to Edmonds, 23 May and 2 June 1939, all in 1/259.

[52]"Diary Notes," 16, 19 Mar. 1939 entries, 11/1939/24b.

[53]LH also argued vigorously against conscription, which Britain instituted in April 1939. Conscription was of course necessary to raise a mass army, the sine qua non of a Continental commitment. See "Free v. Compulsory Service," text prepared for 24 Apr. 1939 debate at Cambridge Union, 12/1939/39–43; "Free v. Compulsory Service," text prepared for 27 Apr. 1939 debate at Oxford Union, 12/1939/44–54. On conscription during this period, including LH's views, see Peter Dennis, *Decision by Default: Peacetime Conscription and British Defence, 1919–39* (Durham, N.C.: Duke University Press, 1972).

[54]"A Reflection," memorandum for the record, 2 Apr. 1939, 11/1939/35b.

[55]See A. J. P. Taylor, *The Origins of the Second World War*, 2d ed. (Greenwich, Conn.: Fawcett, 1961). See also William Roger Louis, ed., *The Origins of the Second World War: A. J. P. Taylor and His Critics* (New York: Wiley, 1972); Gordon Martel, ed., *The Origins of the Second World War Reconsidered: The A. J. P. Taylor Debate after Twenty-five Years* (Win-

which he would stick with throughout the war, that amounted to appeasement.

What policy prescriptions did Liddell Hart advocate in the wake of Czechoslovakia's incorporation into the Third Reich? He repeated the same arguments he had used before the fall of Prague. He continued emphasizing the utility of collective security, despite his earlier admission that Munich, if not Abyssinia, had undermined that option. He continued to disparage the military option, as in this memorandum written just a week before the war began: "Apart from the possibility of some radically new means, real pressure on Germany can only be exerted by the slow process of economic and moral blockade. In the long run it might prove more effective than any military efforts—while its moral effect should be felt all the sooner if France and Britain refrained from such an offensive as would tend to stiffen the fighting spirit of the German people as a whole."[56] He could scarcely have placed much faith in the economic lever after he had argued at the time of Munich that the loss of Czechoslovakia would make it virtually impossible for Britain to put significant economic pressure on Germany. Yet, he repeated the old arguments.

Of course there was a second dimension to Liddell Hart's approach to dealing with Hitler: convincing the Germans that aggression does not pay, given the power of defense on the modern battlefield. A special effort to achieve this aim in the last year of peace would seem to have been called for. After all, signs of war abounded, and apparently Liddell Hart had grave doubts about the utility of collective security. But there is no evidence he tried at any point in the 1930s to ensure that his ideas received widespread attention in Germany. His writings from the period often leave the impression he was more concerned about the French and British taking the offensive than about deterring the Third Reich.[57] It is difficult to understand why he did not strive to convince German leaders that offense does not pay.

The final crisis came in August 1939 when Hitler began making demands over Poland. Liddell Hart's reactions were consistent with

chester: Allen & Unwin, 1986). For other examples of the Taylor argument in LH's writings, see "Diary Notes," 20 Mar. 1939 entry, 11/"1939/24b; "Reflections—from Diary Notes and Memoranda," 19 Apr. 1939 entry, 11/1939/25; "Reflection," memorandum for the record, 1939, 11/1939/114b; LH to Esmé Wingfield-Stratford, 5 Oct. 1942 and 6 Sept. 1949, 1/757; LH to John Brophy, 7 Sept. 1941, 1/112; *Defence of Britain*, 24, 46; *History of the Second World War*, chap. 1; *Memoirs* 2:214. See also Taylor to LH, 1 Oct. 1959, and LH to Taylor, 5 Oct. 1959, both in 1/676.
[56]Copy in *The Current of War* (London: Hutchinson, 1941), 142–47, quotation on 144. See also LH, "Strategic Problems of Europe"; LH to Edmonds, 23 May 1939, 1/259.
[57]B. Bond makes the same point in *Liddell Hart*, 98, 114.

his reactions to the second Czechoslovakian crisis. He remarked in his diary on the day war broke out: "It is impossible to deny . . . the comparative reasonableness of Hitler's suggested terms for a settlement with Poland," clearly implying Britain should seek to deal, as at Munich.[58] The nature of Hitler's demands aside, he recognized Poland was incapable of standing up to the Third Reich alone and Britain and France could offer little help in the short term. He concluded:

> Facing these strategic realities soberly, the question should be weighed whether the Polish Government is justified in calling on its subjects to sacrifice themselves for what they are bound to lose in any case, and whether the British and French Governments are justified in encouraging it to fight for what they themselves are unlikely to be able to regain for Poland. Any sacrifice may be better than surrender, but is it worthwhile if the surrender—of the object for which the war is fought—is seen to be inevitable before fighting begins?[59]

Little wonder, Hugh Dalton, one of a handful of strong opponents of appeasement in the Labour party, wrote him on the eve of the war: "It is ironical that now, when 'The Times' [which essentially mirrored the government's position on foreign policy], in my view, is shaping very much better, you should have become an appeaser!"[60]

Liddell Hart was well aware, however, that it was probably too late to avert war. "If it is too late," he argued,

> the best course would be to base our action on the gradual effect of economic blockade and moral boycott, abstaining from such an offensive, both on land and in the air, as would tend to consolidate the fighting spirit of the German people while exhausting our own resources in a vain effort. To think and talk of "victory" in such a war would be the most dangerous of delusions. In the actual circumstances, the more that our action demonstrates repugnance and the less it resembles pugnacity the more effective it is likely to be, and the best chance it offers of our civilization surviving the issue.[61]

Once the war began, he continued to repeat these same arguments along with his claim about the overwhelming superiority of the defense.[62] In the first weeks of the war his arguments about defense were directed at Britain and France, for he feared they might strike into

---

[58]"Diary Notes," 1 Sept. 1939 entry, 11/1939/75b.
[59]*Current of War*, 145.
[60]Dalton to LH, 31 Aug. 1939, 11/1939/85.
[61]*Current of War*, 147.
[62]See, for example, the three pieces in ibid., 151–68.

Germany while the Wehrmacht was occupied in Poland. He wanted to make sure the Allies did not launch any offensives. Thus, he wrote on 9 September,

> a declaration that we were renouncing military attack as a means of combating aggression would be a far-sighted move, strengthening our moral position, while forestalling the otherwise probable growth of derision abroad and disillusionment here. . . . It would set us free to develop economic and moral pressure to the utmost, and to make the best disposition of our military forces to meet any German attempt to break our "sanitary cordon." It would throw on the Germans the responsibility of taking the offensive, with all its disadvantages.[63]

Liddell Hart was actually very interested in reaching a negotiated settlement with Hitler during the Phoney War, the period between the fall of Poland and the German attack in the West. He actually wrote an article in March 1940 in which he expressed hope that Hitler would recognize "the proved strength of modern defence" and consent to a disarmament agreement abolishing offensive weapons,[64] maintaining:

> It may be thought that Hitler's lack of these weapons [tanks and heavy artillery] in 1935 was the reason why he thus proposed their abolition. But it is worth special note that at the end of his speech of October 6 last [1939], after the defeat of Poland, he renewed his proposal for a general disarmament agreement apparently on the same lines. It seemed by far the most promising point of his peace proposals, but it passed almost unnoticed in the Allied countries.[65]

Liddell Hart must have been desperate to avoid a land war in Europe. All hope ended on 10 May 1940.

What general conclusions can be drawn from this discussion? Liddell Hart paid little attention to the Japanese threat in the Far East and less to the Italian one in the Mediterranean. He was somewhat concerned about the Abyssinian crisis, but it was the Spanish Civil War among the crises not involving Germany that really worried him. That was the only crisis of the interwar period, Czechoslovakia included, where he exhibited any willingness to take concrete measures to protect British interests, and his worry proved unfounded because Franco remained neutral after assuming power. Liddell Hart's view of the German

[63]Ibid., 156–57.
[64]Ibid., 164–68. See also LH, "The Best Guarantee against Aggression," memorandum for the record, 27 Feb. 1940, 11/1940/10.
[65]*Current of War*, 168.

threat—at least as reflected in his writings—appears to have varied markedly over the course of these crises. Three phases in his thinking can be discerned. He seems not to have been alarmed by the German threat before 1938—not by the Rhineland crisis, not by the problem with Austria, not by German rearmament. To support his efforts to keep Britain from accepting a Continental commitment, he even began arguing in the mid-1930s that Hitler's decision to expand the German army was actually weakening it, making it a less than formidable fighting force (chap. 5). This claim, expounded often, certainly did not make him sound like an alarmist in those years.

The second phase covers 1938, the year of the first Czechoslovakian crisis. He was very concerned about German control of Czechoslovakia, an eventuality he believed would markedly alter the strategic balance. Although he was not firmly convinced Hitler was so aggressive he would move to take all of Czechoslovakia, he was not blind to that possibility either. His ambivalence was naturally reflected in his mixed view of appeasement.

His assessment of the German threat appears to have changed radically in the spring of 1939, after the Chamberlain government decided to accept a Continental commitment. He argued in this third phase that Hitler's demands were reasonable and British pressure on Hitler was pushing Europe to the brink of war. Paradoxically, just as the Chamberlain government and many other Britons were concluding that the German threat was far more malign than previously assumed, Liddell Hart began moving in the opposite direction. This shift, I argue later, he made mainly for tactical reasons, not because of any major reassessment of the Third Reich's intentions. Nevertheless, his writings convey the impression that only during the course of 1938 and early 1939 did he take the German threat seriously and even then he was not sure Hitler was bent on aggression.

As for Liddell Hart's policy prescriptions, he was not willing to threaten the use of military force to resolve any of the crises or to deter further adventurism by the fascist states. He never prescribed a policy likely to lead to armed conflict. The Spanish Civil War was the only crisis where he called for any concrete measures on Britain's part, and then he argued for sending limited amounts of arms to the Spanish government well after the conflict had begun. The rhetoric in his *Memoirs* notwithstanding, Liddell Hart was unwilling to make a stand against Hitler. The circumstances surrounding his departure from the *Times* in late 1939 illustrate this point. It is sometimes incorrectly assumed that he left because of differences with the editors over the paper's proappeasement line. He did have some differences with them over appeasement in 1938, although it was mainly disagreement over Spain that soured relations during that year.[66] Regardless, he continued to write for the *Times* when it was staunchly proappeasement, and he also maintained close relations with the Chamberlain government throughout the period that it advocated appeasement. He left the *Times* in late 1939 well after that paper, as well as the government with which it was so closely identified, had moved away from appeasement to support a policy of threatening Hitler with direct military force. Liddell Hart's break with the *Times* was due in good part to the fact that he could not support its new editorial policy, the cornerstone of which was a Continental commitment.[67] Simply put, Liddell Hart could not support a foreign policy predicated on the threat to use military force against Hitler.

Liddell Hart's preferred foreign policy relied on rhetorical support for collective security along with a campaign to persuade possible aggressors about the supremacy of defense on the modern battlefield. He did not argue vociferously for collective security before 1938, when there was actually a chance it might have worked, for example, during the Abyssinian crisis. He only began to stress its merits during the Czechoslovakian crisis of 1938,[68] when he surely realized it was not a serious option. Probably Liddell Hart also realized his best hope of stopping the Third Reich was to convince its leaders that World War II would look much like World War I because of the supremacy of defense, and this probably explains why he was so deeply concerned about events in Spain as well as *The Times*'s description of battlefield developments in that conflict. A fascist victory in Spain, seen by many as a laboratory for the next war, could well be interpreted as evidence that offense pays.

Liddell Hart's campaign to deter the Third Reich by stressing the power of modern defense met with little success. It was evident by 1939 that Europe was rapidly moving toward another war in which England would be deeply involved. Liddell Hart simply went on em-

[66]See their correspondence (3/108), which actually shows LH had few disagreements with his editors through 1937 (see 3/105–3/107). For LH's account of his relationship with the *Times* during 1938, see *Memoirs* 2: chap. 4.

[67]See his correspondence for 1939 with his editors at the *Times* (3/109). See also "Diary Notes," 27 Aug. 1939 entry, 11/1939/75b; *Memoirs*, 2:236–37, 258–59; Iverach McDonald, *The History of the Times: Struggles in War and Peace, 1939–1966* (London: Times Books, 1984), 5:43–45; Donald McLachlan, *In the Chair: Barrington-Ward of the Times, 1927–1948* (London: Weidenfeld & Nicolson, 1971), 154–67.

[68]The prominence of collective security in his writings during and after the first Czechoslovakian crisis *and* his corresponding lack of interest in that policy option before 1938 is illustrated by comparing *Europe in Arms* (1937) with *Defence of Britain* (1939). The former hardly mentions collective security, while the latter places considerable emphasis on it.

phasizing the wisdom of collective security and the superiority of defense over offense, although curiously he never made any special effort to reach Germany with that message. At the same time, however, he added a new wrinkle: he began to define away the German threat. He started writing about the reasonableness of Hitler's demands while maintaining that Britain's decision to stand up to Hitler was likely to provoke, not deter, him. Effectively, Liddell Hart began to embrace appeasement in the months immediately before the war began.

This might appear at first glance to be a case of incredible naiveté on his part. This is surely not the case. After all, Liddell Hart was well aware of the potential danger posed by the Third Reich before 1939, and as late as 16 March 1939 he commented, "To my mind, the most ominous aspect of Germany's invasion of Czecho-Slovakia is not its evidence of her aggressive designs—which should have been clear to anyone before this."[69] Surely he changed his description of the German threat after the Polish guarantee (31 March 1939) not because of any fundamental reassessment of Hitler's intentions but for tactical reasons: a desperate wish to avoid British involvement in another European war. The essence of the problem Liddell Hart faced was that recognition of the real danger presented by the Third Reich almost axiomatically led to a foreign policy based on the threat of military confrontation. This conclusion, in turn, meant that Britain would have to build military forces, including a large army, for use against Germany. Early in 1939 large portions of the British elite finally began to recognize the danger at hand, and appropriately, the government began a crash program to expand its military, especially its army. Out of sheer desperation, apparently, Liddell Hart began to redefine the threat to try to undercut the need for a military buildup for the Continent. In the final analysis, Liddell Hart's thinking about foreign policy was driven by his deep-seated commitment to see that Britain never repeat its World War I experience on the Western Front.

LIDDELL HART DURING WORLD WAR II

The start of the war marked the beginning of a long and dark period in Liddell Hart's life. Brian Bond, who knew Liddell Hart well, notes that in later years, "he seldom spoke spontaneously about the war years." His *Memoirs* stop with the Fall of France. He was only forty-three when the war began, and he was certainly knowledgeable in the

---

[69]"Diary Notes," 16 Mar. 1939 entry, 11/1939/24b.

extreme about military affairs. One would have expected him to be close to the decision-making hub throughout that conflict, much as he had been during the 1930s, but this was not the case. From that time, there are many signs of his precipitous decline in stature. His diaries for the war years show he had little contact with the generals and politicians who directed the war in London; in fact he moved to the countryside shortly after the war began. His isolation is also reflected in his correspondence files. He corresponded mainly with friends who were themselves outsiders. Even here, however, relations were not always smooth; his good friends sometimes found his arguments unpersuasive. For example, Liddell Hart wrote in October 1942 to Esmé Wingfield-Stratford, a faithful correspondent during the war years: "I feel rather sad that your earlier trust in my judgment . . . has waned to the extent it has."[70]

Probably the only prominent insider he was in regular contact with during the war was his long-standing friend Gen. Frederick "Tim" Pile, who was head of Anti-Aircraft Command from 1939 to 1945. Even here, there is evidence of how far Liddell Hart's standing in Britain had plummeted; Pile told him soon after the Fall of France that he was coming under severe criticism in the War Office.[71] Liddell Hart wrote back: "I have already had various indications of the way the wind was blowing. . . . There seems to be similarities, if also differences, with the way that Haldane was treated in the last war." He then offered to work for Pile "in an advisory or inspectory capacity."[72] Pile was a loyal friend, but even he could not employ Liddell Hart at this juncture.

Another good indicator of how far Liddell Hart had fallen is found in the reviews of his books from the war years. Whereas his pre– and post–World War II books were widely and almost always favorably reviewed, those from the war years were not widely reviewed and frequently met with a hostile reception.[73] Consider, for example, this April 1941 review of *The Current of War*:

> This volume is not a book but merely a collection of newspaper articles, competitive essays and confidential memoranda, gathered together from the dusty files of the past 20 years. Most of it is entirely antiquated and obsolete; its main prophecies have been shown by recent events to have

[70]B. Bond, *Liddell Hart*, 121; LH to Wingfield-Stratford, 5 Oct. 1942, 1/757.
[71]Pile to LH, 16 June 1940, 1/575. All their correspondence is in 1/575.
[72]LH to Pile, 22 June 1940. See also Pile to LH, 26 June 1940.
[73]The books LH published during the war and the files containing the reviews: *Dynamic Defence* (London: Faber, 1940), 9/18/4; *Current of War*, 9/19/8; *This Expanding War* (London: Faber, 1942), 9/20/7; *Thoughts on War* (London: Faber, 1944), 9/22/7; *Why Don't We Learn from History?* (London: Allen & Unwin, 1944), 9/21/4.

been false: its leading principles have been decisively discredited. Captain Liddell Hart has striven to maintain his reputation for prescience and profundity by omitting considerable sections of many of the selected articles, and by adding introductions and footnotes intended to show that, although apparently he was wrong in what he said, he was really right. The result is much confusion and complete bewilderment. As a guide to the future Captain Liddell Hart has ceased to count.[74]

It is hard to imagine a reviewer treating him like this in the 1930s. He was not only criticized in book reviews but also attacked in newspaper articles, books, and speeches.[75] His fall was sudden. He had been at the peak of his career in late July 1939, when *The Defence of Britain* was lavishly praised throughout the world. Then the war came, and his ideas about continuing to try for an accommodation with Hitler were largely ignored. He remarked in his diary on 8 September 1939, "It is less than two months ago that the 'Defence of Britain' was published, and its warnings . . . were greeted in every quarter as obvious common sense. One expression of opinion after another [now] shows complete disregard of the warnings, and an urge to march to battle in the same old way—'Blood has gone to their heads'."[76]

The start of the war in itself did not seriously damage Liddell Hart's reputation, although his views began to be treated with considerable skepticism. It was the Fall of France that delivered the first serious blow. The German victory showed that Liddell Hart's claims about the overwhelming superiority of the defense and the futility of offense were simply wrong. A comment from the memoirs of Hugh Dalton highlights this point:

Some of us who were taking a special interest in Defence saw a good deal at this time of Liddell Hart. . . . We valued his knowledge, his judgment, his quick intelligence and his personal contacts. . . . I lost confidence in him, perhaps unfairly, in 1940 when France fell. For he had been maintaining stoutly the thesis, both in speech and writing, that in the conditions of modern war the Defence, on the ground, had a great advantage

[74]"A Depressing Prophet," rev. of *The Current of War*, by LH, *National Review*, 116 (Apr. 1941): 494.
[75]See, for example, Ivor Halstead, *The Truth about Our Tanks* (London: Lindsay Drummond, 1943), 11; Irving M. Gibson [A. Kovacs], "Maginot and Liddell Hart: The Doctrine of Defense," in Edward Mead Earle, ed., *Makers of Modern Strategy: Military Thought from Machiavelli to Hitler* (Princeton, N.J.: Princeton University Press, 1943), 375–85; and esp. LH's correspondence with the press for 1940 and 1941, in sec. 6 of his papers.
[76]"Diary Notes," 11/1939/75b. For an illustration of the heights to which LH's reputation had risen by the summer of 1939, see the photo spread "Liddell Hart at Home: Off-Duty Shots of a Great Military Scientist," *Bystander*, 2 Aug. 1939, 172–73; also rev. of *Defence of Britain* by V. S. Pritchett in ibid., 183.

over the Attack, which could only succeed with a tremendous superiority of force.[77]

Critics at the time were also quick to point the error out.[78] The Allies' stunning defeat demonstrated conclusively as well that the Chamberlain government and those closely associated with it—like Liddell Hart—had not just failed to deter Hitler but failed to provide a way to thwart his armies in the event deterrence collapsed. Not only was Britain now involved in another world war, but she had also suffered a catastrophic defeat that left her in an extremely precarious strategic position. It is hardly surprising that the reputations of virtually everyone affiliated with those failed policies were badly damaged. Liddell Hart, who had in *The Defence of Britain* linked himself with Hore-Belisha's policies at the War Office, was no exception.

There was another reason, however, why Liddell Hart remained in the political wilderness during the war: his views about the nature of the German threat and his policy prescriptions for dealing with the Third Reich were antithetical to those of the vast majority of Britons. He was an archcritic of the Allies' policy of unconditional surrender and favored instead a negotiated settlement with Hitler.[79] This was certainly not a totally implausible idea in the early stages of the war, when Britain stood alone against Germany; but he continued to argue for reaching an accommodation with Hitler even after the Soviet Union and the United States had entered the war on Britain's side and it was clear Germany would be decisively defeated.

He offered two arguments in support of his case. The first and least controversial was that total defeat of Germany would result in Soviet domination of the Continent, which was certainly not in Britain's interest.[80] The second and much more controversial argument was that Hitler was basically a reasonable statesmen led astray by the Allies. This argument, which first appeared after the Polish guarantee of March 1939, became a staple during and after the war. Consider this excerpt from a letter he wrote in October 1942: "The profound psychological truth of experience [is] that 'burglars do not commit murder' unless they are deprived of any way out. . . . Hitler was remarkably reluctant to get into war—considering his military assets—and . . . he repeatedly tried to get out of it from the first afternoon onwards . . . it

[77]*The Fateful Years: Memoirs, 1931–1945* (London: Muller, 1957), 175.

[78]See, for example, A. Rhinoceros [someone from the War Office], letter, *New Statesman and Nation,* 7 Sept. 1940, 234; and see Pile to LH, 22 June 1940, 1/575.

[79]See B. Bond, *Liddell Hart,* chap. 5; also Paul Addison, "Lloyd George and Compromise Peace in the Second World War," in A. J. P. Taylor, ed., *Lloyd George: Twelve Essays* (London: Hamilton, 1971), 361–84.

[80]LH to Wingfield-Stratford, 22 Apr. 1944, 1/757.

is in accord with the underlying doubts revealed in *Mein Kampf.*"[81] To
sell this argument, which was essential if he was to convince others of
the viability of a negotiated settlement, he defended the Third Reich
against charges it was a barbaric regime. This excerpt, for example,
comes from a letter he wrote to his good friend John Brophy in August
1944, by which time there was widespread evidence that the Third
Reich was systematically murdering Jews:

> In brief, the trend of the evidence in the last century seems to suggest that
> the most dangerous quality among Germans in general, is not their sup-
> posed special degree of aggressiveness, but their docility and tractability.
> That is the psychological problem to which we should wisely address
> ourselves.
>
> You are on safer grounds when you speak of the pre-war Nazi con-
> centration camps. These certainly provided abundant evidence for an
> indictment. (Even so, I had rather a shock when a number of friends of
> mine among German refugees told me, after their release from internment
> in 1940, that, on balance, they had found the Nazi ones preferable to our
> own!) The most reliable evidence we have up to now is, naturally, that
> which comes from the areas of Europe which our forces have already
> redeemed from German occupation. And here, as well as in the case of
> the Channel Islands, it is to be noted that the behaviour of the Germans
> was much more "correct" and restrained than we had imagined.[82]

His remarkable comments comparing German and British concentration camps point out that in addition to defending the Third Reich
throughout the war, he also was critical of British institutions and
British policy on the homefront. He often talked about totalitarianism
in Britain, implying that the situation was at least as bad in Britain as in
Nazi Germany. He was not above arguing, for example, that Britain
had the equivalent of the Gestapo at Whitehall.[83] Brophy was undoubtedly correct when he told him, "You have taken to applying two
different standards to British and German" behavior.[84]

This sad story might seem to suggest that Liddell Hart had anti-
democratic views and was at least sympathetic to fascism, that he was
even an anti-Semite. After all, his friend Fuller was a rabid anti-Semite

[81]Ibid., 5 Oct. 1942.
[82]LH to Brophy, 9 Aug. 1944, 1/112. On public knowledge of the Holocaust in Britain
during the war, see Walter Laqueur, *The Terrible Secret: Suppression of the Truth about
Hitler's 'Final Solution'* (Boston: Little, Brown, 1980), and Bernard Wasserstein, *Britain and
the Jews of Europe, 1939–1945* (Oxford: Clarendon, 1979).
[83]LH to Wingfield-Stratford, 5 Oct. 1942, 1/757. See also B. Bond, *Liddell Hart*, 126; LH,
The Other Side of the Hill, rev. and enlarged ed. (London: Cassell 1951), 12–13.
[84]Brophy to LH, 30 July 1944, 1/112.

and a fascist.[85] There is no evidence to this effect. On the contrary, Liddell Hart was a staunch defender of democracy and a person with remarkably few prejudices.[86] He was, moreover, if anything, a philo-Semite. There are no instances I know of in his massive files where he speaks disparagingly of anyone because of religion, race, or ethnic background. He was in that regard a tolerant and decent man.

How then could he have defended the Third Reich even after its barbarousness became known? How could he have continued to support the claim that Hitler was a reasonable and responsible statesman? This is an especially intriguing question when one considers that he appears to have been cognizant of the potential danger posed by the Third Reich throughout 1938. His doubts about appeasement, after all, grew out of his belief that Hitler probably could not be placated with diplomatic concessions. The answer, I believe, is straightforward and by now a familiar one: his opposition to fighting another world war was so deep seated, so all-consuming, that it forced him to *change* his views on the nature of Nazi Germany and adopt a position that can most charitably be described as shameful. Even while that war raged, his one overriding aim was to cut it short through a negotiated settlement.

---

[85]See Anthony J. Trythall, *'Boney' Fuller: The Intellectual General, 1878–1966* (New Brunswick, N.J.: Rutgers University Press, 1977), chap. 8.

[86]See LH to Fuller, 6 May 1937, 1/302; "Power and Freedom," memorandum for the record, 9 May 1937, 11/1937/39; "The Universal Pattern of Self-made despotic Rulers throughout History," memorandum for the record, 12 May 1937, 11/1937/40; "B.H.L.H. Special Diary Notes, 1934," 27 Feb. entry, 11/1934/1c; untitled note, 6 Sept. 1934, 11/1934/14; "Thoughts Jotted Down—to Be Expanded," memorandum for the record, 4 Aug. and 6 Nov. 1936 entries, 11/1936/2-25c; "'Woman Wanders—the World Wavers' or Woman and the World-quake," *English Review* 59 (Sept. 1934): 312. As this last piece (ibid., 310–25) shows, however, LH had very traditional views about women and was firmly opposed to the feminist movement of his day.

[7]

Liddell Hart's Role in Policy Making

Along with the detailed examination of the substance of Liddell Hart's military thought in the interwar period and the factors behind the formation of his principal theories, there has also been some discussion of his role in the policy-making process, but not the systematic examination required. This chapter fills that need, before I turn, in chapter 8, to my final aim: to show how Liddell Hart rescued his badly stained reputation after World War II.

To assess Liddell Hart's role in the policy-making process during the interwar period requires answers to three sets of questions. First, what were his policy prescriptions during those years? Second, what influence did he have on German policy before World War II? Did he have any meaningful influence on official British policy? Were his policy proposals and warnings ignored, as he suggests, or did he wield influence in official circles? Third, what were the consequences of his policy views? Did he offer sound advice about how to prevent World War II?

I have already said a great deal about the first question. For example, I outlined Liddell Hart's thinking about the threat posed by the Third Reich, as well as his policy prescriptions for meeting that threat, in considerable detail in the previous two chapters. I also compared his views with official policy. Two critical issues, however, remain: Was he cognizant of the formidable military threat presented by the Wehrmacht as well as Allied weaknesses? Did he anticipate what would happen in the spring of 1940?

Liddell Hart attempted after World War II to make the case he foresaw the Fall of France. Others have repeated it. According to Michael Howard, for example, "Nobody should have known better than Liddell Hart in 1939 that Britain's Allies were likely to be defeated. Probably nobody *did* know better."[1] It is, however, my view that he did *not* anticipate the Fall of France. All available evidence indicates that by the late 1930s he firmly believed in the military positions he had staked out, even though it is probable that in the mid-1930s, when he first began to shift his views about the blitzkrieg and the relative balance of French and German fighting power, he was aware that the change was for expediency, not because he actually believed the new positions he was staking out.

Some sketchy evidence supports this claim of expediency. Liddell Hart wrote a revealing note in December 1934, around the time his first article on the growing power of defense appeared.[2] The main theme in this note is the difficulty of challenging orthodox ideas because "the direct assault of new ideas sets upon its own resistance." He thus concluded that his theory of the indirect approach, which was initially conceived as a way of winning wars, actually had much broader application, that in fact it was "something that lies at the root of practical philosophy." He argued that "reflection leads one to the conclusion that the indirect approach is a law of life in all spheres—and its fulfilment, the key to practical achievement in dealing with any problem where the human factor is predominant, and where there is room for a conflict of wills." This philosophical memorandum, coupled with what we know about the profound change in his military views that took place at this point, suggests that he was consciously shifting his approach. There is also in this note an important passage that hints that Liddell Hart was not abandoning the blitzkrieg because his thinking about armored strategy per se had changed but for expediency in the service of a higher cause: "My personal difficulty, at present, is to reconcile my belief in the practical value of this principle [of the indirect approach] with ever developing passion for truth." He evidently saw a conflict between the new ("indirect") approach he intended to take and "the truth." I believe this problem concerned the fact that he would have to abandon his previous views on armored war and the relative fighting capabilities of the French and German armies, which he surely must have believed at the time, to keep Britain from another bloodbath on the Western Front.[3] There is certainly no evidence his

---

[1] Michael Howard, "Liddell Hart," *Encounter* 34 (June 1970): 41. A. J. P. Taylor claimed likewise in "A Prophet Vindicated," rev. of *Memoirs*, vol. 2, by LH and *The Theory and Practice of War*, ed. Michael Howard, Observer, 31 Oct. 1965, 27.

[2] Untitled note, 20 Dec. 1934, 11/1934/32. The article was "Speed!—and More Speed!—in War," *New York Times Magazine*, 2 Dec. 1934, 3–18; a close reading supports my argument.

[3] LH wrote to his son Adrian after World War II, "I have found myself that life becomes

change of thinking in the mid-1930s resulted from careful analysis, as when he moved away from his theory of infantry tactics to become a proponent of blitzkrieg.

Regardless of what Liddell Hart thought in the mid-1930s about the validity of his new strategic views, he apparently became convinced of their correctness with the passage of time. And there *was* some evidence to support his new positions. For example, the French army was developing mechanized divisions in the mid-1930s, which he could point to as a positive development. Also, he had a long-standing belief that large conscript armies were highly inefficient on the battlefield, and the German army certainly grew in size under Hitler (chap. 5). More important, however, he was so deeply committed by the late 1930s to keeping Britain out of the next war that he probably could not allow himself to have doubts about his new views, with the result that he completely misjudged the course of events in the spring of 1940. This conclusion is supported by the flaws in his claim that he anticipated the Fall of France.

There is no evidence in Liddell Hart's public writings or archives to sustain his case. There is no private correspondence or memorandum to indicate he had private views that differed from his public ones.[4] Had such evidence existed, would he not have cited it in his *Memoirs*? Nor can one conclude he held different views in private but simply did not write them down, for that supposition does not square with the way he worked. He compulsively committed his thoughts to paper.

It would, moreover, have been the height of irresponsibility for Liddell Hart, had he anticipated the problems that led to the Fall of France, not to let key policy makers know. And Liddell Hart was not irresponsible. He cared deeply about his country; that is why he worked so passionately to keep Britain out of war. Although he often exercised bad judgment in those final years before the war, it is hard to imagine him remaining silent about glaring weaknesses in the Allies' deterrent posture. If nothing else, correcting those problems would have facilitated deterrence, which was, after all, one of his principal goals. Liddell Hart surely would have done his utmost to alert responsible leaders had he had any inkling of what was going to happen in May 1940.

---

an unavoidable series of compromises between one's ideals and one's circumstances. It is a vain hope to seek solutions for our problems in any direct way, but the indirect approach turns out to be a philosophy as well as a strategy" (quoted in the transcript of Robert Pocock's BBC radio program, "Liddell Hart: The Captain Who Taught Generals," a copy of which is in *Listener*, 28 Dec. 1972, 892).

[4]LH hinted *after* the war that he had privately warned the French about weaknesses in their defenses; see LH to Edward Mead Earle, 24 Apr. 1946, 1/255/6. No evidence supports this claim.

There is not a whit of evidence, however, that he spoke with anyone about such matters. All available evidence instead indicates he was confident about the Allies' prospects for meeting a German attack.

Finally, Liddell Hart's assessment of the German offensive as it unfolded in mid-May 1940 (see the concluding section of chap. 5) demonstrates that he did not foresee the outcome. Even after the newspapers had reported that the Allies were in grave danger, he continued to maintain that they would halt the German attack. He expected the Allies to pull off another "miracle of the Marne" as they had done in World War I. He had completely lost sight of the fact that the tank, properly deployed, would lead to victory.

The common belief is that during the interwar years British and French policy makers refused to listen to Liddell Hart's sage advice, while the German generals paid careful attention to his military theories, the result being the stunning German victory of May 1940. Although I have already offered much evidence to challenge both the specific claim that British policy makers rejected his advice and the general claim that he was a voice in the wilderness during the 1930s, these matters demand consideration in greater detail. First, though, there is a subject that has received little attention: Liddell Hart's influence on the German generals.

LIDDELL HART AND THE GERMAN GENERALS

It is widely assumed that the German generals, especially the famous armored commanders, owed Liddell Hart a great intellectual debt, for they adopted his ideas about blitzkrieg and produced a handful of brilliant victories in the early years of the war. This story is simply not true and is largely a myth Liddell Hart created after World War II to help rescue his blemished reputation. How he built this myth belongs to the next chapter; here, I simply want to challenge the claim that he significantly influenced the development of thinking about the blitzkrieg in Germany.

It is difficult, however, to determine how well known Liddell Hart's ideas were in Germany during the 1930s. He knew personally very few influential Germans, in or out of uniform, in this period. There are certainly pieces of evidence that indicate some of his ideas were well-known in Germany. For example, Sir Maurice Hankey, the powerful executive secretary of the Committee on Imperial Defence, told him in 1933 that he had "heard from a high military authority in Berlin . . . that your's and Fuller's writings are widely read and eagerly awaited

throughout the German army."[5] His books were also frequently reviewed in popular German journals and newspapers.[6] In late July
1939, when Germany was pressuring Poland for concessions, German
authorities went to considerable length to emphasize that Britain and
France could do nothing to help Poland. The Nazi propaganda machine maintained Britain and France were incapable of launching an
offensive and would have to confine themselves to a defensive posture. As the *New York Times* correspondent in Berlin noted, "The authorities adduced for that argument and widely circulated in the German press are, first, Captain B. H. Liddell Hart, described as 'the
greatest military critic of Germany,' and Alfred Duff Cooper, former
First Lord of the Admiralty."[7] But aside from this evidence, there are
no grounds for concluding Liddell Hart had much impact on the German policy debates of the 1930s. Scholars of the period, for example,
have produced no evidence of his influence.

Let us focus, however, on the specific issue of whether Liddell Hart
influenced German thinking about the blitzkrieg. The basic charac-
teristics of Liddell Hart's writings about armored war raise serious
doubts about his purported influence. As I have shown, his ideas on
blitzkrieg, written when he was just beginning to establish his reputation, were never comprehensively laid out in a single article, much less
in a book. How likely is it, then, that the German generals learned
about blitzkrieg from his writings? Liddell Hart was apparently aware
of this problem. He told Chester Wilmot in May 1953 that with regard
to the "adoption [of his ideas on 'the expanding torrent'] in tank doctrine, both here and in Germany, that was produced not from any one
exposition of it in a book, but rather by constant reiteration of the
keynote in my current articles commenting on maneuvers etc."[8] The
"current articles" were mostly in the *Daily Telegraph*,[9] and in none of
them did he explicitly lay out his early thinking about armored doctrine. That he rarely referred to these articles himself in later years
would suggest he did not look upon them as a primary source for his
views.

Furthermore, there is Liddell Hart's abandonment of his progressive

---

[5]Hankey to LH, 27 Dec. 1933, 1/352. See also Andrew Thorne to Hankey, 22 Mar. 1946, 13/45.

[6]See, for example, the many German reviews of *The Defence of Britain* (London: Faber, 1939) in 9/17/9.

[7]Otto D. Tolischus, "Reich Press Hails Submarine Fleet," *New York Times*, 26 July 1939, 8.

[8]LH to Wilmot, 14 May 1953, 9/24/30.

[9]Copies in sec. 10 of his personal papers.

ideas on armored warfare in the 1930s in favor of the argument that offense is futile on the modern battlefield, a message he constantly repeated. If the German generals, especially Heinz Guderian and Erich von Manstein, had been disciples of Liddell Hart, they would have held far different views about Germany's prospects against the Allies.[10] After all, Liddell Hart's writings in the 1930s were designed to retard not facilitate thinking about the blitzkrieg.

If Liddell Hart was indeed influential in Germany, it was probably for his ideas on the power of the defense. After the war, Fritz Bayerlein, a German general who had served under both Guderian and Rommel, told Liddell Hart, "Your books: 'The future of infantry', 'Dynamic defense', 'When Britain goes to war', [and] 'Europe in arms' gained our recognition especially whilst your standard work 'The strategy of indirect approach' was still unknown to us at that time."[11] None of these books contains any of his early writings on the blitzkrieg. *Europe in Arms* and *When Britain Goes to War* actually contain some of his key writings on the supremacy of the defense. The German generals could not have found support for their progressive ideas on armored warfare in these books. Fuller told Liddell Hart in 1935, after a visit to Berlin, that he had seen copies of Liddell Hart's book on T. E. Lawrence in German and that he had been told *The Future of Infantry* had been translated and had attracted the attention of "the Second in Command of the S.A."[12] These books do not contain any of his writings on the blitzkrieg either.

Could the channel for transmitting his ideas about the blitzkrieg have been direct personal contact with German generals? This too seems unlikely. He had limited contact with German military leaders during the interwar years and none with the famous generals with whom his name was later linked: Guderian, Rommel, and Manstein. His principal contacts were field marshals Werner von Blomberg and Walter von Reichenau, neither of whom he knew very well. Both were generally progressive thinkers about tank warfare, but there is no indication he discussed his ideas on blitzkrieg with them.[13] He implies in his *Memoirs* that they picked up on his ideas about deep strategic penetration when they translated *Sherman* into German, but as I have

[10]On the views of Guderian and Manstein, see John J. Mearsheimer, *Conventional Deterrence* (Ithaca, N.Y.: Cornell University Press, 1983), chap. 4.

[11]Bayerlein to LH, 15 Feb. 1950, 9/24/50.

[12]Brian Bond, *Liddell Hart: A Study of His Military Thought* (London: Cassell, 1977), 219.

[13]Correspondence with Reichenau in 9/24/87; no correspondence with Blomberg, whose only contact with LH appears to have been at the 1932 Disarmament Conference; see *Memoirs* 1:171–72, 200–203; LH, "Talk with Gen.-Lt. von Blomberg—8/3/32," memorandum for the record, 11/1932/9.

shown, there is no discussion of deep strategic penetration in *Sherman* or any of his writings from the interwar years.[14] In his memorandum for the record after his *only* conversation with Blomberg, Liddell Hart makes no mention of blitzkrieg; in fact, he wrote of this meeting: "What had particularly struck him in my 'Foch' etc. was its stress on the power of the defensive and on the possibilities of the elastic defensive. Said he was correcting the orthodox obsession with the offensive in his training."[15] Liddell Hart did not put this quotation in his *Memoirs*.[16] The best case that can be made is that progressive thinkers in the Wehrmacht were able to pick up some of Liddell Hart's early insights on armored war and build on them while wisely rejecting his writings from the 1930s. If this supposition were true, one would expect some corroborating evidence to have surfaced *after* the war. Liddell Hart's extensive interviews with many of the defeated German generals produced no such evidence.[17] In *The German Generals Talk* (1948), where Liddell Hart reports on those postwar interviews, he does not bring forward any evidence of the purported influence.

Liddell Hart's fortunes began to change in late 1949 when he made contact for the first time with Guderian and the family of the late Field Marshal Rommel. He soon became deeply involved in the publication of Guderian's memoirs (*Panzer Leader*) and the editing of *The Rommel Papers*. It is these two famous generals, and to a lesser extent Manstein, he used to make the case that he had influenced the development of the blitzkrieg in Germany. The Manstein case was difficult to make. Manstein had not been an armor advocate during the interwar years, so he could not have been influenced by Liddell Hart's writings on blitzkrieg during that period. He had, however, been deeply involved in the planning for the German attack in the West.[18] He had actually been the principal architect of the famous plan that called for moving the German army's main axis of attack from northern Belgium to the Ardennes area. Liddell Hart, who was well aware of this fact, alleged after the war that Manstein had gotten the brilliant idea of locating the

[14]*Memoirs* 1:171–72; see also *Memoirs of General William T. Sherman* (Bloomington: Indiana University Press, 1957), xiv; LH, Introduction, *From Atlanta to the Sea*, by William T. Sherman, ed. LH (London: Folio Society, 1961), 14–15.
[15]"Talk with Gen.-Lt. von Blomberg."
[16]LH wrote *after* the war of that meeting: "He told me he had been greatly impressed by the exposition of Sherman's technique [deep strategic penetration] in my book and was applying it in the training of the troops under his command" (*Memoirs of General William T. Sherman*, xiv). This is not borne out by the memorandum. See also *The German Generals Talk* (New York: Morrow, 1948), 23, where LH claims it was Blomberg's interest in his ideas about offensive strategy "which first brought us into contact."
[17]Records of these interviews in 9/24 of his personal papers.
[18]See Mearsheimer, *Conventional Deterrence*, chap. 4.

main attack in the Ardennes area from his writings (more on this in chap. 8). Manstein, however, refused to endorse this claim, which there is no evidence to support.

The matter of Liddell Hart's influence on Rommel during the inter-war years is straightforward. During this period Rommel was an infantry officer who was actually hostile to Guderian's claims about the tank's revolutionary potential. To quote Liddell Hart: "Prior to the war, he had been such a keen infantryman that he had opposed the ideas of those who preached the gospel of tank warfare."[19] Moreover, he was not involved, as Manstein had been, in the planning of the German offensive in the West. Thus Liddell Hart could only try to show he had influenced Rommel *during* the war. There was no link between Rommel and Liddell Hart that had bearing on the German victory in France.

The case for Liddell Hart's influence therefore rests on Heinz Guderian, whom Liddell Hart once called "the prime minister of *Blitzkrieg.*"[20] Guderian not only had been one of the principal architects of Germany's panzer forces but had also been an important contributor to the planning that led to the Fall of France. Here is an interesting story. There are two critical paragraphs in the English version of Guderian's memoirs, *Panzer Leader*, that indicate Liddell Hart had a significant impact on the development of Guderian's thinking about the blitzkrieg:

It was principally the books and articles of the Englishmen, Fuller, Liddell Hart and [Gen. Giffard] Martel [a British tank expert], that excited my interest and gave me food for thought. These far-sighted soldiers were even then trying to make of the tank something more than just an infantry support weapon. They envisaged it in relationship to the growing motorisation of our age, and thus they became the pioneers of a new type of warfare on the largest scale.

I learned from them the concentration of armour, as employed in the battle of Cambrai. Further, it was Liddell Hart who *emphasized the use of armoured forces for long-range strokes, operations against the opposing army's communications, and also proposed a type of armoured division combining panzer and panzer-infantry units.* Deeply impressed by these ideas I tried to develop them in a sense practicable for our own army. So I owe many suggestions of our further development to Captain Liddell Hart.[21]

[19]*German Generals Talk*, 46–47.
[20]LH, ed., *The Rommel Papers*, trans. Paul Findlay (New York: Harcourt, Brace, 1953), xx.
[21]*Panzer Leader*, trans. Constantine Fitzgibbon (London: Joseph, 1952), 20, emphasis added.

This is a remarkable statement, not only because Guderian says Liddell Hart had been a major influence on his thinking about the blitzkrieg, but more specifically because he seems to say he picked up the idea of deep strategic penetration ("long-range strokes") from him. This admission certainly undermines my argument that Liddell Hart did not understand the importance of the deep strategic penetration until after World War II. The second paragraph appears to be the crucial piece of evidence that shows direct responsibility.

There is, however, more to this story. The second paragraph did not appear in the German version of *Panzer Leader*.[22] Only the first paragraph is found there. Liddell Hart, who was deeply involved in the editing of the English version of Guderian's memoirs, was not satisfied with the first paragraph's terse acknowledgment; he suggested Guderian provide for the English version some additional words about Liddell Hart's influence. Liddell Hart indicated what he thought should be said, and Guderian accepted the proposal. Specifically, Liddell Hart wrote Guderian on 6 April 1951:

> I appreciate very much what you said in the [first] paragraph. . . . So, I am sure, will Fuller and Martel. It is a most generous acknowledgment. But because of our special association, and the wish that I should write the foreword to your book, people may wonder why there is no separate reference to what my writings taught. You might care to insert a remark that I *emphasized the use of armoured forces for long-range operations against the opposing army's communications, and also proposed a type of armoured division combining panzer and panzer-infantry units*—and that these points particularly impressed you. A suitable place for such a remark . . . would be. . . . I should appreciate it if you felt inclined to insert a sentence or two.

Guderian responded with a letter on 23 April that included the famous second paragraph, which repeats almost verbatim the key points from Liddell Hart's letter.[23] It is perfectly clear from this correspondence that this key paragraph cannot be taken as legitimate evidence of Liddell Hart's influence on Guderian. The case for his influence must therefore rest on the first paragraph.

There is no reason to doubt the legitimacy of the first paragraph, as there is no evidence that Guderian wrote it at Liddell Hart's prompting. Moreover, Guderian briefly indicated in *Achtung-Panzer*, written in the mid-1930s, that he recognized that Liddell Hart, along with Fuller

---

[22]Heinz Guderian, *Erinnerungen eines Soldaten* (Heidelberg: Vowinckel, 1951), 15.
[23]LH to Guderian, emphasis added; Guderian to LH, both in 9/24/62.

and Martel, were the principal proponents of mechanization in Britain.[24] Guderian was obviously familiar with Liddell Hart's name and at least the broad outlines of his early thinking about tanks. Liddell Hart was widely recognized as an advocate of mechanization in the 1920s, and Guderian was Germany's principal advocate of developing powerful armored forces. Guderian told Liddell Hart after the war, "I think that I first read your articles about the year 1923/24. I read 'When Britain Goes to War,' 'The Future of Infantry,' and 'The Remaking of Modern Armies,'"[25] the last containing some of Liddell Hart's early writings on the blitzkrieg. The first paragraph is *not* however an indication of significant influence, which is what Liddell Hart solicited. It indicates that Liddell Hart's writings, along with those of other British armor advocates, helped stimulate Guderian's interest in tank warfare and contributed in an unspecifed way to his early thinking about the blitzkrieg. This is not insignificant by any means, but it does not support the claim Guderian was Liddell Hart's disciple.

There is no evidence elsewhere to support the claim of significant influence. Guderian never indicated, until the questionable paragraph, that Liddell Hart's writings had been very important for his intellectual development. For example, Guderian described the development of his interest in tank warfare in one of his first letters to Liddell Hart without mentioning Liddell Hart's name in discussing the evolution of his thinking about blitzkrieg.[26] Furthermore, Kenneth Macksey, in his excellent biography of Guderian, could find no evidence that Liddell Hart had had substantial influence on that panzer general's thinking. In fact Guderian's elder son told him:

> As far as I know it was Fuller who made the most suggestions. Once before the war my father visited him. Fuller was almost certainly more competent as an active officer than Captain B. H. Liddell Hart. . . . At any rate my father often spoke of him [Fuller] while I cannot remember other names being mentioned at the time [before 1939]. . . . The greater emphasis upon Liddell Hart seems to have developed through contacts after the war.[27]

Again, significant influence is unlikely simply because Liddell Hart wrote so little about the blitzkrieg. Evidence supporting this argument

[24]Heinz Guderian, *Achtung-Panzer!: Die Entwicklung der Panzerwaffe, ihre Kampftaktik und ihre operativen Möglichkeiten* (Stuttgart: Union Deutsche Verlagsgesellschaft, 1937), 136. The publisher reissued this book under another title, *Die Panzerwaffe*, in 1943.

[25]Guderian to LH, 19 Mar. 1949, 9/24/62. It is also clear he was familiar with LH's *Europe in Arms* (London: Faber, 1937); see Heinz Guderian, *Die Panzertruppen: Und ihr Zufammenwirfen mit den anderen Waffen* (Berlin: Mittler & Gohn, 1938), 14, 47.

[26]Guderian to LH, 14 Dec. 1948, 9/24/62.

[27]Kenneth Macksey, *Guderian: Creator of the Blitzkrieg* (New York: Stein & Day, 1976), 62; see also idem, *The Tank Pioneers* (London: Jane's, 1981), 118, 137, 155–56, 216.

is found in *Achtung-Panzer*. Guderian mentions Liddell Hart's name in the text along with those of Charles de Gaulle, Fuller, and Martel, but he does not list any of Liddell Hart's works in the bibliography, while he does cite the relevant works of the other three.[28]

Finally, although Liddell Hart clearly had some influence on Guderian's thinking in the 1920s, the general surely rejected Liddell Hart's writings from the 1930s on the supremacy of the defense.[29] Had Guderian been a Liddell Hart disciple in 1939, he undoubtedly would have argued against launching an offensive in the West. Instead, he argued forcefully that an armored offensive would succeed against the Allies.[30] Thus Liddell Hart's influence concerning blitzkrieg was probably operative only in the 1920s and not a major factor in shaping Guderian's thinking. In conclusion, I find no basis for the widely accepted claim that Liddell Hart had marked influence on the development of thinking about the blitzkrieg in Germany during the interwar years and that the German offensive of May 1940 was essentially a case of his disciples putting his theories into practice.[31]

LIDDELL HART'S INFLUENCE IN BRITAIN DURING THE 1930S

It is commonly accepted that Liddell Hart was an isolated individual whose views throughout the interwar period were largely ignored by British policy makers, the generals in particular. His lack of influence, so the argument goes, was mainly because his personal views were diametrically opposed to official policy. For example, it is widely assumed the British and French generals refused to listen to his sage advice about armored war because they had very different ideas about how to defend against a German offensive in the West. The result was the Fall of France, which Liddell Hart, the rejected prophet, had "to watch as a mere onlooker."[32]

It should be amply clear now that Liddell Hart's position in the policy-making process bears little resemblance to the conventional wisdom. He was well integrated into British policy-making circles throughout the entire interwar period, and his views not only were

---

[28]Guderian, *Achtung-Panzer*, 214.

[29]It seems reasonable to assume that if Guderian was familiar with *When Britain Goes to War* (London: Faber, 1935) and *Europe in Arms*, he was aware of LH's claims about the supremacy of the defense.

[30]See Guderian, *Panzer Leader*, chap. 5; Mearsheimer, *Conventional Deterrence*, chap. 4.

[31]Although LH focused on making the case that the Germans' offensive successes were markedly influenced by his writings, he also maintained that their defensive strategy was based on his ideas from the 1930s; see, for example, LH to Esmé Wingfield-Stratford, 5 Oct. 1942, 1/757. There is no evidence to support this claim.

[32]*Memoirs* 1:281.

taken seriously but often matched official policy. By his own admission, senior officers paid serious attention to him during his years as an army officer; he was certainly not ignored by policy makers after he left the army and joined *The Daily Telegraph;* and in fact, he was in constant contact with Britain's military elite throughout the late 1920s and early 1930s. Once he moved to the *Times*, he was certainly an integral part of the foreign policy establishment. In light of his *Times* position and his close working relationship with Hore-Belisha, it is difficult to see how anyone could consider him an outsider. In January 1938, while Liddell Hart was helping Hore-Belisha reorganize the army, the editor of the *Daily Telegraph* remarked to him, "I hear they have made you C.I.G.S. now." That same month a cabinet minister asked him, undoubtedly with tongue in cheek, "As C.I.G.S. what advice would you give to the Cabinet about the course to be adopted in the Far East?"[33] One month earlier, after he congratulated Maj. Gen. Clive Liddell (no relation) on his recent appointment as adjutant general, the general remarked, "I have an idea that you are responsible for it."[34] It is probably no exaggeration to claim that as a result of his partnership with Hore-Belisha, Liddell Hart was for a brief period of time "the unofficial C.I.G.S."[35] In short, Liddell Hart was simply not an isolated figure in Britain, either during the 1920s or the 1930s.

The question still remains, however: How much influence did Liddell Hart exert on official British policy during the 1930s? To say policy makers paid serious attention to his views says little about the extent of his influence, and that is difficult to measure. Without a government position (of course as unofficial advisor to Hore-Belisha for about a year, he certainly had an effect on the secretary of state's thinking) he did not participate directly in the policy debates within the Chamberlain government. Instead, his influence had to come largely from his writings, which certainly received widespread attention, and his contacts with particular individuals.

Influence is convincing others to change their views or leading the thinking about a new issue and helping shape the way others think about it. Liddell Hart did not have much influence in Britain during the

[33]LH, "How People Talk," memorandum for the record, 14, 25, Jan. 1938 entries, 11/1938/19b.

[34]LH, "Talk with General Liddell (Lunch, with Me, at the Athenaeum)—31.12.37," memorandum for the record, 11/1937/108. It is apparent from *Memoirs* 2:49, 68, 70, that the general's suspicions were correct.

[35]The commissioner of customs used this phrase to describe LH; see "How People Talk," 21 Jan. 1938 entry. See also LH, "Correspondence with Various Officers regarding Army Reform," memoranda for the record, 11/1933/50–108. LH viewed himself at this point as a very important figure; see, for example, "Adam. 9th January, 1938," memorandum for the record, 11/1938/7.

1930s. Seldom did he grasp an emerging issue and shape others' thinking. His views were usually consistent with official policy or with the views of a particular group of influential people. Not the iconoclast he later portrayed himself as, he was in fact highly regarded during the 1930s because he often told people what they wanted to hear. Comments from two well-known senior officers about Liddell Hart's *Europe in Arms* reinforce this point. Marshal of the Royal Air Force Viscount Trenchard wrote him shortly after the book was published: "The words you have written are what I, if I had the power to write, should like to have written myself . . . it is splendid." Maj. Gen. Sir John Kennedy had similar words of praise for the book: "It is full of things which I have always wanted to say but couldn't express myself . . . you present an almost unanswerable argument against the folly of a future war—I only hope it will reach all the warmongers in the world."[36] Liddell Hart's book mainly reinforced, albeit in a powerful way, these officers' basic inclinations. The many reviews of *Europe in Arms*, almost all favorable, show that the views of Kennedy and Trenchard were hardly atypical. In fact the reviews of Liddell Hart's various books from the 1930s show his core views were widely shared by his fellow countrymen.[37]

Let us look at this matter of influence from a different perspective by briefly contrasting Liddell Hart's thinking in the 1930s about policy issues with the official view. Consider the Continental commitment, which Liddell Hart opposed throughout the decade. During that entire period there was little enthusiasm for such a commitment within the British government; it was only with great reluctance that the Chamberlain government accepted it in early 1939. Moreover, there was little enthusiasm within the army for making a commitment to fight on the Continent. Liddell Hart wrongly believed the generals were anxious to raise an army for use in Europe and were pushing hard for a policy decision to allow that buildup.[38] Most generals did recognize, to their credit, that if a war broke out on the Continent, Britain was sure to be

[36]Trenchard to LH, 8 Mar. 1937, and Kennedy to LH, 22 Feb. 1937, both in 9/15/8. See also favorable comments in Gen. William E. Ironside to LH, 9 Mar. 1937, 1/401; Neville Chamberlain to LH, 8 Mar. 1937, 1/519/1; Chamberlain to Leslie Hore-Belisha, 1/519/2.
[37]For reviews, see 9/10/18, 9/15/8, 9/17/9.
[38]On the army's attitude, see Brian Bond, *British Military Policy between the Two World Wars* (New York: Oxford University Press, 1980), chaps. 7–11; also idem, *Liddell Hart*, 106; Norman H. Gibbs, *Grand Strategy*, Vol. 1 (London: Her Majesty's Stationery Office, 1976), xxi, 451–52; Michael Howard, *The Continental Commitment: The Dilemma of British Defence Policy in the Era of the Two World Wars* (Harmondsworth: Penguin, 1974), 106–7, 119. For two examples of LH's fear that the army desired a Continental commitment, see his "Talk with Field Marshal Sir C. J. Deverell, 12.11.36," memorandum for the record, 13 Nov. 1936, 11/1936/99; LH to Robert Barrington-Ward, 19 Dec. 1936, 3/106.

drawn into it and would in all likelihood have to raise another mass army.[39] Despite this fatalistic view, military leaders throughout the 1930s were unwilling to argue forcefully that Britain should prepare an army for the Continent. In short, Liddell Hart's position on this important matter was widely shared by British policy makers, including many army generals. His writings about a Continental commitment were well-received because he was "preaching to the choir."

Consider Liddell Hart's views on the choice between offensive and defensive strategies. He believed the generals were firmly committed to building an offensively oriented army and had little appreciation of the power of defense. The interwar generals actually exhibited little enthusiasm for offense. The idea that Liddell Hart was locked in battle in the 1930s with a coterie of generals who favored offense and believed the tank or some other weapon provided the means to a quick and decisive victory bears little relation to what happened in those years. Liddell Hart's views on the power of defense and those of the majority of generals were similar.[40] The British officers who believed the tank had the potential to give renewed life to the offense were in the minority: they also were invariably those Liddell Hart trusted most because of the ties he developed with them in the 1920s, when he too believed that the tank was an offensive weapon. The absence of significant disagreement between Liddell Hart and the majority of generals over the question of offense versus defense is illustrated by their respective views on the crucial issue of whether the Allies should have launched an offensive against Germany in the period between 1 September 1939 and 10 May 1940. The Allies' behavior immediately before the war and during the Phoney War was actually in close accord with Liddell Hart's thinking about the futility of offense.[41] He was naturally very pleased the Allies opted to remain on the defensive, and he had no complaints about the state of the Allies' defensive positions during the Phoney War.

Liddell Hart did voice misgivings about appeasement during the Czechoslovakian crisis of 1938. Nevertheless, he did not call upon the government to abandon that controversial policy, undoubtedly be-

[39]See, for example, Deverell's comments in LH, "Talk with Field Marshal Sir C. J. Deverell, 12.11.36"; Kennedy to LH, 23 Sept. 1937, 1/417; Gen. Sir Frederick Maurice, letter, *Times*, 29 Oct. 1937, 17; Gen. Sir Clement Armitage to Barrington-Ward, 8 Dec. 1936, 3/106.
[40]See B. Bond, *British Military Policy*. On the British generals' views about the tank and its implications for the battlefield, ibid., 130–32.
[41]On Allied thinking about military strategy against Germany, see Brian Bond, *France and Belgium, 1939–1940* (London: Davis-Poynter, 1975); Mearsheimer, *Conventional Deterrence*, chap. 3; Barry R. Posen, *The Sources of Military Doctrine: France, Britain, and Germany between the World Wars* (Ithaca, N.Y.: Cornell University Press, 1984), chaps. 3–5.

cause he had no alternative. He simply expressed doubts about the efficacy of appeasement. The concept of influence has no relevance here, where he was not trying to change existing policy.

Liddell Hart had so little influence in Britain throughout most of the 1930s, not because he was an isolated figure with views antithetical to the government and the military, but because his views were mostly consistent with official thinking. He was an important figure, not because he wielded real influence, but because he was a spokesman for the views of the majority of his countrymen. It was only in the last months of the twenty years' peace, when his country began preparing for a possible war with the Third Reich, that Liddell Hart's views diverged from the mainstream. It was only then he tried to exercise real influence. Fortunately, he failed.

THE CONSEQUENCES OF LIDDELL HART'S IDEAS

Because Liddell Hart's thinking about the blitzkrieg per se cannot be linked to the Fall of France or any other event in the early years of World War II, an evaluation of the consequences of his military theories must focus on his arguments about the manifest advantages of defense on the modern battlefield, which he trumpeted in the years after Hitler came to power. There would not have been a war in the West in 1940 if the policy makers in each of the European states had known of and accepted Liddell Hart's claims about the supremacy of the defense. The Germans, after conquering Poland, would have remained behind the Siegfried Line, while the Allies would have stayed behind the Maginot Line. The Allies' actions, of course, were fully consistent with Liddell Hart's preachings about the futility of offense. It was the Germans who ultimately rejected the logic of his position and launched an attack. There were actually some German generals who held views not altogether unlike Liddell Hart's,[42] and they adamantly opposed Hitler's call for an offensive in the West.[43] What is particularly ironic is that it was senior officers like Guderian and Manstein, who were later depicted as Liddell Hart's disciples, who rejected his reasoning about the futility of offense and instead maintained that the Wehrmacht could quickly win against the Allies. Had these purported disciples paid serious attention to his writings, the course of the early part of the war might have been quite different.

[42]See, for example, Ritter von Leeb, *Defense,* trans. Stefan T. Possony and Daniel Vilfroy (Harrisburg, Pa.: Military Service, 1943).
[43]See Mearsheimer, *Conventional Deterrence,* chap. 4.

One might argue that although Liddell Hart was unsuccessful in his attempt to deter the Third Reich, the effort was worthwhile if not noble. This is not the case because the Allies' ability to deal with the Nazi threat was seriously impaired by their adoption of policies he promoted—avoidance of a Continental commitment and no Allied development of an offensive option—both of which made it very difficult to deter Germany. We will never know whether there was any way Britain could have avoided a major war with Germany. We do know Liddell Hart's policy prescriptions precluded employment of the best strategy for achieving that outcome. They not only weakened deterrence but also left the British army unprepared for war in the event deterrence failed.

Allied shortcomings cannot simply be blamed on Liddell Hart. It is rare that a single person is responsible for the successes and failures of a modern nation-state's national security policy. Liddell Hart held no important policy-making position and was simply not one of the principal guiding forces behind British foreign and military policy in the 1930s. But by contributing to building and maintaining a solid consensus on how to deal with the Third Reich, which lasted until early 1939, he surely earned a small share of the blame, even if others bear the principal responsibility for failing to deter Hitler.

The size and shape of the British army was determined in large part by Britain's position on a Continental commitment. Had this commitment been accepted it would have been necessary to maintain a formidable standing army well trained for war on the Continent and capable of rapidly increasing its size upon mobilization. Without this commitment, only a small army suited for police actions in the Empire, and incapable of fighting a major European war, was required. Britain's conscious decision in December 1937 not to prepare for a European land war and hence to neglect her army, coupled with the fact the army had been given very little money in preceding years, had a devastating effect on the army. It fell into such a state of disrepair that some doubted whether it could even handle its policing tasks in the Empire.[44] It was in a woeful state when a Continental commitment was finally accepted in early 1939. Unfortunately, the army had only five months to rectify the problem before the war broke out and only thirteen months to prepare for the German attack in the West. Critics are certainly correct when they claim the British army was not prepared to meet the Wehrmacht on the battlefield. Liddell Hart, of course, attributed this unfortunate situation to leadership by Colonel Blimps

---

[44]For a graphic description of the state of the British army in the late 1930s, see *Time Unguarded: The Ironside Diaries, 1937–1940*, ed. Roderick Macleod and Denis Kelly (New York: McKay, 1962); see also B. Bond, *British Military Policy*, chaps. 10–11.

rather than to the political decision not to prepare, a decision Liddell Hart firmly supported.

There is no question but that Liddell Hart was aware that rejecting a Continental commitment would keep the army small and weak. Field Marshal Deverell, when he was the CIGS, told him at least twice that his writings against a Continental commitment in the *Times* "had increased his difficulties a hundred per cent in getting money from the Government for the Army. They led the ministers to argue that 'only policemen were needed.'" Liddell Hart's close friend Tim Pile told him shortly after the 22 December 1937 cabinet meeting that Hore-Belisha had "told the Cabinet that by the new army policy he would 'save millions' on tanks." Here we see evidence of the real reason there were only a handful of tanks in the British army when the war began. In this same vein, General Martel, the British tank advocate, asked Liddell Hart in late November 1938 if he "might do something to modify the effect" of a recent letter in the *Times* arguing "that the army was not wanted for use on the continent." Martel feared this letter, which was written by a prominent army officer, "might lead the Government to put a check on the tank programme—in particular the new heavy Christie tanks." Two weeks later, General Edmonds told him, "Hore-Belisha has killed the Army as a profession. We shall NOT do so well next time."[45] Liddell Hart was not sympathetic to these arguments. A small and weak army would curb temptation to use it on the Continent.

One might argue that although Liddell Hart did not favor building a field force, he made a worthy contribution by helping to get the army to focus on building a formidable ground-based air defense system. Liddell Hart was, as his *Memoirs* reflect, a staunch advocate of spending what little money was in the army's pot on these forces. No one would argue in principle against allocating money to build an effective ground-based air defense system, especially in Britain during the late 1930s when there was considerable concern about a German air attack. Spending on air defense, however, invariably cut into the small amount of money available for the infantry and armored units that would form the nucleus of any force sent to the Continent. Thus there was tension in the army throughout the late 1930s over whether to spend on air defense or more traditional fighting units. Deverell told

[45]LH, "Talk with Sir Cyril Deverell—29.6.37," memorandum for the record, 30 June 1937, 11/1937/56, and LH, "Talk with Field Marshal Sir C. J. Deverell," memorandum for the record, 13 Nov. 1936, 11/1936/99; see also LH, untitled note, 6 Nov. 1936, 11/1936/96. LH, "Talk with Pile—30.12.37," memorandum for the record, 11/1937/107. LH, "Talk with Brigadier G. Le Q. Martel," memorandum for the record, 28 Nov. 1938, 11/1938/122; regarding the original letter, see J. Burnett-Stuart, letter, *Times*, 28 Nov. 1938, 15; Brig. Gen. J. E. Edmonds to LH, 17 Dec. 1938, 1/259.

Liddell Hart as early as December 1936 that "the demands of anti-aircraft defence were endangering the needs of the Army itself." Gen. Percy Hobart, an armor advocate and close friend of Liddell Hart, told him in May 1938 that there was a feeling throughout the army that antiaircraft "claims must not be allowed to interfere with building a large field army." Earlier that year, Pile, head of the Anti-Aircraft Command from 1939 to 1945, told Liddell Hart that Gort, who was then CIGS, was blocking improvements in antiaircraft defenses "because of fear of subtracting from his expeditionary force." Liddell Hart was well aware of the sharp tension between these two missions. He wrote to Barrington-Ward at the *Times* in May 1938: "I am growing increasingly concerned at the rate of progress in the Army. . . . The most depressing aspect of all is the Air defence of this country. Here the subconscious desire for a large field army, again, is a powerful factor."[46]

Given this tradeoff, Liddell Hart could, by advocating spending money to improve Britain's air defenses, hope to keep the ground forces impoverished. Liddell Hart's bitter foe General Montgomery-Massingberd, in a public speech shortly before the Germans struck in the West, emphatically condemned him for contributing to this weakness:

> We have now got three expeditionary forces and it is largely due to him and people like him that those expeditionary forces are not as fully equipped as they should be.
>
> I should be very sorry to be in that man's place and to have that on my conscience. He accuses Earl Haig and the British generals of losing lives in the last war, but I wonder how many lives are going to be lost in this war because of the teaching of that man and of people like him.[47]

A small, weak British army would be not only largely unprepared to engage the highly efficient Wehrmacht in battle but also unlikely to deter Hitler. Any chance of deterring the Third Reich would depend on robust fighting forces along the Western Front that would make it extremely difficult for the Wehrmacht to win a quick and decisive victory. Liddell Hart, with his rhetoric about the supremacy of the

[46]LH was concerned, though by no means deeply worried, about a German air offensive (chap. 4, n. 22 and attendant text). LH, "Talk with the C.I.G.S. (Sir Cyril Deverell) (at His Flat) Sunday Morning—6.12.36," memorandum for the record, 11/1936/118; LH, "Lunch with Hobart—24.5.38," memorandum for the record, 11/1938/58; LH, "Pile—12th and 13th March 1938," memorandum for the record, 11/1938/29; LH to Barrington-Ward, 24 May 1938, 3/112; see also ibid., 9 Feb. 1938, 3/108; LH, "Outline of the Opposition to the Development of the Anti-Aircraft Defence of Great Britain," memorandum for the record, 30 July 1938, 11/1938/89.

[47]Excerpts from this speech are from the 29 Apr. 1940 *Lincolnshire Echo*, copy in LH's personal papers, 6/1940/5; see also LH, "Note," 4 May 1940, 11/1940/29.

defense and the futility of offense, correctly understood the importance of convincing the Germans that victory on the battlefield was highly unlikely, but he was not willing to go beyond rhetoric and urge on the Allies the force buildup necessary to back it up. He preferred to let the French stand alone on the Western Front. Not only was it clear from World War I that France alone was no match for the powerful German army, but two developments had further weakened France's position by the late 1930s. First, the disparity between France and Germany in economic strength and manpower, two very important ingredients of military success, had widened between the early 1920s and the late 1930s.[48] Second, France and the Soviet Union were not able to form an alliance in the 1930s like the one developed before 1914; if France were to present Hitler with the threat of a two-front war, she would have to rely on the small and quarrelsome states of Eastern Europe—not a promising alternative.

Liddell Hart certainly was not unfamiliar with the argument that Britain could bolster deterrence if she accepted a Continental commitment and built the requisite field force to back up France. During the Czechoslovakian crisis of 1938 he examined the question of whether a clear-cut British pledge to support France before 1914 might have prevented World War I.[49] His conclusion is quite surprising: "While no verdict can be passed with certainty, the general trend of the evidence offers a strong probability that a clear statement of Britain's intentions, had it been possible, would have prevented the war—by prompting the German Government to restrain the Austrians in time."[50] Nevertheless, despite some indications to the contrary in 1938 and early 1939 (chap. 6), Liddell Hart could not bring himself to accept the logical consequence of this argument and endorse a Continental commitment. He was, in short, unwilling to back up his oft-repeated claim that a German offensive would fail. This unwillingness could only weaken the prospects of deterrence.

The discussion up to now has focused on deterring the Third Reich from striking into France by building up forces along the Western Front. The Allies were also concerned about deterring Germany from

---

[48]See H. C. Hillmann, "Comparative Strength of the Great Powers," in Arnold Toynbee and Frank T. Ashton-Gwatkin, eds., *The World in March 1939* (London: Oxford University Press, 1952), 366–507; Robert J. Young, *In Command of France: French Foreign Policy and Military Planning, 1933–1940* (Cambridge, Mass.: Harvard University Press, 1978), chap. 1.

[49]See LH, "Talk with Dr. G. P. Gooch (Editor of British Documents on the Origins of the War)—19.3.38," memorandum for the record, 11/1938/34; LH, "The Neutrality Issue in 1914," memorandum for the record, 21 Mar. 1938, 11/1938/36b, rptd. in his "Strategy and Commitments," *Fortnightly* 143 (June 1938):645–48, and in *Defence of Britain*, 70–74.

[50]"Strategy and Commitments," 647.

attacking in the East, not only as an end in itself, but also because such a move would have significant implications for their own position in the West. The French and British did not want to allow Hitler to knock out their allies in the East, consolidate his position, and then turn virtually all his forces against them. If war was inevitable, they much preferred to force Germany to fight a two-front war. The Germans, of course, had a long-standing fear of a two-front war and preferred to deal with their adversaries in turn. Deterrence was therefore much more likely to obtain if Germany recognized she could not expect to fight on a single front.

Germany's opponents on both flanks needed an offensive capability to insure a two-front war. That capability would make it very difficult for Germany to strike against one opponent without unleashing an offensive by the other, thus producing a two-front war. If instead both or even one of Germany's principal adversaries were wedded to a strict defensive strategy and made no provision for launching an offensive, then Germany would be able to deal with one opponent at a time. The argument here is not that the Allies simply needed to adopt an offensive strategy, for if the Germans had struck first in the West, the Allies undoubtedly would have wanted to remain on defense and not repeat the mistake of 1914. They needed an offensive option in case Germany struck first in the East. The Allies, of course, had a defensive strategy in the late 1930s and were therefore unable to threaten Hitler when he moved against Czechoslovakia in 1938 and Poland in 1939. They allowed him, in effect, to consolidate his gains in the East and then turn most of his military might against them. Of course, after the Wehrmacht defeated the Allies, Hitler turned it against the Soviet Union.

Liddell Hart was well aware of the deterrent value of forcing the Third Reich to contemplate a two-front war, as his deep concern about German control of Czechoslovakia showed. Nevertheless, he staunchly opposed adopting an offensive strategy for use in case Hitler struck first in the East. He emphasized throughout the Czechoslovakian crisis, for example, that a French offensive in support of the Czechs would not successfully resolve the crisis. He was so dedicated to dissuading the Allies from countenancing any form of offense that, although he understood the importance of threatening Hitler with a two-front war, he simply could not urge the Allies to develop the military strategy necessary to make that threat a real one. It is not clear that even this strategy would have deterred Hitler. It is apparent, however, that a policy providing for an offensive option had a better chance than Liddell Hart's purely defensive strategy, which allowed Hitler to deal with his adversaries piecemeal.

The argument that although there is much to be said for these criticisms of Liddell Hart, they must be tempered by the realization that the available options were greatly limited by the British generals' overwhelming incompetence—that these generals simply could not be trusted with a large and powerful army that might be used for offensive purposes—can be easily dismissed. The generals who headed the British army in the 1920s and 1930s were not the troglodytes Liddell Hart so successfully portrayed them as in later years. On the contrary, as I have shown, they were generally a competent lot, and there is reason to believe they could have developed a formidable army that could have been used to put significant pressure on Hitler, should he threaten war in the East, or to defend against a Wehrmacht attack in the West.

[8]

The Resurrection of
a Lost Reputation

Liddell Hart's concern with avoiding another World War I became
moot after the Fall of France. That calamitous defeat in the spring of
1940 and the question of who bore ultimate responsibility became the
new focus of his attention and remained so until he died in 1970. The
viselike grip World War I had on his thinking was finally broken by the
event he described as "a world-shaking disaster which changed the
course of history for the worse."[1] Unlike the Great War, however, in
which he had virtually nothing to do with the course of events, the Fall
of France badly damaged Liddell Hart's reputation. He faced a major
task: to rescue that reputation in the face of a mountain of damning
evidence. Over the next twenty-five years, he met that challenge.

The effort revolved around two closely related questions: Did he
foresee the Allied defeat in May 1940? and Who in Britain bore responsibility for that disaster? The question of responsibility boiled down, in
Liddell Hart's view, to a choice between him or the generals. He placed
all the blame on the generals and pictured himself as a prescient
thinker who foresaw the events of May 1940 but was ignored by British
and French military leaders, while the German generals listened to
him. Liddell Hart was of course already in the habit of heaping scorn
on the British military.

The campaign to purvey this account actually began before France
had even surrendered to Germany, although it only achieved success
well after World War II had ended.[2] The publication of his *Memoirs* in
1965 was the crucial event in the selling of his version of what trans-

---

[1]*Memoirs* 2:280. He rarely wrote again about World War I after the Fall of France; the
only major article I know of is "The Basic Truths of Passchendaele," *Journal of the Royal
United Services Institution* 104 (Nov. 1959): 433–39.
[2]See Brian Bond, *Liddell Hart: A Study of His Military Thought* (London: Cassell, 1977),
132. See also LH, "The German Invasion of the West: The Basic Factors," *Union: The*

pired in the 1930s. His success at convincing readers that his account was true prompts two important questions. How did he actually sell his recountal of the past and what devices did he use to convince a wide audience? Why were his efforts so successful in the face of so much evidence to the contrary?

THE SELLING OF THE MYTH

Liddell Hart used four principal techniques to rescue his tarnished reputation. First, he maintained he was unable for sound security reasons to reveal in his public writings the full truth about Allied weaknesses and German strengths in the late 1930s. He claims in his *Memoirs*, for example, that he wrote in a "guarded way . . . because I knew that what I wrote would receive close attention in Germany, so that exposure of any weaknesses that were not obvious might tend to precipitate the dangers that I foresaw."[3] There is no evidence to support this claim. Had he known of these weaknesses, he could have communicated his insights privately to government officials, but there is no evidence he did. Furthermore, this claim contradicts his often-repeated assertion that he clearly pointed out Allied deficiencies before the debacle but no responsible policy makers listened.

The second and more important technique was selfish manipulation of the historical record. He used evidence selectively, quoting from articles and books that supported his argument while ignoring those that made him look foolish. He emphasized his writings from the 1920s while ignoring many articles from the late 1930s. For example, he hardly discusses his views about the supremacy of the defense in *Memoirs*. He mentions only once his famous "Defence or Attack?" series in the *Times* in October 1937, and even then he does not tell the reader what he said in those articles about the balance between defense and offense.[4] A reader of *Memoirs* unfamiliar .with the debates of the late

---

Monthly Forum of the New Commonwealth Institute (July 1940): 193–205; LH, *Dynamic Defence* (London: Faber, 1940)—two early attempts to defend himself.

[3]*Memoirs* 2:202; also 204, 242–43; LH to Edward Mead Earle, 24 Apr. 1946, 1/255/6; ibid., 19 Sept. 1947, 1/255/11; LH, *This Expanding War* (London: Faber, 1942), 10.

[4]He briefly discusses in his *Memoirs* most of the *Times* articles from the 1930s in which he laid out his views on the supremacy of the defense, but there is barely any indication of his views on the offense–defense equation. The appropriate references are "The Army To-day" series of November 1935, discussed *Memoirs* 1:294–98; "The Army under Change" series of October–November 1936, discussed *Memoirs* 1:379–81; "The Attack in Warfare" article of 10 Sept. 1937, discussed *Memoirs* 2:21, 24–28; the famous "Defence or Attack?" series of October 1937, discussed *Memoirs* 2:58.

1930s about how Britain should deal with the Third Reich would have no inkling Liddell Hart maintained an extreme position about the superiority of the defense. Instead, he spends considerable space discussing the blitzkrieg, leaving the reader to conclude he was forcefully arguing for that strategy throughout the interwar period.

Liddell Hart's efforts to downplay his prewar writings about the superiority of the defense and to emphasize his early writings on the blitzkrieg began well before he published his *Memoirs*. Consider, for example, two books he wrote during World War II. In *The Current of War* (1941) he reprinted two of his principal articles on armored warfare from the 1920s in the opening chapters. He had rarely mentioned these articles during the 1930s. His subsequently published *Thoughts on War* (1944), a compilation of selected quotations from his pre–World War II writings, scarcely mentions the manifest advantages of defense over offense and emphasizes his early writings about the blitzkrieg and the indirect approach, which are treated as synonymous military theories.[5]

He used the same technique with his writings about the French army. He ignored his articles from the 1930s, where he presented a positive view of French military capabilities, and stressed instead his writings from the 1920s, where he described the contrary view. He reprinted in *The Current of War*, for example, the series of critical articles he wrote for the *Daily Telegraph* in 1926, which were also published in *The Remaking of Modern Armies* (1927). He often referred to these articles in the years after World War II, a ploy that created the illusion of prescience.[6]

Liddell Hart not only used evidence selectively but also made claims and inferences that are at best highly questionable and at worst simply not true. Moreover, he was not above manufacturing evidence to support his cause, behavior I have given evidence of in previous chapters—for example, his claim after World War II that when he met Field Marshal Blomberg in 1932, the German leader was particularly impressed by his ideas on deep strategic penetration and blitzkrieg. Blomberg, according to Liddell Hart, said he was applying those ideas to the training of the German army. In fact, Liddell Hart's memorandum for the record on that meeting shows Blomberg was actually struck by Liddell Hart's ideas on the power of defense and was in the process of "correcting the orthodox obsession with the offensive in his

[5]See two other examples of this technique in *Dynamic Defence*, 57–64; "German Invasion of the West," 203–5.

[6]*The Current of War* (London: Hutchinson, 1941), 83–91. For references to these articles, see, for example, LH to editor, *New York Herald Tribune*, 5 Nov. 1948, 9/24/16; LH, "Appeasement in the Thirties," transcript of lecture for BBC Home Service Programme, written Apr. 1963, delivered Sept. 1963, 12/1963/1; *Memoirs* 2:127.

training."[7] Recall, for example, the matter of Liddell Hart asking Guderian to add the critical second paragraph to *Panzer Leader* and his describing himself after the war as an archfoe of appeasement who favored standing up to Hitler over Czechoslovakia.

There are many other examples of Liddell Hart twisting the historical record that I have not discussed. Not surprisingly, he was sometimes identified after World War II as an advocate of the defense à outrance. For example, the editors of *Infantry Journal*, an American magazine, wrote in 1949, "In the years preceding World War II, Captain Hart gained some distinction as an advocate of the idea that in modern war the defense was much stronger than the offense." Liddell Hart responded with a letter containing this remarkable statement: "European soldiers would be amused to hear that I am mainly known in the USA as an advocate of defense. To them I was known primarily, from 1920 on, as the exponent of armored attack and of the future *Blitzkrieg* methods."[8] The truth is reflected in a comment made to Liddell Hart shortly after the Fall of France by his good friend Pile:

> You recognize that Tiny [the nickname for Field Marshal Ironside, who was the CIGS for the first nine months of World War II] and I suppose all his following criticise you for your statements of the power of defence . . . they do not argue even moderately fairly, they just say that you deny that attack is ever possible and therefore you have ruined the offensive spirit of the British and indeed the French armies. At the moment, all our failures are attributed to this lack of offensive spirit.[9]

Another American wrote in the *New York Herald Tribune* that the doctrine he "had helped implant in Allied minds after the first world war drew its lessons from static trench warfare." In a letter to the editor, Liddell Hart denied this, emphasizing that he "often repeated the prophecy that 'in the future we shall not again witness the stagnation of trench warfare owing to the new mobility brought in by the tank, the caterpillar tractor, the aeroplane.'" This was probably true in the 1920s, but it was definitely not true in the 1930s; in February 1939 he wrote, "While nothing can be certain, it would appear . . . that trench warfare is likely to recur in any larger European war of the near future."[10] One of his principal goals in the late 1930s was, after all, to

---

[7]"Talk with Gen.-Lt. von Blomberg—8/3/32," memorandum for the record, 11/1932/9.

[8]Editors' biographical sketch, *Infantry Journal* 64 (Mar. 1949): 31; LH, letter, ibid. (June 1949): 52–53.

[9]Gen. Frederick Pile to LH, 22 June 1940, 1/575.

[10]William Harlan Hale, "Meeting of Military Minds," rev. of *The German Generals Talk*, by LH, *New York Herald Tribune*, Weekly Book Review, 26 Sept. 1948, 2. LH to editor, ibid., 5 Nov. 1948, 9/24/16; LH, letter, *World Review* 6 (Mar. 1939): 65.

convince his readers that World War II would repeat World War I, which was of course characterized by "static trench warfare."

He also harped on the theme that the British and French armies were defeated in 1940 because they had failed to heed his warnings. "The defence of the West," he argued in *Memoirs*, "collapsed through blind neglect of the weaknesses that had been pointed out so clearly."[11] He seems to imply that he pointed out these deficiencies, which contradicts his claim that he could not do so without alerting the Germans. "The plain fact is that the reception that my reasoning found in British and French military councils was the reverse of enthusiastic."[12] The theme "I told you so," which is so prominent in *Memoirs*, actually appeared in *Dynamic Defence*, the first book he published after the Fall of France. Its *Times Literary Supplement* reviewer remarked, "Captain Liddell Hart is dynamic all right, though the number of times that he says 'I told you so' is astonishing in so slim a volume."[13]

To cite a specific example, Liddell Hart claimed after the war that he had foreseen the German breakthrough in the Ardennes: "The German *Panzers* broke through in the very sector I had pointed out as likely."[14] He even went so far as to claim the Germans, Manstein in particular, got the idea of locating their main attack in that area from his writings. Neither claim can stand up to serious scrutiny.[15] Although he occasionally mentioned the Ardennes in his writings, he never said the Germans were likely to place a main axis of advance in that area, nor do his writings expound on the virtues of doing so.[16] He did briefly note, when discussing the 1918 American offensive on the Western Front, that "the impassability of the Ardennes has been much exaggerated."[17] He did not, however, develop this point in subsequent writings nor argue it had implications for a future war. He actually did

[11]*Memoirs* 2:270; also 53–54, 280–81; LH, "Churchill in War," *Encounter* 26 (Apr. 1966): 16.

[12]LH to editor, *New York Herald Tribune*, 5 Nov. 1948, 9/24/16. See also LH to Earle, 24 Apr. 1946, 1/255.

[13]"New Techniques of War: Captain Liddell Hart's Analysis," rev. of *Dynamic Defence*, by LH, *Times Literary Supplement*, 16 Nov. 1940, 574.

[14]LH to editor, *Time*, 5 Nov. 1948, 9/24/16. See also *Memoirs* 1:237, 379; 2:202–4, 265–66.

[15]See B. Bond, *Liddell Hart*, 232–33.

[16]For LH on the Ardennes, see *The Decisive Wars of History: A Study in Strategy* (Boston: Little, Brown, 1929), 89, 166, 225; *The Defence of Britain* (London: Faber, 1939), 216–19; *Foch: Man of Orleans* (London: Eyre & Spottiswoode, 1931), 383; *A History of the World War, 1914–1918* (London: Faber, 1934), 577; *The Real War, 1914–1918* (London: Faber, 1930), 461; *Reputations* (London: Murray, 1928), 23, 28; *Through the Fog of War* (New York: Random House, 1938), 8, 126, 316, 320.

[17]*Real War*, 461. See also *History of the World War*, 577; *Decisive Wars of History*, 225. LH claimed after the war that he had expounded on the virtues of the Ardennes as an area

discuss the military situation in the Ardennes in his 1939 *Defence of Britain* (216–19); he had recently toured that area. He wrote nothing about the danger of the Germans' placing a main axis of advance in that region and described the Allies' prospects in that obstacle-ridden area in very favorable terms. Finally, as I go on to discuss later, his claim that the Germans got their idea of striking through the Ardennes from him is simply not true.

Another example of evidence manipulation concerns Charles de Gaulle and Paul Reynaud, who maintained in the 1930s that France should develop an armored force with significant offensive capability.[18] They believed France needed the capability to attack Germany, should Germany strike first into Eastern Europe, for they correctly understood the importance of confronting Germany with a two-front war problem. Liddell Hart implies in *Memoirs* that he was in agreement with de Gaulle and Reynaud—for example, that when he came across de Gaulle's *Army of the Future* in 1935 he was "delighted to find" de Gaulle calling for "a mechanised striking force of professional soldiers."[19] Liddell Hart might have liked de Gaulle's emphasis on building a small armored force dominated by professional soldiers, although there is no evidence to that effect. It is almost inconceivable, however, that he would have welcomed a French armored force with a potent offensive capability.[20] He dreaded a French strike into Germany and made a concerted effort to discourage the French army from adopting an offensive strategy. For example, when he was contemplating a limited Continental commitment in 1938, he insisted it be tied to a French promise not to launch an offensive.[21]

---

for an armored offensive in *Real War* and *Decisive Wars of History*; see LH, "The Ardennes as a Potential Route for Mechanised Forces: Historical Note," memorandum for the record, 14 Dec. 1948, 11/1948/28; also LH to Earle, 24 Apr. 1946, 1/255. This is not the case.

[18]See P. C. F. Bankwitz, *Maxine Weygand and Civil-Military Relations in Modern France* (Cambridge, Mass.: Harvard University Press, 1967), chap. 4; Gen. Charles de Gaulle, *The Army of the Future* (London: Hutchinson, n.d.); Robert A. Doughty, "De Gaulle's Concept of a Mobile, Professional Army: Genesis of French Defeat," *Parameters*, 4, no. 2 (1974): 23–34.

[19]*Memoirs* 1:274; see also 2:126–27; LH, "Appeasement in the Thirties."

[20]LH actually outlines the views of Reynaud and de Gaulle in *Defence of Britain*, 203–6 but without indicating what he thinks. Although his principal writings from the 1920s on the French army reveal an interest in seeing that army evolve into a highly professional mechanized force, there is no mention of the need for an offensive capability; see, for example, *The Remaking of Modern Armies* (London: Murray, 1927), chaps. 15–18; *Current of War*, chap. 5. His writings from the 1930s, however, contain little on the need to create such a mechanized force; instead they express satisfaction with the state of the French army in those years.

[21]LH, "The Defence of the Empire," *Fortnightly* 143 (Jan. 1938): 29.

Other important examples of Liddell Hart's manipulation of the historical record also bear mentioning. These cases, however, are best discussed in the context of his other two techniques for rescuing his reputation. The third was calculated characterization of his relationship to British, German, and Israeli military leaders. To pin the blame for the Fall of France squarely on the British (and French) generals, he pictured them as incompetent and unwilling to listen to his ideas. The resulting deep gulf between him and the Allied generals naturally served to absolve him of responsibility for that momentous defeat.

He had a different objective with the Wehrmacht: to portray the German generals in highly favorable terms and then link himself with the most highly regarded among them. This identification with the Wehrmacht worked to elevate his standing in the eyes of students of military affairs. More specifically, it helped him make the case he had foreseen the events of May 1940 and that in fact the German generals had won that victory by employing a strategy they learned from him. His ultimate goal was straightforward: to convince others that the roots of the great German victory could be traced back to him; that not only was he not responsible for the Allied defeat, but he bore much of the credit for the German victory.

Liddell Hart had made the point a number of times during the war that the German generals had paid attention to his prewar writings on blitzkrieg, "and, having grasped its significance, they made haste to provide the necessary means for translating it into reality. The month of May 1940 witnessed its fulfillment."[22] After the war, he had the opportunity to try to find some hard evidence of his influence. He struck up a close relationship with a number of German generals soon after the war ended. Most of them were in captivity at the time, and some were in desperate straits. Liddell Hart went out of his way to help them. Brian Bond summarizes his efforts on their behalf:

> Liddell Hart made himself a leading champion of the captured German generals in the five years or so after the ending of the Second World War in the sense that he campaigned in the Press for better prison conditions and against their being tried as war criminals. In private he behaved with great generosity towards them, sending them cigarettes, tobacco, food parcels and copies of his books and articles. In particular hard cases he put

---

[22]LH, "Tortoise to Tank," *World Review* 9 (Sept. 1940): 21. See also LH to Esmé Wingfield-Stratford, 5 Oct. 1942, 1/757; LH, *This Expanding War*, 258.

himself to even further trouble, supplying the ailing Rundstedt with a mattress and securing the transfer of Manstein's wife and son to the home of the Field Marshal's sister in the French-occupied zone.[23]

Most important, however, were his efforts to help them resurrect their soiled reputations. First, he went out of his way to assist them in getting their memoirs and other writings published in English. He was especially helpful to Guderian.[24] Liddell Hart effectively acted as Guderian's literary agent and then played such an important role in producing the English version of Guderian's memoirs that the publishers decided to identify him as the book's editor. Liddell Hart quashed this idea, probably so as not to raise doubts about the validity of Guderian's praise of him.[25]

Second, he presented a most favorable view of the generals in his own writings and often defended them in public, bolstering their reputation for moral rectitude and praising their performance on the battlefield. The Wehrmacht's reputation had been badly stained by its active participation between 1941 and 1945 in the enormous horrors perpetrated by the Third Reich in Eastern Europe and the Soviet Union,[26] and this Liddell Hart worked to correct. His principal vehicle was *The German Generals Talk* (1948), where he described the generals as basically rational and decent men pitted against a madman bent on leading Germany to ruin. "They were essentially technicians," he wrote, "intent on their professional job, and with little idea of things outside it. It is easy to see how Hitler hoodwinked and handled them, and found them good instruments up to a point." When accused by one reviewer of having an "overdeveloped sense of fair play [that] blinds him to the moral rottenness of the men he so assiduously whitewashes," he responded that it was "remarkable . . . the extent to which they managed to maintain a code of decency that was in con-

---

[23]*Liddell Hart*, 227–28. Gen. Frido von Senger describes the essence of the relationship LH struck up with numerous German generals: "In the [prisoner of war] camp we were also visited 'collectively' by the distinguished military writer, Captain B. H. Liddell Hart, who was so well-disposed towards the Germans, and with whom I have since developed a friendship that is not merely professional. Several times I have enjoyed the hospitality of his home" (*Neither Fear nor Hope: The Wartime Career of General Frido von Senger und Etterlin, Defender of Cassino*, trans. George Malcolm [New York: Dutton, 1964], 353).

[24]See, for example, the voluminous correspondence between the two on the publication of *Panzer Leader* (9/24/37; 9/24/38; 9/24/42). LH also tried to help generals Geyr von Schweppenberg and Adolf Heusinger get their memoirs published in English; see LH to Robert Lusty, 27 Apr. 1951, 9/24/42.

[25]A copy of the proposed jacket cover with LH featured as the book's editor is in 9/24/42; see also LH to V. W. Morrison, 18, 20, 28 Dec. 1951, and Morrison to LH, 19 Dec. 1951, all in 9/24/42.

[26]See chap. 1, n. 34.

stant conflict with Nazi ideas."[27] He also strove, through public as well as private channels, to preclude prosecution of the generals for war crimes. When that failed, he worked hard to help them win acquittal.[28]

Liddell Hart tried to shore up their reputation as battlefield commanders and military strategists, as Robert Vansittart's comments about *The German Generals Talk* point out: "It is suggested that the omniscient German generals were continually prevented from having their own way, and, but for the blundering interventions of an ex-corporal, the results of the war might have been different." We also see this ploy in *The Rommel Papers*, where Liddell Hart describes the generalship of Rommel, who was already very highly regarded in the West, in the most laudatory terms. It is hard to disagree with the reviewer in the *Spectator* who noted that the book "needed an editor less wedded to the idea of his hero's invincibility in all but the most impossible conditions of war."[29]

Liddell Hart must have realized he could go a long way toward salvaging his own tarnished reputation by linking himself closely with the German generals. His first such effort was *The German Generals Talk*, a book describing the retrospective views of the Wehrmacht commanders and based largely on his postwar interviews with those generals. The book, which was widely reviewed at the time and remains a classic, served to show a close connection between Liddell Hart and the generals; his name is certainly sprinkled liberally throughout the book's many reviews.[30] Liddell Hart subtley alludes to this link in the text, as when discussing the German plan employed against the Allies in the spring of 1940:

> The inner story of how the plan was changed is an extraordinary one. It was only by degrees that I got on the track of it. From the outset the German generals were very forthcoming in telling me about the military operations—such professional objectivity is a characteristic of theirs. Most

[27]LH, *The German Generals Talk* (New York: Morrow, 1948), x; see also LH, *The Other Side of the Hill*, rev. and enlarged ed. (London: Cassell, 1951), 12–13. "The German Generals Oblige," rev. of *The German Generals Talk*, by LH, *Manchester Guardian*, 22 Apr. 1948, 4. LH, letter, ibid., 29 Apr. 1948, 4.
[28]On the extent of his efforts, see 9/24/155–202; also B. Bond, *Liddell Hart*, 180–88.
[29]Robert Vansittart, "My Reply to the German Generals," *Sunday Dispatch*, 13 Oct. 1946, 6, a response to a serialized version of *German Generals Talk* in the *Sunday Dispatch* in 1946. Nigel Nicolson, "Partisan for Rommel," rev. of *The Rommel Papers*, ed. LH, *Spectator*, 24 Apr. 1953, 506. Chester Wilmot, commenting on *The Rommel Papers*, told LH: You should have "restrained your enthusiasm a little more in the introduction and in the footnotes" (Wilmot to LH, 13 May 1953, 1/753).
[30]For the reviews, see 9/24/18.

of them, I found, were old students of my military writings, so that they were all the more ready to talk, and exchange views. (112–13)[31]

When the book was serialized in Britain in the *Sunday Dispatch,* the newspaper's editors introduced the book with the following words: "The Germans knew all about Liddell Hart. They had been close students of his books on strategy and tactics before the war. Therefore they were willing to talk freely, frankly, and fearlessly to one whose great reputation they acknowledged."[32]

Liddell Hart naturally used other means to link himself with the German generals. The most well-known German generals of World War II in the English-speaking world are probably Guderian, Manstein, and Rommel, all renowned for their masterful handling of large armored forces. Liddell Hart edited the personal papers of Rommel and wrote an introduction for the book. He also wrote introductory essays for Guderian's and Manstein's memoirs as well as for a handful of other books concerned with the German army. Jay Luvaas nicely characterizes this situation: "Indeed, it almost has become a rule of the publisher's trade for any English translation of the memoirs of a German general to include an introduction by this well-known advocate of mobile warfare."[33] Thus it became easy for a student of World War II— especially one concerned with the Wehrmacht—to assume Liddell Hart had a close relationship with the German generals.

Still, the real key for him was concrete evidence that he had had significant influence on German thinking about the blitzkrieg in the years *before* the war, hard facts that would support a claim the generals had truly been his disciples. He needed evidence that showed his prewar writings had influenced the German plan to defeat the Allies in the West, but in *The German Generals Talk* Liddell Hart does not point to a single instance of a German general claiming such an influence. Liddell Hart had to manufacture the evidence. This is a serious charge,

---

[31]See also 23, 100, 185, 280; *Other Side of the Hill,* 9–13.

[32]"Hitler's Generals Tell All," *Sunday Dispatch,* 8 Sept. 1946, 1. Lengthy excerpts from the book appeared in the *Sunday Dispatch* on 8, 15, 22, 29 Sept. and 6 Oct. 1946.

[33]Jay Luvaas, *The Military Legacy of the Civil War: The European Inheritance* (Chicago: University of Chicago Press, 1959), 225. See LH, Introduction, *The Rommel Papers,* ed. LH, trans. Paul Findlay (New York: Harcourt, Brace, 1953), xiii–xxi; LH, Foreword, *Panzer Leader,* trans. Constantine Fitzgibbon (London: Joseph, 1952), 11–15; LH, Foreword, *Lost Victories,* by F. M. Erich von Manstein, ed. and trans. Anthony G. Powell (Chicago: Regnery, 1958), 13–16; also LH, Foreword, *The Schlieffen Plan,* by Gerhard Ritter, trans. Andrew Wilson and Eva Wilson (London: Wolff, 1958), 3–10; LH, Foreword, *The German Army and the Nazi Party, 1933–1939,* by Robert J. O'Neill (New York: Heineman, 1966); LH, Foreword, *Neither Fear nor Hope,* 5–7.

I know, but the evidence warrants it. His effort was focused largely on Guderian, Manstein, and Rommel.

Liddell Hart's effort to picture Manstein as his disciple revolved around the latter's crucial role in developing the plan that led to Germany's stunning victory in the spring of 1940. Liddell Hart's claim that Manstein got his brilliant idea of placing the Wehrmacht's main axis of attack in the Ardennes area from his writings appears in a memorandum for the record from Liddell Hart's files:

> The notion that my teachings were "proved wrong" in 1940 has become comic in view of the fact that Guderian, who made the decisive break-through, called himself my "disciple" and "pupil"—while Manstein, who conceived the plan of the tank stroke through the Ardennes, has stated that the idea came to him from an article of mine in which I had pointed out the possibilities of an armored move in the Ardennes.[34]

Liddell Hart repeats this claim in *Memoirs* (2:202–4). There is no supporting evidence, however, and Manstein refused to endorse the claim.

The first reason for skepticism is that Liddell Hart wrote nothing before the war about the virtues of striking through the Ardennes, so there was nothing for Manstein to have read. A second reason is the significant body of personal correspondence between the two on the planning of the 1940 offensive; not once does Manstein mention that Liddell Hart's writings had any influence on his thinking.[35] In fact the correspondence shows no influence before 1945, nor do Manstein's memoirs, *Lost Victories*, show any.

The final and best reason for not believing Liddell Hart is the field marshal's reaction to Liddell Hart's attempt to insert a sentence about this matter in a biography of him. Liddell Hart was deeply involved in the effort to stop Allied authorities from prosecuting Manstein as a war criminal, and when this failed, he worked tirelessly to help win acquittal.[36] In the process, he became friendly with Reginald T. Paget, Manstein's British lawyer. Paget wrote a book about his client, which appeared in late 1951. On 12 April 1951, Paget wrote Liddell Hart, "I have included [in the book] the following sentence: 'Captain Liddell Hart, he [Manstein] says, had suggested in an article written before the war

---

[34]"Attack and Defence," memorandum for the record, n.d., filed under memoranda written in 1948, 11/1948/32.

[35]Correspondence in 9/24/71. See esp. LH to Manstein, 29 Dec. 1947, 10 Jan. 1948, 2 Apr. 1949; Manstein to LH, 7, 25 Jan., 24 Feb. 1948, 14 Feb. 1950.

[36]See, for example, LH, "Manstein Trial—Correspondence, Notes and Cuttings," 9/24/176–181; LH's correspondence with Reginald T. Paget (1/563) and Manstein (9/24/71). See also B. Bond, *Liddell Hart*, 184–86.

that an armoured thrust through the Ardennes was technically possible.' I think this is alright."[37] It was not all right. Liddell Hart wrote
back to Paget on 1 May 1951:

> The sentence which you quoted at the start of your letter of the 12th is
> quite neat and effective—(the typist, however, has put "he says" instead
> of "he said".) An alternative way of putting it might be: "He had been
> impressed, he said, by an article of Captain Liddell Hart's arguing that an
> armoured thrust through the Ardennes was technically possible." That is
> only for your consideration, and either would do—many thanks.[38]

Liddell Hart's alternative, unlike Paget's original, clearly implies that
Manstein had gotten his brilliant idea from Liddell Hart. There is,
unfortunately, no further correspondence between Liddell Hart and
Paget on this matter in Liddell Hart's files, and Liddell Hart never
raised the issue directly with Manstein. There is, however, in the files a
memorandum for the record that shows Paget attempted to change the
key sentence to reflect Liddell Hart's suggestion, but Manstein refused
to go along:

> Paget subsequently told me that Manstein raised objection to such a defi-
> nite statement of what he had told Paget privately—so in the published
> version of the book the sentence was revised to read: "Captain Liddell
> Hart, he said, had suggested in an article before the war that an armoured
> thrust through the Ardennes was technically possible."[39]

Of course, there is no evidence Liddell Hart suggested any such thing,
but more important is that Manstein effectively rejected Liddell Hart's
effort to portray him as a disciple.[40]

Liddell Hart found Guderian more cooperative on the matter of in-
serting the paragraph acknowledging Liddell Hart in the English version of his memoirs. I suggest he was repaying Liddell Hart for his
assistance and generosity. Liddell Hart worked hard on *Panzer Leader*.
When Guderian offered to give him a share of the profits, Liddell Hart

[37]Paget to LH, 12 Apr. 1951, 1/563. I could find no evidence as to why Paget inserted
this sentence, but I deduce that he did so at LH's prompting because Paget would not
have reached this conclusion on his own. He was not a military expert, and there were,
as I have said, no writings for him to have been aware of. Reginald T. Paget, *Manstein:
His Campaigns and His Trial* (London: Collins, 1951).
[38]LH to Paget, 1 May 1951, 1/563.
[39]"Later Note," n.d., copy in 9/24/71 and 9/24/124. Actual quotation in Paget's *Manstein*, 22. See also B. Bond, *Liddell Hart*, 237, n. 32.
[40]The final wording in Paget's *Manstein* thus undercuts LH's citation of the book in
Memoirs 2:204 as evidence Manstein had gotten the idea of locating the main axis in the
Ardennes from his prewar writings.

wrote a very nice letter back saying he could not take any money unless he was assured that Guderian was financially well off.[41] It might be an exaggeration to argue that Liddell Hart was obsequious in his correspondence with Guderian, but the fact is he came very close to being so. Guderian's letters have that same flavor. When Liddell Hart issued a revised and enlarged version of *The German Generals Talk* (*The Other Side of the Hill,* 1951), he devoted all of chapter 5 to Guderian, whereas the original version, written before they met, contained no such chapter. Is it too much to conclude these two understood that each had much to gain by praising the other?

There is a further aspect of this case that merits discussion. Liddell Hart's 6 April 1951 letter to Guderian must have been a cause of concern to Liddell Hart. After all, the letter shows he had asked Guderian to add the famous second paragraph to *Panzer Leader.* Moreover, it shows Liddell Hart had written the most important part of that crucial paragraph—not the kind of information he would want others to know about. It appears he permanently removed his copy of that letter as well as Guderian's 23 April 1951 response from his files and pretended they never existed. Let me lay out the basis for this charge.

An American graduate student wrote the translator of *Panzer Leader* in March 1968, asking why the famous second paragraph was not in the German version of the memoirs.[42] He was writing a dissertation on the development of the German Panzerwaffe, and he had an obvious interest in knowing about the origins of that paragraph. The translator forwarded the letter to Liddell Hart, who wrote back to the student in April 1968, telling him he could only find the letters he had sent to the publisher and the translator—transmitting the second paragraph. He said nothing about his 6 April 1951 letter to Guderian and the latter's 23 April response. In fact he said, "There is nothing about the matter in my file of correspondence with Guderian himself except . . . that I thanked him in a May 18, 1951 letter for what he said in that additional paragraph."[43]

It is possible the letters were accidentally lost, but unlikely given their importance. Also, there appear to be few examples of missing correspondence from Liddell Hart's files. He usually had his secretary make multiple copies of important letters he wrote or received and then distribute the copies among different files in his papers. Consider this comment by the archivist who put Liddell Hart's papers in order after his death: "Not only did Liddell Hart throw virtually nothing

[41]LH to Guderian, 26 Feb. 1951, 9/24/42.
[42]Richard T. Burke to Constantine Fitzgibbon, 6 Mar. 1968, 9/24/38.
[43]LH to Burke, 2 Apr. 1968, 9/24/38.

away, but particularly from 1945 onwards he had anything he considered to be important duplicated. Some of the duplicates were kept together in readiness for sending to interested parties, but most were distributed throughout the archive in an effort to maintain a wide variety of overlapping subject, chronological, personal, business and correspondence files by the selective use of available carbon copies."[44] From what we know about the state of his personal papers, there should have been copies of these letters somewhere among them. The matter of losing the letters aside, it is virtually inconceivable that he did not recall those letters and the gist of what they contained; the issue was just too important to have forgotten. Moreover, whenever Liddell Hart received an accolade from someone, he invariably spread the word to others with whom he corresponded. The one exception to this rule is the letters on the second paragraph of *Panzer Leader*.

This episode establishes that he did not want to acknowledge the existence of those two letters and that the letters were probably missing from his files by April 1968. It is also apparent from his correspondence files that he made no effort in the remaining two years of his life to get copies of those letters from Guderian's family, which he could have done if so inclined. It is difficult to believe he did not remove these letters from his personal papers. Copies of the letters were put back in Liddell Hart's personal files in the late 1970s. Kenneth Macksey, a military historian who had been a friend of Liddell Hart's, discovered the letters in the mid-1970s when going through Guderian's personal papers. Macksey had previously examined Liddell Hart's own files and knew the correspondence was missing (personal communication, 20 July 1985 and 15 September 1987). He gave copies of both letters to Brian Bond, who inserted them in the Liddell Hart papers. Bond, of course, had no idea the two letters existed until they were shown to him by Macksey (personal communication, 9 July 1985 and 24 September 1987).

Finally, there is the Rommel case, which actually resembles the Guderian story. Because Rommel was an opponent of the Panzer divisions during the interwar years and not involved in the planning of the German offensive that led to the Fall of France, Liddell Hart could only hope to show he had significantly influenced Rommel *during* the war. A successful effort of this sort would not of course directly support Liddell Hart's contention that he had helped produce the German victory in the West. Nevertheless, there were obvious advantages to

---

[44]Stephen Brooks, "Liddell Hart and His Papers," in Brian Bond and Ian Roy, eds., *War and Society: A Yearbook of Military History* (London: Croom Helm, 1977), 2:129.

portraying Rommel, who was immensely popular in the English-speaking world, as a disciple.

There were, however, two problems. Rommel had died in 1944, and his extensive wartime writings did not support the claim he had been Liddell Hart's disciple. Rommel had mentioned Liddell Hart only once in those writings and then merely to comment on an article of Liddell Hart's he had read in mid-1942: "After the battle I came upon an article by the British military critic, Liddell Hart, which ascribed the shortcomings of the British command during the African campaign to the British generals' close association with infantry warfare. I had the same impression."[45] Despite this unpromising situation, Liddell Hart managed to link himself with Rommel—so closely, in fact, that he would claim and others would repeat that Rommel, like Guderian, was his disciple. The making of this myth warrants careful examination not only because the effort involved several individuals and key moves but also because the Rommel story so nicely complements many of the points in the Guderian and Manstein cases.

Brig. Gen. Desmond Young, a British army officer who was finishing a biography of Rommel and who had been in contact with the Rommel family, asked Liddell Hart in November 1949 if he would be interested in editing the English edition of Rommel's personal papers.[46] The Rommel family apparently thought Liddell Hart would be a good choice. Liddell Hart responded to Young's query with two questions: Was the Rommel family certain they wanted him as editor? and What evidence was there of Liddell Hart's influence on Rommel?[47] Young's response implied an affirmative answer to the first question. Regarding the second question, Young wrote that Frau Lucie-Maria Rommel (the field marshal's wife) and Manfred Rommel (his son) had told him, "Rommel was always deeply interested in your writings."[48] Liddell Hart shortly thereafter opened a correspondence with the Rommel family by writing directly to Frau Rommel. After praising the late field marshal, he wrote:

> I was very interested to hear from Desmond Young that you had told him that your husband had studied my writings with such keenness before the war. . . . So I should much appreciate anything more you can tell me about his reading of my books, and any comments he made on them.[49]

[45]*Rommel Papers*, 203.
[46]LH to Young, 15 Nov. 1949, 1/776. It is clear from this letter that Young first raised the matter with LH in a telephone conversation, of which there is no record; the letter follows up that conversation.
[47]LH to Young, 29 Nov. 1949, 1/776.
[48]Young to LH, 3 Dec. 1949, 1/776.
[49]LH to Lucie-Maria Rommel, 16 Dec. 1949, 9/24/24.

Manfred Rommel, responding for his mother, wrote back:

> My father valued you very much and I know, that he read one or more books of your hand, when he became commander of the seventh armoured division in France. In North-Africa he studied the articles, you wrote during the war. I was too young and too much layman to keep in memory my father's accounts on your books, and my mother knew naturally since a long time your name and the fact, that you were teaching modern principles of warfare, but she is not able to say special things.[50]

Manfred Rommel also enclosed two short extracts from his father's wartime papers. Each made reference to the fact British policy makers had rejected the innovative ideas about mechanized warfare developed between the world wars by "British military critics." There was no mention of Liddell Hart's name in either extract. Manfred Rommel then told Liddell Hart what Gen. Fritz Bayerlein, an officer who had served under Rommel during the war and who was very involved in getting Rommel's papers published in Germany, had said about the extracts:

> General Bayerlein said to me, that my father means you and general Fuller in this sentences and that my father and he had the opinion that the British would have been able to prevent the greatest part of their defeats, if they would have paid more attention to . . . you and general Fuller before the war.

Liddell Hart immediately wrote back to Manfred Rommel, thanking him for the letter.[51] He did two things in his letter that merit attention. He asked Manfred Rommel if he would rewrite in German the above paragraph containing General Bayerlein's comments, so that he could get an "exact translation," which shows how serious Liddell Hart was about gathering accolades. He also told the field marshal's son that Guderian had recently referred to himself as Liddell Hart's "disciple in tank affairs." This was more than the usual case of spreading the word when he received an accolade from a famous person. Here he was actively seeking to develop evidence that Rommel had been his disciple, and the Guderian quotation can be seen as a hint as to what he hoped to hear about Rommel. He was not to be disappointed.

General Bayerlein, who had not corresponded directly with Liddell Hart up to this point, wrote to him for the first time on 15 February

---

[50]Manfred Rommel to LH, 28 Dec. 1949, 9/24/24. I have made no attempt to improve the spelling, grammar, or syntax of any of the lengthy quotations used in this discussion of the Rommel case.

[51]LH to Manfred Rommel, 9 Jan. 1950, 9/24/24.

1950. Bayerlein, who because he was very close to the Rommel family had probably been following the correspondence between Manfred Rommel and Liddell Hart, wrote:

> During the war in many conferences and personal speeches with . . . Rommel we discussed your military works that gained our admiration. We recognized you as a military author who made the greatest impression on the Fieldmarshall and who highly influenced his tactical and strategical conceptions. As the former Chief of Staff to Rommel I can state not only Gen Guderian but Rommel too could be called your "pupil" in many respects.[52]

Liddell Hart immediately wrote back to Bayerlein, thanking him for this information and asking the general if he would put those key sentences into German so he could have them retranslated into English. Liddell Hart, always so careful about accolades, was almost surely trying to find the quotation that showed him in the most favorable light. He sent the German version of Bayerlein's statement to two different translators![53] The main point, however, is that Liddell Hart now had a piece of evidence that would allow him to make the case that Rommel, like Guderian, had been his disciple. He now had to find a means of getting this information into the public domain.

Shortly before Liddell Hart received Bayerlein's initial letter, he had asked Brigadier General Young, who was then preparing a new edition of his *Rommel*, if he would incorporate into the book's existing appendix of selections from Rommel's writings the two extracts from Rommel's papers that Manfred Rommel had sent him. Because his name is not mentioned in either extract, Liddell Hart, writing to Young on 21 February 1950, provided a footnote to accompany the extracts: "Here are two short passages from Rommel's papers. I appreciated your readiness to insert them among the 'appendix' extracts in your U.S. and other fresh editions. I enclose both the original German and the translation I had of them. I have also roughed out a footnote which would make their significance clearer—if you care to use it, or adapt it as you think fit."[54] It is clear from Liddell Hart's correspondence that he received Bayerlein's important 15 February 1950 letter almost immediately after he mailed this 21 February letter to Young.[55] He quickly sent another letter to Young, also dated 21 February, repeating what Bay-

---

[52]Gen. Fritz Bayerlein to LH, 15 Feb. 1950, 9/24/50.

[53]LH to Bayerlein, 21 Feb. 1950, 9/24/50. Copies of both translations and the relevant correspondence in 9/24/50.

[54]LH to Young, 21 Feb. 1950, 1/776. LH, at Young's prompting, had just written a favorable review of Young's book; "Genius and Gentleman," rev. of *Rommel*, by Desmond Young, *Listener*, 2 Feb. 1950, 212.

[55]LH's next letter to Young supports this point; copy in 1/776.

erlein had said in his letter about Liddell Hart's purported influence on Rommel. Not surprisingly, Baylerlein's comments were incorporated into the footnote that appeared in the new edition of Young's book:

> General Bayerlein says that Rommel was here referring to General Fuller and Captain Liddell Hart. Speaking of the latter, Bayerlein also states that his theories of armoured warfare "made the greatest impression on Field-Marshal Rommel, and highly influenced his tactical and strategical conceptions . . . not only General Guderian but Rommel too could be called Liddell Hart's 'pupil' in many respects."[56]

The first sentence of this note basically repeated the words Manfred Rommel had written in his first letter to Liddell Hart, while the remaining part of the note was extracted from Bayerlein's initial letter to Liddell Hart. Young also inserted in the body of his book a new sentence that claimed Rommel and Guderian "had . . . studied the writings of General Fuller and Captain Liddell Hart with more attention than they received from most British senior officers."[57]

Liddell Hart's next step was to approach Bayerlein about placing basically the same footnote in the forthcoming German version of the Rommel papers, which would, of course, contain the same extracts Young had inserted in his book's appendix. Bayerlein was finishing his editing of the Rommel papers for publication in Germany when Liddell Hart wrote him. After pointing to the section in the papers where Rommel talked about "British military critics," Liddell Hart posed the following question to Bayerlein: "I should like to know whether you would be agreeable to putting an explanatory footnote on the lines of the enclosed to that particular page. As you will see, it embodies what you wrote previously. Such a footnote would help to explain the significance of the Field-Marshal's remark, and I should naturally appreciate it."[58] Unfortunately, there is no copy in Liddell Hart's papers of the footnote he wrote for Bayerlein, but it is clear from Liddell Hart's letter to Bayerlein and from subsequent correspondence that the footnote published in *The Rommel Papers* is the one Liddell Hart sent Bayerlein.[59] It reads:

> Note by General Bayerlein—Rommel was here referring to Captain Liddell Hart and General Fuller. In his opinion the British could have avoided

[56]Desmond Young, *Rommel: The Desert Fox* (New York: Harper, 1951), 248; originally pub. as *Rommel* (London: Collins, 1950). The first extract and footnote were inserted onto 274 of the 1950 ed. The second extract is on 254 of the 1951 ed. and was inserted onto 279 of the 1950 ed.

[58]LH to Bayerlein, 30 Apr. 1950, 9/24/50.

[59]See esp. LH to Ronald J. Politzer, 31 Jan. 1953, 9/24/23.

most of their defeats if only they had paid more heed to the modern
theories expounded by those two writers before the war. During the war,
in many conferences and personal talks with Field-Marshal Rommel, we
discussed Liddell Hart's military works, which won our admiration. Of all
military writers, it was Liddell Hart who made the deepest impression on
the Field-Marshal—and greatly influenced his tactical and strategical
thinking. He, like Guderian, could in many respects be termed Liddell
Hart's "pupil." (299)

The text of this footnote, of course, is essentially an embellished version of the footnote he wrote for Young's book. Again, Liddell Hart
combined words from Manfred Rommel's first letter with an extract
from Bayerlein's initial letter and made very plain what he wanted
Bayerlein to say.

What is particularly interesting about this episode is that although
Bayerlein accepted Liddell Hart's proposal, he did *not* include all of the
proposed footnote in the German version, *Krieg ohne Hass*.[60] He omitted the last three sentences, which essentially repeat the words *he* had
written in his 15 February letter about Liddell Hart's marked influence
on Rommel's thinking. Thus, the footnote in *Krieg ohne Hass* reads:
"Rommel was here referring to Captain Liddell Hart and General Fuller. In his opinion the British could have avoided most of their defeats if
only they had paid more heed to the modern theories expounded by
those two writers before the war."[61] Bayerlein had chosen not to include the sole piece of information (of which he himself was the
source) that could be used to support the claim that Rommel had been
Liddell Hart's pupil. There is no correspondence in Liddell Hart's files
that deals directly with why Bayerlein omitted the latter part of the
proposed footnote. We can guess that Bayerlein was unwilling to repeat for public consumption a claim he knew was not true. This dis-
crepancy between the English and German versions of Rommel's papers is strikingly similar to the Guderian case. The question at this
point, however, is: How did Liddell Hart manage to get the entire
footnote published in *The Rommel Papers*?

Krieg ohne Hass was published on 15 November 1950, more than two
years before publication of the English version. On 30 January 1953 the
English publisher wrote Liddell Hart that the following footnote would
be placed in *The Rommel Papers*:

PUBLISHER'S NOTE The following footnote by General Bayerlein appeared in the German edition *Krieg ohne Hass* and indicates why the Rom-

---

[60]On Bayerlein's consent, see Bayerlein to LH, 11 May 1950, 9/24/50.
[61]Erwin Rommel, *Krieg ohne Hass*, ed. Frau Lucie-Maria Rommel and Generalleutnant
Fritz Bayerlein (Heidenheim: Heidenheimer Verlagsanstalt, 1950), 241.

mel family were particularly anxious that Capt. Liddell Hart should write an Introduction to, and edit, the English edition:—

Rommel was here referring to Captain Liddell Hart and General Fuller. In his opinion the British could have avoided most of their defeats if only they had paid more heed to the modern theories expounded by those two writers before the war.[62]

The publisher had understandably decided to repeat what Bayerlein had said in *Krieg ohne Hass* and to precede it with a brief publisher's note. Liddell Hart, who was the editor of the English version, immediately objected.[63] He insisted, first of all, that the part of the "proposed" footnote that Bayerlein had omitted be included in *The Rommel Papers*. Furthermore, he realized that it would then no longer be possible to claim in the publisher's note that the subsequent footnote had "appeared in" *Krieg ohne Hass*, so he mandated that the words "was written for" be substituted for "appeared in." The publisher acceded to his demands. Thus, the final publisher's note starts with "The following footnote was written by General Bayerlein for the German edition *Krieg ohne Hass* . . . " (299). The remainder of the footnote contains the entire text of the proposed footnote that Liddell Hart forwarded to Bayerlein. In other words, it contains the claim that Rommel was Liddell Hart's pupil.

Several points are in order here. First, the publisher's note is inaccurate. Bayerlein did not write the footnote that appeared in *Krieg ohne Hass;* Liddell Hart wrote it and asked Bayerlein to insert it. Second, Bayerlein chose *not* to include the crucial second part of that footnote in the German version, yet Liddell Hart's version of the publisher's note implies he did include it. Finally, the decision to modify the footnote that appeared in *Krieg ohne Hass* for *The Rommel Papers* was made by Liddell Hart and officials at Collins, the English publisher, apparently without Bayerlein's knowledge, for the files show no indication it was brought to his attention.

But was there any basis in fact for the discipleship Liddell Hart was working so hard to prove? It is almost surely the case that Rommel knew, even before World War II, that Liddell Hart was a powerful and well-respected military analyst in Britain, for Liddell Hart's reputation was international well before that war. It is even possible Rommel mistakenly believed Liddell Hart was a staunch proponent of blitzkrieg throughout the interwar years. It may be true, as Bayerlein claimed, that he thought the British army would have performed much better in

[62]Politzer to LH, 30 Jan. 1953, 9/24/23.
[63]LH to Politzer, 31 Jan. 1953, 9/24/23. This file contains a good deal of correspondence on this matter.

World War II if its leaders had listened to what he thought were the teachings of Liddell Hart. None of this, though, pertains to whether Rommel was a devoted student of Liddell Hart's *during* World War II.

He almost certainly was not. Other than the one passage in Bayerlein's letter, there is no other confirming evidence. Rommel's extensive papers reveal no such evidence, and no officer who served with Rommel, save Bayerlein, ever mentioned that such an influence existed. In the end even Bayerlein would not include his private claim in the published version of Rommel's papers. There was Manfred Rommel's statement to Liddell Hart that when his father "became commander of the seventh armoured division in France," he read at least one of Liddell Hart's books. Thus the seventh armoured division's participation in the Germans' great victory in France in the spring of 1940 might invite speculation that Liddell Hart's writings had some positive effect on how Rommel conducted his division in that campaign. But Rommel assumed command of that division on 15 February 1940, a little less than three months before the Wehrmacht attacked in the West.[64] During the entire period of the Phoney War (September 1939–May 1940), not to mention the last five years of the 1930s, Liddell Hart was forcefully making the case that the defender had a great advantage on an armored battlefield and that a German offensive in the West was *very* unlikely to succeed. If Rommel read Liddell Hart's books of this period, their main argument was hardly applicable to his task. Furthermore, Liddell Hart wrote little about armored warfare during the war, so there was not much for Rommel to learn from the post–1940 writings.[65] Finally, after having carefully watched the German panzer divisions perform in Poland and after having participated in the battle of France, Rommel had the basis for his *own* firm understanding of armored warfare. In sum, I find no case that Liddell Hart's writings influenced the development of Rommel's thinking about armored warfare.[66]

Why, then, was the Rommel family, and especially Bayerlein, willing to provide Liddell Hart with questionable information about his purported influence on the late field marshal? I believe the answer to be quite straightforward. They recognized Liddell Hart could do much

[64]Young, *Rommel*, 66.
[65]See, for example, the articles he wrote between 1940 and 1945, in sec. 10 of his papers.
[66]Rommel was deeply involved in the study of infantry tactics during the years before World War II. His most famous work is his 1937 book, *Infanterie Greift an*, first published in the United States as *Infantry Attacks*, trans. Lt. Col. G. E. Kiddé (Fort Leavenworth, Kans.: Infantry Journal, June 1944). Liddell Hart, of course, produced a substantial body of literature on infantry tactics in the early 1920s. It is in this realm where one would expect to find influence, but there is no evidence Rommel was aware of, much less influenced by, Liddell Hart's writings about infantry tactics.

to advance their efforts to present a highly favorable picture of Rommel to the English-speaking world. At the same time, however, they understood they would have to say something about Liddell Hart's positive influence on the field marshal. Desmond Young subtly made this point to Manfred Rommel by telling him the prospective book containing his father's writings "will be very widely reviewed in the British and American Press, if only because there will be a general desire to see how far your father's views and Captain Liddell Hart's writings on the conduct of modern war support each other."[67] Liddell Hart made it perfectly clear that he was looking for evidence that Rommel had been influenced by his writings. In effect, a de facto bargain was struck: Liddell Hart would describe Rommel as a brilliant general with few faults; Bayerlein and the Rommels would tell Liddell Hart that the field marshal had been his dutiful student.

This pattern is clearly reflected in the initial correspondence between Liddell Hart and the Rommel family. When Young first contacted Liddell Hart about editing the Rommel papers, he almost certainly (there is no record of this phone call, but subsequent correspondence bears out the supposition) told him that Rommel had had much trouble in his career with "general staff officers" and therefore the family wanted to ensure that the editor of the English version not slight Rommel in favor of his adversaries' viewpoint. Possibly the Rommel family was familiar with *The German Generals Talk* and had interpreted Liddell Hart's favorable treatment of so many former staff officers as reason to question his suitability for editing the papers. Liddell Hart moved to assuage any such fears in his first letter to Frau Rommel.[68] He heaped praise on Rommel and then apologized for not saying enough kind words about her husband in *The German Generals Talk*, a mistake he attributed to what he had been told by officers from the general staff. Then he proceeded to raise the matter of his purported influence on the late field marshal. He told Rommel's widow how "very interested" he was to hear about this link and said that he would "much appreciate anything you can tell me about his reading of my books, and any comments he made on them."

Manfred Rommel's response on behalf of his mother is revealing. First, he tells Liddell Hart, "As Germans we are much engaged [indebted?] to you, because you have given your authority to the task of representing in an objective way the events [that] happened during the last war." He also made it clear he was concerned about his father's enemies from the general staff but said he recognized Liddell Hart

[67]Young to Manfred Rommel, 10 Mar. 1950, 9/24/23.
[68]LH to Frau Rommel, 16 Dec. 1949, 9/24/24.

would be an ally on that crucial issue. Then he turned to answer the question about his father's interest in Liddell Hart's writings, providing him with the previously described response.[69] Thus we see the linking of the two sides' causes.

The publication of the entire footnote in *The Rommel Papers* gave Liddell Hart a basis for his claim that Rommel, like Guderian, had been his disciple. The importance of this lengthy footnote to Liddell Hart's effort to rescue his reputation is highlighted by a letter he wrote to the book's publisher shortly after resolution of the dispute about what to include in the crucial footnote:

> Many thanks for your letter of yesterday, and your confirmation . . . that Bayerlein's footnote on Page 299 will be printed in full. . . .
>
> I appreciate the motive that inspired your cut—the desire to avoid giving critics an opening. But if the main part of Bayerlein's footnote had been omitted, that would have blunted the point of your proposed "Publisher's Note". Moreover, his statement is obviously of significance for history, besides being of value to me. (It has made an immediate and striking impression in France, as it had already done in America when printed in Desmond Young's book.)
>
> It would be both wrong and foolish to suppress evidence of such key importance historically merely in deference to the English convention of mock modesty—which actually is the worst kind of humbug; and utterly different from real humility.
>
> But the Publisher's Note you originally drafted was an excellent accompaniment to Bayerlein's, and as you are still planning to enlarge other footnotes or fit in fresh ones I don't see why you can't fit in those few lines, either before or after the 8–9 lines of Bayerlein's.
>
> In any case, it would be worth emphasizing Bayerlein's testimony, and the Rommel family's consequent reason for wanting me to edit the Papers, in advance publicity about the book and notes you send out with the various copies—as Amiot-Dumont has done in France. I had thought that you would probably do so on the wrapper and pamphlet for booksellers—particularly after what you said when you urged the importance of my providing a quote for Chester's [Wilmot] book [*Crusade in Europe*] last year. Bless you![70]

Reviewers of *The Rommel Papers* of course picked up on the Rommel–Liddell Hart connection. For example, Sir Brian Horrocks, the well-known World War II general, wrote that Liddell Hart's "editing is somewhat reminiscent of a benevolent housemaster recounting the exploits of a favourite pupil. It is all a little puzzling until, in a footnote

[69]Manfred Rommel to LH, 28 Dec. 1949, 9/24/24.
[70]LH to Politzer, 4 Feb. 1953, 9/24/23. See also ibid., 5 Feb. 1953.

on page 299, General Bayerlein lets us in on the secret." The *Times* reviewer went so far as to argue that Liddell Hart was not qualified to edit the papers *because* he had had so much direct influence on Rommel, and one cannot fairly judge his own pupil.[71]

I do not mean to overemphasize the importance of the paragraph in *Panzer Leader* and the footnote in *The Rommel Papers*, for Liddell Hart's effort to rescue his reputation was a comprehensive one. Those two short panegyrics played, nevertheless, a major role in his attempt to rewrite the historical record. Consider, for one example, this excerpt from the dissertation of the student who queried Liddell Hart about the origins of the famous second paragraph in *Panzer Leader*:

> But while Liddell Hart, like Fuller, went unappreciated by many of the British Army leaders in the years prior to World War II he was not ignored by German military men. Heinz Guderian acknowledged himself to be "one of [Liddell Hart's] disciples in tank affairs." General Fritz Bayerlein reported Liddell Hart's great impression on Field Marshal Erwin Rommel, while *Panzer* General Hasso von Manteuffel cited Liddell Hart in March, 1949, as "the creator of modern tank strategy."[72]

LIDDELL HART AND THE ISRAELI ARMY

The Wehrmacht is not the only military with which Liddell Hart is closely associated in the minds of students of war. It is also widely assumed he had significant influence on the development of military thinking in Israel and that many of the most impressive victories of the Israeli Defense Force (IDF) were the result of applying his theory of the indirect approach. Liddell Hart himself argued that the Israelis, not the Germans, were his "best pupils of all."[73] He writes, for example, in *Memoirs*, "From the time I met the budding leaders of Israel I found there a grasp of military problems and new military ideas comparable

[71]Lt. Gen. Sir Brian Horrocks, "The Rommel Myth," rev. of *The Rommel Papers*, ed. LH, *Sunday Times*, 19 Apr. 1953, 6; "German Generals," rev. of *The Rommel Papers*, ed. LH, *Times*, 25 Apr. 1953, 8. There was one critical reviewer, however, who asserted that LH and the German generals were polishing up each other's soiled reputation for mutual benefit. Milton Shulman, a journalist and popular historian, called the relationship an "amiable daisy chain of mutual admiration"; see "This Fervent Friend of the Wehrmacht: Enough of Him!" rev. of *The Rommel Papers*, ed. LH, *Sunday Express*, 19 Apr. 1953, 4. Copies of the reviews in 9/24/32.

[72]Richard T. Burke, "The German 'Panzerwaffe', 1920–1939: A Study in Institutional Change" (Ph.D. diss., Northwestern University, 1969), 87. Burke's footnote to this passage naturally includes reference to the famous two paragraphs in *Panzer Leader* and the lengthy footnote in *Rommel Papers*.

[73]Quoted in Tuvia Ben-Moshe, "Liddell Hart and the Israel Defence Forces: A Reappraisal," *Journal of Contemporary History* 16 (Apr. 1981): 373.

to that of the Germans, and in some respects surpassing theirs."[74] Liddell Hart's overall reputation was certainly enhanced by the perception of close ties with the Israelis, who, along with the Germans, are widely considered the master practitioners of the blitzkrieg. This relationship, however, was not central to the restoration of his lost reputation, for the Israeli connection had little to do with his career in the 1930s, the period for which the historical record presented an obstacle.

There is ample reason for skepticism about Liddell Hart's influence on the Israeli military, as Tuvia Ben-Moshe's work shows.[75] It is his writings on the indirect approach that are said to have markedly influenced Israeli military thinking, and it is during the 1940s that this influence is said to have had its greatest impact. To start with, the vagueness of the concept of the indirect approach makes it both hard to imagine what the IDF could have operationalized and possible to ascribe every Israeli military triumph to that approach. Proving an influence requires a link between Liddell Hart's concrete ideas and the formulation of Israeli military doctrine.

The most important evidence in Liddell Hart's favor, according to Brian Bond, is "the tributes of several distinguished soldiers and scholars." These are generally loosely worded accolades and, as Bond notes, "What needs more careful examination . . . are the sources, extent and nature of this influence. It is simply not good enough, as some enthusiastic but historically unsophisticated interviewers and journalists have done, to attribute all the Israelis' success to their skillful employment of the indirect approach as inculcated by Liddell Hart."[76] Like the German case, however, there is little evidence beyond ex post facto tributes. For example, Ben-Moshe, who as part of his extensive research on this subject in Israel, looked at old issues of the periodical *Ma'arakhot*, which carries articles on important theoretical military topics, concluded:

> A complete and thorough review of what was published in this periodical "aiming at indoctrination" shows that from 1939 to 1949 not a single article appeared by Liddell Hart dealing with "Indirect Approach." Indeed, up to the publication of Herzog's article in 1950, there was not a single article by anyone at all dealing with the subject of "Indirect Approach." . . . Thus it can be affirmed with certainty that no particular

---

[74]*Memoirs* 2:183. See also LH, "Strategy of a War," *Encounter* 30 (Feb. 1968): 17.

[75]Ben-Moshe, "Liddell Hart and the Israel Defence Forces." Brian Bond tends to ascribe more influence to LH than Ben-Moshe, but he provides abundant evidence for Ben-Moshe's position; see *Liddell Hart*, chap. 9. These two works contribute heavily to my subsequent discussion.

[76]B. Bond, *Liddell Hart*, 238.

attention was paid to Hart nor was there any stress on his ideas in this official military training periodical.[77]

Yigael Yadin, an important military figure in the 1940s and early 1950s, is considered the person most responsible for spreading Liddell Hart's ideas within the Israeli military during the 1940s. As Ben-Moshe notes, Yadin claims "that when he was responsible for training in the years 1940–43, he taught and even translated chapters from Hart's books." Ben-Moshe, who researched this claim, writes, "I have been able to find no evidence in support of this statement";[78] moreover, the available evidence "indicates very strongly that Hart's 'best pupils' in fact knew very little about him in the war whose operations are praised to the skies as signal examples of 'Indirect Approach.' "[79] Probably the best case for Liddell Hart's influence is that his writings were useful for a few Israelis in triggering some thoughts about war, as at least two generals have claimed,[80] though the lines of influence have never been described. There is simply no evidence to support Ariel Sharon's claim that Liddell Hart was "the greatest teacher of all of us."[81] This was another myth manufactured to enhance Liddell Hart's reputation.

Why would certain Israelis cooperate in creating this myth? Let me propose a plausible explanation. Israeli military prowess is now taken for granted. Students of war often name the Wehrmacht and the IDF as the two most formidable military machines of the twentieth century. This was not always so. Israeli fighting power was not accorded special recognition until the stunning victories of June 1967. Before that, the IDF's status was nothing special, although it had performed well in the War of Independence and the 1956 War. As Liddell Hart wrote in 1965, "The army of Israel was of such recent creation that conventional military minds in the West tended to regard it as a body of amateurs."[82] This lack of respect, coupled with the fact that in the years between 1948 and 1967 Israel was a fledgling state trying to establish its legitimacy with other states, would have made praise from Liddell Hart very attractive. He was, after all, probably the most well-known and highly respected military writer in the world. And sing their praises he did: "Liddell Hart made no pretence of impartiality where Israeli mili-

---

[77]Ben-Moshe, "Liddell Hart and the Israel Defence Forces," 375.

[78]Ibid., 374.

[79]Ibid., 376.

[80]Generals Yadin and Haim Laskov, in interviews with Brian Bond; see *Liddell Hart*, 245–46.

[81]Quotation from an inscribed photograph displayed in the Liddell Hart Centre for Military Archives, King's College, University of London.

[82]*Memoirs* 2:183.

tary affairs were concerned; indeed his attitude rather resembled that of a proud headmaster praising successive generations of pupils who not only carried off the prizes but improved upon his own teaching." The informal quid pro quo called for the Israelis to shower lavish praise on Liddell Hart and go out of their way to lend credence to the claim they were his disciples. The Israelis had little difficulty living up to their end of the bargain, the overall success of which is nicely captured by Bond's description of Liddell Hart's only visit to Israel, in 1960:

> Liddell Hart's visit . . . as a guest of the Government was something of a triumphal tour. He was hailed by the Press as "the greatest military expert of our time", "the Clausewitz of the 20th Century" and "the Pope of theory", while *he in return* was quick to laud his hosts as his best disciples and the most brilliant soldiers in the world. He had interviews with all the "top brass", including discussions over the map with Laskov [the chief of staff of the IDF] and his Vice-Chief, Rabin, and with the Prime Minister, Ben Gurion.[83]

DEALING WITH POTENTIAL RIVALS

Two people besides Liddell Hart are frequently considered to have had significant influence on German thinking about the blitzkrieg between the world wars: Charles de Gaulle and J. F. C. Fuller. Liddell Hart's fourth technique was to challenge their influence. *The National and English Review* published an article in 1958 that described de Gaulle as "the most original military thinker of the 1930s."[84] He was also credited with having had considerable influence on Guderian. These two claims, often made in the years after 1940, raised Liddell Hart's ire, and he made a practice of challenging them.[85] He stressed that de Gaulle could not have influenced Guderian because Guderian himself had said that it was not until 1937 that he read de Gaulle's *Army of the Future* and by then the organization of the panzer division was in place. De Gaulle's treatise, in Guderian's own words, "did not exercise any influence on the development of the Panzertruppen." There seems no reason to challenge this claim. Liddell Hart could not, however,

---

[83]B. Bond, *Liddell Hart*, 242; see also "Strategy of a War," 16–20. B. Bond, *Liddell Hart*, 260, emphasis added.

[84]"Charles De Gaulle," 151 (Oct. 1958): 138.

[85]See, for example, LH to Harvey A. DeWeerd, 20 Apr. 1944, 1/234; LH to John Brophy, 17 Aug. 1942, 1/112; LH to George Orwell, 8, 16 Aug. 1942, 1/557; LH to Earle, 24 Apr. 1946, 1/255; LH, letter, *National and English Review*, 151 (Nov. 1958): 198–99; LH, letter, *Times Literary Supplement*, 18 July 1942, 355; LH, letter, *Times*, 9 July 1942, 5.

argue that de Gaulle did not have progressive ideas about armored warfare because the evidence shows otherwise. He concentrated instead on arguing that de Gaulle had gotten these ideas from British advocates of blitzkrieg, implying, of course, himself: "DeGaulle's one short treatise on mechanized forces and warfare was not written and published until 1934, whereas British writers had been expounding the theory for fifteen years previously. DeGaulle's borrowings from them were even more specific than Guderian's—but he was much less honest than Guderian in acknowledging his indebtedness."[86]

There is another case where Liddell Hart suggests that de Gaulle borrowed an important idea from him, and it involves his false assertion (discussed earlier) that in the 1930s he had shared with de Gaulle and Reynaud the view that France should build an armored force with a potent offensive capability. There too he implied that de Gaulle got this idea from him, although there is no supporting evidence. He writes, for example, in *Memoirs*, "I had originally urged the need for this [a mechanized spearhead of professional soldiers] in my 1927 articles on that Army and in *The Remaking of Modern Armies*—an argument which had been taken up in the last two years by Lieutenant-Colonel de Gaulle in a striking little book . . . and by Paul Reynaud in Parliament" (2:127).[87] The effect is to lessen de Gaulle's status as a military thinker by showing that his important ideas were largely derivative. As Liddell Hart told George Orwell, from whom he had exacted an apology for having "accepted too readily the legend" that the Germans had borrowed their tank theories from de Gaulle, "The real point is that the use of mobile armoured forces was a British conception—conceived and developed in this country long before it was appreciated anywhere else."[88] This argument, while it detracted from de Gaulle's reputation, elevated Liddell Hart's.

This discussion of Liddell Hart's purported influence on de Gaulle, coupled with the previous discussion of his supposed influence on the Germans and the Israelis, suggests that Liddell Hart hoped to show that the success of virtually all the famous armored commanders in the West owed something to him. To complete the picture, there was Gen. George Patton. According to Stephen Brooks, the archivist who arranged Liddell Hart's papers after his death:

[86]Letter, *National and English Review*. See also *German Generals Talk*, 91; *Other Side of the Hill*, 121–22. LH never adduced any evidence to support his claim that de Gaulle had borrowed ideas from British writers.
[87]See also *Current of War*, 91; *Memoirs* 1:274; LH, "Appeasement in the Thirties."
[88]Orwell to LH, 12 Aug. 1942, 1/557; LH to Orwell, 16 Aug. 1942, 1/557. See also LH to Orwell, 8 Aug. 1942, 1/557.

In 1948 Liddell Hart wrote a note about two meetings he had with Patton in 1944. Briefly the note says that on his first visit Patton was despondently talking about having to return to slow 1918-style warfare in France. Liddell Hart reminded him about Sherman's campaigns, and "I think the indirect argument made some impression. At any rate, when I spent another evening with him in June, just before he went over to Normandy, he was no longer talking about 1918 methods, but on much bolder lines." The implication here is clearly that Liddell Hart's little talk did the trick; but this is really pure conjecture. Looking back now to the original notes which Liddell Hart made at the time of these two meetings . . . there is certainly a reference to Sherman in the first note, but as Liddell Hart recorded it it is in the second one that Patton talks of returning to 1918 methods. . . . Evidently the note written in 1948 does not tally with the notes made at the time.[89]

Fuller was a more difficult case. Liddell Hart owed a great intellectual debt to Fuller, one he never publicly acknowledged. Fuller, after all, was responsible for converting Liddell Hart into an armor advocate, and he also significantly influenced his early thinking about blitzkrieg. They were good friends in the years after World War II, and because they had quarreled during the interwar period, Liddell Hart probably did not want to do anything to rupture the friendship.[90] Moreover, if anyone had a legitimate claim to have influenced the German panzer generals, it was Fuller.[91] For these reasons Liddell Hart was apparently willing to share credit with Fuller, as reflected in the correspondence on de Gaulle's influence on the Germans, where Liddell Hart talked not about his influence per se but about the influence of "British writers."

Nevertheless, Liddell Hart did diminish Fuller's importance while elevating his own. He argued in his *Memoirs*, published the year before Fuller died, that there were fundamental differences in their early views about the blitzkrieg:[92] Fuller advocated an all-tank army, while he called for armored forces that incorporated the other combat arms, and while he understood the importance of the deep strategic penetration, Fuller did not and instead called for a deep tactical penetration. These two matters—combined arms operations and deep strategic

[89]Brooks, "Liddell Hart and His Papers," 138. Also on LH's discussing his influence on Patton, see *German Generals Talk*, 23; *Memoirs of General William T. Sherman* (Bloomington: Indiana University Press, 1957), xvi.

[90]See B. Bond, *Liddell Hart*, 30; Anthony J. Trythall, *'Boney' Fuller: The Intellectual General, 1878–1966* (New Brunswick, N.J.: Rutgers University Press, 1977), 155–57, 159–60, 199–200; LH's correspondence with Fuller, 1/302.

[91]See Trythall, *'Boney' Fuller*, 203–5, and recall the quotation from Guderian's son in chap. 7 of this book.

[92]See *Memoirs* 1:90–91; also LH, "The Development of Armoured Infantry—'Tank Marines,'" memorandum for the record, 1948, 11/1948/36a.

penetration—are among the most important issues in how to effect a blitzkrieg. They were, after all, at the heart of the crucial second paragraph Liddell Hart wrote for Guderian's *Panzer Leader*.

World War II, especially the German experience, established that the deep strategic penetration was the central element in the blitzkrieg and that an all-tank army was a fundamentally bad idea. The British army actually suffered in the early stages of the war for approximating that ideal.[93] So Liddell Hart clearly lined himself up on the right side of these two debates, while placing Fuller on the wrong side. The inference, of course, was that the Germans and Liddell Hart were in agreement on these crucial issues while Fuller's views were similar to those of the British generals. The reader of *Memoirs*, however, is not left to infer; Liddell Hart tells them:

> [I]n the nineteen-thirties most of the R.T.C. [Royal Tank Corps] leaders, especially Hobart, tended to discount the need for such accompanying artillery and swung strongly in favour of Fuller's concept that an armoured force should be an 'all-tank' force rather than an 'all-mobile' force. Thus when war came the British pattern of armoured division lacked a balanced composition, in contrast to the German one as developed by Guderian, who had chosen to follow an earlier British idea [Liddell Hart's, of course]. As all too often happens, a heavy penalty was paid for the conflict of vested interests. (1:103)

Liddell Hart's claims notwithstanding, there is no evidence from the interwar period of disagreements about armored war. Liddell Hart did not discuss the subject of deep strategic penetration, nor did he mention differences between them over the exploitation phase of the blitzkrieg. A careful examination of their writings produced no evidence of differences.[94] Furthermore, there is no discernible difference in their views on the need for integrating infantry and artillery into large-scale armored units. Contrary to what Liddell Hart implied *after* World War II, *before* that conflict he occasionally came close to advocating an all-tank army, whereas Fuller often emphasized that infantry and artillery would not disappear from the battlefield.[95]

---

[93]See chap. 2, n. 68.

[94]What did Fuller think of LH's views on the superiority of defense over offense? Fuller challenged this claim on at least one occasion during the late 1930s (see Brian H. Reid, *J. F. C. Fuller: Military Thinker* [London: Macmillan, 1987], 192), although he apparently wrote little on the subject. This is not surprising, as he was primarily concerned during this period with fascist politics, not armored war. See ibid., chap. 8; Trythall, *'Boney' Fuller*, chap. 8.

[95]On LH's flirtation with the idea of an all-tank army, see chap. 2. For Fuller's views on the use of infantry and artillery, showing there was little difference between them on this matter, as well as that of deep strategic penetration, see Brian H. Reid, "J. F. C. Fuller's Theory of Mechanized Warfare," *Journal of Strategic Studies* 1 (Dec. 1978): 295–312.

Fuller expressed his views on armored war in 1932 in his famous *Lectures on F.S.R. III*. Liddell Hart twice commented on that book in 1932. He discussed it in an article he wrote for the *Daily Telegraph* and in a letter he wrote to the *United Services Review*, commending that periodical for running a favorable review of Fuller's book. In neither case did he criticize any of Fuller's ideas. He also sent Fuller a copy of the *Daily Telegraph* column with an accompanying note.[96] He offered no criticism of Fuller's views on armored war in that letter or apparently anywhere else during the interwar period.[97] Simply put, Liddell Hart manufactured these differences after the war to denigrate Fuller's influence while inflating his own.[98]

SUCCESS OF THE RESCUE EFFORT

It was in the mid-1960s that Liddell Hart's efforts to rescue his blemished reputation attained fulfillment. He and Fuller were awarded the Royal United Services Institution's prestigious Chesney Gold Medal in October 1963. At the awards ceremony Liddell Hart was profusely praised for, among other things, his foresight and his influence on the German generals. He was then knighted in 1966. The crucial year for him, however, was 1965, the year both of his seventieth birthday and of the keystone of his success, the publication of his *Memoirs*, which, in A. J. P. Taylor's words, were "greeted with almost deafening praise."[99] The *Memoirs*, of course, are almost exclusively

96"Armies of the Future: Tanks Instead of Men," *Daily Telegraph*, 19 July 1932, 8; letter, *United Services Review*, 29 Dec. 1932, 4314. LH to Fuller, 19 July 1932, 1/302.

97I could find no evidence in their extensive correspondence (1/302) of any discussion of the concept of deep strategic penetration, much less mention of their purported differences. There *is* a lengthy memorandum in LH's files (11/1932/49) titled "Notes on Fuller's 'Lectures on F.S.R. III' (Operations between Mechanized Forces) 1932"; it contains the same key points found in *Memoirs*. The cataloguing of the document implies it was written in 1932, but there is no date on the memorandum; 1932 is the date Fuller's book was published. I believe it was written *after* the war because there are no references to it in LH's other correspondence from the period, as there surely would have been about so significant a statement of his views.

98The importance LH ascribed to this task is reflected in Anthony Trythall's description of his first and only meeting with LH. Trythall, who was writing a biography of Fuller, notes, "*Almost immediately* I was given some notes which Liddell Hart had made on Fuller's 'Lectures on FSR III'—notes outlining the differences between them in the '30s" (Lt. Col. Anthony J. Trythall, "Liddell Hart: Some Thoughts and Memories," *Journal of the Royal United Services Institution* 115 [June 1970]: 71), emphasis added. LH's success at purveying this myth is reflected in Trythall, *'Boney' Fuller*, 200, 226–28.

99See "Award of Chesney Gold Medals," *Journal of the Royal United Services Institution* 109 (Feb. 1964): 68–72. A. J. P. Taylor, "A Prophet Vindicated," rev. of *Memoirs*, vol. 2, by LH and *The Theory and Practice of War*, ed. Michael Howard, *Observer*, 31 Oct. 1965, 27.

concerned with detailing Liddell Hart's version of the events leading to the Fall of France.

The *Memoirs* were published in England by Cassell, which published two other books in 1965 that contributed to the resurrection of Liddell Hart's reputation. The first was Jay Luvaas's *The Education of an Army*, which contained a very laudatory chapter on Liddell Hart.[100] Luvaas, an extremely close friend of Liddell Hart's,[101] made many of the same points that would soon appear in the *Memoirs*, which is not surprising because Liddell Hart "emended in detail" the chapter on himself in Luvaas's book.[102] Cassell also published *The Theory and Practice of War*, a book edited by Michael Howard, another close friend of Liddell Hart's.[103] This book, which was actually a festschrift presented to Liddell Hart on his seventieth birthday, contained essays by a host of distinguished people: Yigal Allon, André Beaufre, Alastair Buchan, Gordon Craig, Norman Gibbs, Henry Kissinger, and Peter Paret, to name some. The essays were dedicated "to a great teacher by a group of his pupils, disciples, admirers and friends" (ix).

The festschrift enhanced Liddell Hart's reputation in two ways. First, the mere fact of being thus honored could not help but raise his overall stature.[104] Second, the book contained three essays that supported Liddell Hart's version of the interwar period: André Beaufre's "Liddell Hart and the French Army, 1919–1939"; Robert O'Neill's "Doctrine and Training in the German Army, 1919–1939"; and "Tim" Pile's "Liddell Hart and the British Army, 1919–1939." These authors were close friends of Liddell Hart's.[105] O'Neill's essay, which focused on the development of thinking about the blitzkrieg in Germany, concluded by quoting the two key paragraphs from *Panzer Leader*.[106] Pile's essay, dealing with the British army between the world wars, was fully con-

---

[100]See Luvaas, "The Captain Who Teaches Generals," in *The Education of an Army: British Military Thought, 1815–1940* (London: Cassell, 1965), 374–424.

[101]Reflected in their extensive correspondence (1/465).

[102]These are Brian Bond's words in *Liddell Hart*, 279; copy of the vetted chapter in 13/4.

[103]*The Theory and Practice of War: Essays Presented to B. H. Liddell Hart on His Seventieth Birthday* (London, 1965). For evidence of their close friendship, see correspondence in 1/384.

[104]See, for example, Louis Morton, rev. of *The Theory and Practice of War*, ed. Michael Howard, *Journal of Modern History* 39 (Dec. 1967): 454–55. Morton concludes: "Liddell Hart has been called 'The captain who teaches generals.' This volume amply supports this observation, but it also provides eloquent testimony to the influence he has had on two generations of military historians" (455).

[105]According to Morton, in these particular essays, "the contribution of Liddell Hart to the development of mechanized war is made abundantly evident" (ibid., 454). For evidence of these friendships, see the following correspondence files: Beaufre (1/49); O'Neill (1/555); Pile (1/575).

[106]Howard, *Theory and Practice of War*, 164.

sistent with Liddell Hart's version of events.[107] Finally, the essence of Beaufre's essay is reflected in its final paragraph: "It is beyond doubt that Liddell Hart's influence has been immense. For my part I have simply tried to show here how that influence, which might have saved us from the catastrophe of 1939–40, was insufficient to change the course of history, at least insofar as the French Army was concerned."[108]

Cassell released *The Education of an Army* in February 1965. The first volume of the *Memoirs* was published in May, and in October the second volume came out with *The Theory and Practice of War*. These last two were frequently reviewed together. The serial publication of these four works, all so important to Liddell Hart's efforts to alter the historical record, all favorably received, solidified the revised assessment of Liddell Hart. Shortly after the publication of the second volume of the *Memoirs*, André Beaufre and Michael Howard discussed Liddell Hart's career on a BBC radio program. Their exchange concluded:

> HOWARD: He emerges as a rather tragic figure, I think; and it is most gratifying that he should have survived, and be celebrating his seventieth birthday now, to see virtually the whole world bearing tribute to his wisdom and foresight and acknowledging his genius as a prophet and guide.

> BEAUFRE: Yes I entirely concur with you.[109]

Liddell Hart had come a long way from the dark years of the 1940s. He had done very well for himself.

---

[107]LH actually helped Pile write this chapter; see Howard to Pile, 8 Sept. 1964; Pile to LH, 10 Sept. 1964; LH to Pile, 16 Sept. 1964; copies in 13/51.

[108]Howard, *Theory and Practice of War*, 141. LH vetted Beaufre's chapter; see LH to Beaufre, 9, 20 Oct. 1964; Beaufre to LH, 15 Oct. 1964; copies in 1/49.

[109]Copy in *Listener*, 23 Dec. 1965, 1028–30. Michael Howard, it should be emphasized, played a key role in 1965 in solidifying the conventional wisdom about Liddell Hart. Not only was he the editor of the aforementioned festschrift, but he also reviewed Liddell Hart's *Memoirs* very favorably in two places; see chap. 1, n. 18 and the attendant text; and Michael Howard, "The Liddell Hart Memoirs," rev. of *Memoirs*, vols. 1 and 2, *Journal of the Royal United Services Institution*, 111 (Feb. 1966): 58–61, which ends: "For the past 20 years Liddell Hart has stuck to . . . teaching, writing, analyzing, above all training a new generation of officers and academics throughout the Western world to apply to military matters his own meticulous criteria of reason and intellectual honesty. As a result his reputation has grown immeasurably. His place in history is secure; not, as he might have wished, as the reformer of the British Army, but as the man who, more than any other in this century, has shown us how to think clearly and sanely about war. And as such the prophet has at last been deservedly honoured in his own country" (61). Howard did, however, temper his judgment with the passage of time; see, for example, Michael Howard, "Liddell Hart," *Encounter* 34 (June 1970): 37–42.

Liddell Hart was successful for several reasons. With the passage of time, memories dull and people lose interest in the details of controversies that no longer have direct policy implications. It therefore becomes easier as time passes to change how people think about a particular event. Liddell Hart's *Memoirs* would not have been as well received in 1945 as they were in 1965. Furthermore, as Brian Bond notes, "by British social custom all is forgiven to mavericks, rebels, outsiders and critics of the Establishment when they reach the age of seventy."[110] These factors undoubtedly help account for Liddell Hart's success at restoring his reputation, but it would be wrong to place too much significance on them. After all, many of the controversies of the 1930s that concerned Liddell Hart are still the subject of heated debate.

The British army, the institution at which Liddell Hart pointed the finger of blame, was an easy target, partly because of the lingering effects of the damage done to its reputation during the interwar years. Most Britons were familiar with the charge that their army was led by "Colonel Blimps" and were therefore predisposed to believe the worst. More important, however, the army never seriously defended itself against his charges. Surveying both the 1930s and the postwar period, it is remarkable how completely Liddell Hart dominated the public debate with his military foes. The military as an institution, not to mention individual generals, rarely contested Liddell Hart in print. Luvaas, writing Liddell Hart soon after publication of *The Education of an Army*, expressed his pleasure at the book's favorable reviews and added, "I thought sure that I would bump up against a bitter old critic who would use the occasion to settle some old score, but no such luck." Liddell Hart probably was not surprised, for it was apparent to him by the late 1940s that he was almost immune to criticism from Europeans and that it was Americans who criticized his writings, as he said in a letter to Henry Steele Commager: "In recent years I have become accustomed to cheap criticism in the American press—in contrast to the general, and increased, respect with which my views are treated in Europe since the war."[111]

Two further points about the British generals are pertinent. First, not only did British officers fail to challenge Liddell Hart's description of the interwar years, but a handful of influential generals contributed to his effort to rewrite history. For example, Gen. Sir John Hackett forcefully articulated the conventional wisdom in his remarks at the cere-

---

[110]B. Bond, *Liddell Hart*, 273.

[111]Luvaas to LH, 27 May 1965, 1/465; LH to Commager, 1 June 1949, 9/24/18. Of the negative reviews of *German Generals Talk* that elicited a written response from LH, the majority appeared in American newspapers and journals; see 9/24/18.

mony where Liddell Hart was awarded the Chesney Gold Medal, and F. M. Lord Michael Carver, a prominent soldier-scholar who was chief of the British Defence Staff in the mid-1970s, did much the same thing in his 1979 Lees Knowles Lectures, subsequently published as *The Apostles of Mobility*.[112] Second, one might have expected Fuller to challenge Liddell Hart's interpretation of what transpired in the years between the wars; yet Fuller seems not to have cared about establishing his place in history. He was the antithesis of Liddell Hart in this regard and thus never bothered to dispute his friend. Adrian Liddell Hart commented during the discussion after a 1978 lecture on his father and Fuller (who was Adrian's godfather): "I think that the difference between the two men was, perhaps, that if they were here today my father would be passionately concerned with what you were saying, both the tributes and the criticisms. He was very much concerned, even as a young man, with what his role in history would be. I wonder, knowing Fuller, whether he would really care a damn what people here said about him!"[113]

Liddell Hart was successful too because he was rarely challenged by students of military affairs. *Memoirs* should have elicited some quarrels; yet few critical words were spoken. This was not an unfamiliar pattern. Throughout his life he was occasionally challenged in private correspondence but rarely in public.[114] No one during the course of the 1930s engaged him in a lengthy public debate, and in later years no one called him to account for his part in the policy debates of the 1930s. This absence of sustained and powerful criticism probably contributed to his great stature during the 1930s, although he undoubtedly would have profited from having had his views challenged more often. In the absence of criticism, he was free to shape the historical record to suit his own purposes.

[112]See "Award of Chesney Gold Medals," 68–69; also relevant is Hackett's address at a memorial service for LH on 20 Apr. 1970, in *Journal of the Royal United Services Institution* 115, (Sept. 1970): 37–38. F. M. Lord Michael Carver, *The Apostles of Mobility: The Theory and Practice of Armoured Warfare* (New York: Holmes & Meier, 1979).

[113]"The Fuller-Liddell Hart Lecture," *Journal of the Royal United Services Institution* 124 (Mar. 1979): 30. Also Fuller, who died in February 1966, was in failing health when *Memoirs* were published in 1965; see Trythall, *'Boney' Fuller*, chap. 10.

[114]The one significant public challenge LH faced during his lifetime is Irving M. Gibson's [A. Kovacs] chapter in Edward Mead Earle, ed., *Makers of Modern Strategy: Military Thought from Machiavelli to Hitler* (Princeton, N.J.: Princeton University Press, 1943), 365–87, written during World War II and critical of LH's military writings from the 1930s. The piece has attracted little attention although the Earle book is widely regarded as a classic. See chap. 1, n. 37, and n. 123 below. Spencer Wilkinson, the first Chichele Professor of the History of War at Oxford, also publicly challenged some of LH's early ideas; see his "Killing No Murder: An Examination of Some New Theories of War," *Army Quarterly* 15 (Jan. 1928): 14–27. LH was occasionally challenged in private; see LH correspondence with Fuller (1/302); J. M. Scammel (1/622); Wilkinson (1/748).

We can only speculate on the causes of this absence of scholarly criticism. To start, there have until recently been few serious students of military affairs. There is now a thriving community of historians, especially in Britain, who focus on military issues; but this community was only emerging in the last decade of Liddell Hart's life. By that time, the accepted thinking on Liddell Hart was so firmly entrenched that it would naturally take some time for the real story to emerge. Only someone thoroughly familiar with the history of the British army in the 1920s and 1930s as well as with Liddell Hart's personal papers could seriously challenge his version of history. Brian Bond, of course, fits that description, and his excellent book on Liddell Hart, as well as his fine work on the British army, helps set the record straight.

Then there is the important matter of Liddell Hart's personal relations with that body of military historians that emerged in England and the United States after World War II: he befriended most of them, as Luvaas testifies:

Few obituaries have mentioned the immeasurable personal debt owed Liddell Hart by students of history the world over. For twenty-five years his house was a Mecca for historians as well as generals and politicians. He never hesitated to make available his famous files, even to an undergraduate wrestling with an honors thesis, and he gladly shared his unrivaled knowledge and his time with others involved in the study of war. He was particularly kind to visitors from America, often at excessive cost to his own leisure and productivity. No inquiry, however trivial, went unanswered, and no error, however small, passed unchallenged. He has been described as the captain who teaches generals: in a very real sense he was also the foremost teacher of a generation of military historians in the United States as well as in Britain.

Those of us who were privileged to receive help and guidance from this unusual man can truthfully say that he encouraged, corrected, and on occasion intervened to give our careers—and our spirits—a generous boost.[115]

The list of those who developed close ties with Liddell Hart includes: Correlli Barnett, Brian Bond, Alastair Buchan, Michael Howard, Alastair Horne, Paul Kennedy, Ronald Lewin, Jay Luvaas, Kenneth Macksey, Richard Ogorkiewicz, Robert O'Neill, Peter Paret, Barrie Pitt, and Donald Schurman. The one exception was John Terraine, who

[115]Luvaas, LH's obituary, *American Historical Review* 75 (June 1970): 1574. See also B. Bond, *Liddell Hart*, 1–4; Howard, "Liddell Hart," 37–42; Kathleen Liddell Hart, Foreword, LH, *History of the Second World War* (London: Cassell, 1970), vii–viii; Robert Pocock, "Liddell Hart: The Captain Who Taught Generals," BBC radio program (transcript in *Listener*, 28 Dec. 1972, 892–96); Trythall, "Liddell Hart: Some Thoughts and Memories," 71–72.

became a bitter foe, for he is a staunch defender of Field Marshal Haig, the ultimate bête noire of World War I for Liddell Hart.[116]

The bonds that developed between Liddell Hart and these scholars worked to his advantage in two ways. First, they insured that when these scholars focused on events in which he had been involved, he would be well situated to make the best possible case for his position. They would know Liddell Hart's side of the story very well, after hearing it from him in person, while almost always being less familiar with how others might recount the same history. Inevitably, the tone and content of their accounts would be affected. Second, respect and friendship would dispose these scholars to accept Liddell Hart's version. Even when they doubted his claims, they respected his deep knowledge and appreciated his friendship and personal generosity. They certainly would not assume the worst about him. I should emphasize that I am not implying in any way that Liddell Hart's scholar-friends were intellectually dishonest, only that all scholars' personal relationships affect the questions they ask and the answers they provide. Thus Liddell Hart's close friendships with these distinguished scholars could only work to his advantage.

Those who did not write about the interwar period were not likely to come across information that challenged their view of Liddell Hart's career; for them, his writings would appear definitive. Consider, for example, Peter Paret's influence on a Ph.D. student at Stanford who for a time considered writing his dissertation on the subject of this book but eventually wrote on a different topic:

> As a graduate student at Stanford University I thought it would be useful to make a detailed examination of the evolution of Liddell Hart's theories with an emphasis on how they had been influenced by his experience in the Great War. My adviser, Peter Paret, pointed out that a great deal of work had already been done in this area, most notably the publication of Liddell Hart's memoirs, and wisely steered me away from this approach.[117]

Paret, whose research did not cover European history in the period between the wars, undoubtedly had no inkling that Liddell Hart's *Memoirs* significantly distorted the record.

---

[116]See, for example, LH, letter, *Times*, 24 Apr. 1963, 13; John A. Terraine, letter, *Times*, 26 Apr. 1963, 15; LH, "The Basic Truths of Passchendaele"; John A. Terraine, "Passchendaele and Amiens: I," *Journal of the Royal United Services Institution* 104 (May 1959): 173–83; idem, "Passchendaele and Amiens: II," ibid. (Aug. 1959): 331–40; their correspondence in 1/683; John A. Terraine, *Douglas Haig: The Educated Soldier* (London: Hutchinson, 1963); idem, *The Western Front, 1914–1918* (Philadelphia: Lippincott, 1965); idem, *To Win a War: 1918, the Year of Victory* (Garden City, N.Y.: Doubleday, 1981).

[117]Harold R. Winton, "General Sir John Burnett-Stuart and British Military Reform, 1927–1938" (Ph.D. diss., Stanford University, 1977), iv.

Of course the real story has begun to emerge, and some of Liddell Hart's scholar-friends, to their credit, took the initial steps in setting the record straight. Kenneth Macksey was the first to raise doubts about the accepted version Liddell Hart helped shape. He suggested soon after Liddell Hart's death that he had rescued his damaged reputation on the backs of the German generals, although he did not develop the suggestion in any detail. In 1981 he published *The Tank Pioneers,* which deals with the development of armored doctrine in the first half of the twentieth century. Although the book pays little attention to Liddell Hart's thinking about tank warfare, it leaves no doubt that the conventional wisdom about him is deeply flawed.[118] Brian Bond's *Liddell Hart* is the first major work to challenge seriously the legacy Liddell Hart created. The book is not a straightforward indictment of the legacy, but Bond challenges many aspects and raises doubts about others. It surely must have been difficult for him to write what is a fairly critical study of a man he admired so much.

Liddell Hart's success at distorting the historical record was also a function of certain qualities in the man himself. He was extremely smart and had an encyclopedic knowledge of military affairs, especially about events that had a bearing on his career. Anyone engaged in debate with him quickly realized that it was intellectual combat with a formidable adversary, as Brigadier General Edmonds told him in the midst of one of their heated disputes: "You are a far more dangerous antagonist than L. G. [Lloyd George]. Which is saying a good deal!"[119]

He was also a highly skillful writer, which is not surprising for one who made his living by writing. Even so, his ability to turn a phrase or make an argument in print was impressive by the standards of the journalistic profession. Moreover, his cause was helped greatly by the fact that he was a prolific author whose views on important subjects had changed over time. He therefore had a veritable grab bag of policy positions he could choose from when challenged on a particular point. Furthermore, the indirect approach, one of his principal military ideas, was such a loosely defined and flexible concept that it could be used to suit almost any purpose. Thus only a person very familiar with his corpus of writings could pin down his ideas and hold him accountable for what he had said at different times.

---

[118]See Macksey's comments in Pocock, "Liddell Hart," 895; also Kenneth J. Macksey, "Fuller and Liddell Hart Reviewed," rev. of *Liddell Hart: A Study of His Military Thought,* by Brian Bond, *Journal of the Royal United Services Institution* 123 (Mar. 1978): 72. See also the numerous favorable references to LH in Macksey's *Armoured Crusader: A Biography of Major-General Sir Percy Hobart* (London: Hutchinson, 1967), a marked contrast to *Tank Pioneers.*

[119]Edmonds to LH, 20 Nov. 1934, 1/259.

Liddell Hart's success in rescuing his reputation was also due to his dedication to the task. He displayed boundless energy, and it is no exaggeration to say that the overriding goal in his life from the Fall of France until his death in 1970 was establishing his place in history. The following anecdotes show just how serious he was about that enterprise. In early 1949 a critical but nevertheless insightful review of *The German Generals Talk* appeared in *Military Affairs,* an American journal. The reviewer, an officer on active duty in the American army who had conducted about five hundred interviews with captured German officers, complained about

> the pernicious effect of Captain Liddell Hart's propensity for putting his own words in other mouths. Not only did I find it extremely irritating but even destructive of the book's validity when virtually every German is made to utter unctuous phrases to the effect that the author's books had taught them all they knew about warfare. The variation on this theme was that the Germans' experience had fully substantiated Liddell Hart's theories on the superiority of the tactical defense and the transcendent value of "indirection." These avowals, I submit, are spurious. . . . The real trouble with *The German Generals Talk* is: They don't talk that way.[120]

An incensed Liddell Hart wrote Dwight Eisenhower explaining why the review was flawed and, moreover, asking whether it would be possible for Eisenhower to see that this officer was punished for his transgression. Eisenhower, of course, refused to cooperate.[121]

The second anecdote concerns a 1957 book about the World War II battle for Monte Cassino by Fred Majdalany. At one point, the author briefly outlines Liddell Hart's prewar views about the supremacy of the defense and then explains why they were proven wrong in the early stages of the war. This discussion, which occupies one page, is accurate and even-handed. Liddell Hart took umbrage and wrote Reginald Paget, the British lawyer who had defended Manstein, asking him about the possibility of filing a libel suit. After Paget told him that he could not help because he was not an expert on libel, Liddell Hart wrote back to Paget, telling him that actually he was "not seriously contemplating a libel action against Longmans [the British publisher] . . . but I would like to shake them up a bit—and if possible

---

[120]Capt. Frank C. Mahin, rev. of *The German Generals Talk,* by LH, *Military Affairs* 13 (Spring 1949): 58. Biographical data on Mahin from ibid.
[121]LH to Gen. Dwight D. Eisenhower, 21 May 1949, 9/24/18; see also LH to Commager, 1 June 1949, 9/24/18. Eisenhower to LH, 11 July 1949, 1/261.

induce them to do something towards correcting the misrepresentation of my views in Majdalany's book."[122]

In sum, Liddell Hart's raw intellectual skills, coupled with his dedication to his task, enabled him to disarm critics and others who identified him with the positions he held in the late 1930s.[123] What is so remarkable is that the critics were almost always right. They were not purveying misinformation. This entire state of affairs is nicely captured in an editorial note in *Infantry Journal* soon after Liddell Hart had written a letter protesting the editors' description of him in an earlier issue as one who had argued before World War II "that in modern war the defense was much stronger than the offense." The note reads:

> The *Journal's* humblest apologies. Our statement was an editorial error which should have been caught and deleted, for we did know better. We have long regretted that a completely erroneous idea of Captain Liddell Hart's actual military thought and recommendation has so long persisted.[124]

[122]LH to Paget, 20, 28 June 1958; Paget to LH, 24 June 1958, 1/563. Fred Majdalany, *The Battle of Cassino* (Boston: Houghton Mifflin, 1957), 25.

[123]For examples of LH's ability to disarm critics and actually turn them into allies, see his correspondence with Paul Addison (2/121), Gen. André Beaufre (1/49), and F. M. Lord Michael Carver (1/153). The best example involves the chapter on LH in the original Earle, *Makers of Modern Strategy* (see chap. 1, n. 37). This piece, which contains some minor errors, is actually a good analysis of LH's thinking in the 1930s. He engaged in an extensive correspondence with the book's editor, Edward Mead Earle, and eventually succeeded in convincing Earle that the chapter's author was fundamentally wrong. See correspondence in 1/255.

[124]For the editor's original description, see *Infantry Journal* 64 (Mar. 1949): 31. For LH's letter, see ibid. (June 1949): 52–53. For the editors' apology, see ibid., 53.

[9]

Conclusion:
Lessons for the Present

Three broad lessons can be drawn from the Liddell Hart story. The first concerns how history influences policy makers, a subject of considerable interest to students of foreign policy.[1] Policy makers invariably have theories (and here I use that term in its broadest sense) about how the world works, for they need frameworks to make sense of the problems they face. In formulating those theories or frameworks, people rely, either intentionally or unconsciously, on the past. Of course the extent to which the past informs thinking varies markedly from person to person. History serves as a rich data base for constructing theories about how the world operates. It is particularly useful when past events appear to provide illuminating parallels with present ones. Historically based theories with policy relevance spring easily from such parallels, especially in foreign and military policy, where the past is studded with major wars and diplomatic events that bear important messages for contemporary policy makers.

Policy makers behave in respect to history according to three general patterns.[2] In the first pattern, *analytic history*, the policy maker behaves like the classic rational actor; he consciously turns to the past for help in understanding the present.[3] History is used to develop generaliza-

---

[1]Robert Jervis, *Perception and Misperception in International Relations* (Princeton, N.J.: Princeton University Press, 1976), chap. 6; Ernest R. May, *"Lessons" of the Past: The Use and Misuse of History in American Foreign Policy* (New York: Oxford University Press, 1975); Richard A. Melanson, *Writing History and Making Policy: The Cold War, Vietnam, and Revisionism*, vol. 6 (New York: University Press of America, 1983); Ernest R. May and Richard E. Neustadt, *Thinking in Time: The Uses of History for Decision-Makers* (New York: Free Press, 1986).

[2]I derived these three patterns from this study of LH and from the general literature on decision-making theory.

[3]On the rational actor model, see Graham T. Allison, *Essence of Decision: Explaining the Cuban Missile Crisis* (Boston: Little, Brown, 1971), chap. 1; John D. Steinbruner, *The*

tions applicable to the present. The policy maker selects historical cases carefully, paying attention to differences between present problems and the historical case. Moreover, he looks for evidence that might disconfirm those generalizations he finds useful. In essence, the policy maker selects historical events to guide him in dealing with contemporary problems, for history cannot provide final answers—only a frame of reference that can deepen understanding of current problems and perhaps clues to solutions.

There are limits to history's usefulness. We have only incomplete information about past events; thus there is hardly ever agreement on interpretation. In short, there are no universally accepted lessons of the past. There are, as well, always differences between past events and present problems, for example, differences in the military technology of two periods or differences in the strategic circumstances of two parties. The rational actor, of course, takes these differences into account, and furthermore, he recognizes evidence that undermines the historical analogy at hand. History may be a valuable tool, but it must be used carefully.

In the second pattern, *omnipresent history*, a policy maker views issues almost exclusively in terms of a specific historical event.[4] He forces the present to conform to his chosen interpretation of the past. He does not acknowledge differences between past and present events that undermine the utility of the past event as a model. In short, there is insufficient give and take between past and present in the decision maker's mind. A narrow slice of history is the dominating variable.

In the third pattern, *selective history*, history has little influence on the decision maker.[5] Although no one is completely unaffected by the past, with this type of policy maker, there is no evidence that history has made any significant or lasting impression or that he has tried to understand the present through the past. Instead, the decision maker bases policy prescriptions on parochial interests that he is doing his utmost to defend. History, however, usually does have a role to play,

---

Cybernetic Theory of Decision: New Dimensions of Political Analysis (Princeton, N.J.: Princeton University Press, 1974), chap. 2.

[4]Jervis, *Perception and Misperception,* chap. 6; Deborah W. Larson, *Origins of Containment: A Psychological Explanation* (Princeton, N.J.: Princeton University Press, 1985); Richard Ned Lebow, *Between Peace and War: The Nature of International Crisis* (Baltimore: Johns Hopkins University Press, 1981); May, *"Lessons" of the Past;* Herbert A. Simon and James G. March, *Organizations* (New York: Wiley, 1958), chap. 6; Janice G. Stein and Raymond Tanter, *Rational Decision-Making: Israel's Security Choices, 1967* (Columbus: Ohio State University Press, 1980); Steinbruner, *Cybernetic Theory of Decision,* chap. 4.

[5]Allison, *Essence of Decision,* chap. 3; Richard W. Cottam, *Foreign Policy Motivation: A General Theory and a Case Study* (Pittsburgh: University of Pittsburgh Press, 1977); Morton H. Halperin, *Bureaucratic Politics and Foreign Policy* (Washington, D.C.: Brookings, 1974).

for once the policy maker's position on an issue is established, he selectively uses history to support that position. His use of history is neither scientific nor unbiased. History serves him merely as a cover for his vested interests. One scholar labels this a "motivated perception" of the past.[6] Not only is the past culled to suit the policy maker's interests, but as obvious lessons from the past prove relevant and threatening, the policymaker does his best to ignore them. Threats to the policymaker's parochial interests must be minimized. With omnipresent history, the past completely dominates the present; here the pattern is reversed, and the past is subordinated to the present.

How did Liddell Hart use history during the interwar period? This question is reducible to the more specific one of How did his thinking about World War I relate to the development of his military theories? During the years immediately after World War I, when Liddell Hart's attention was focused on infantry tactics and armored strategy, his thought is best characterized as analytic history. He made an impressive effort to study systematically the lessons of World War I and come up with a comprehensive theory of infantry tactics. He was also receptive to criticism. He sought others' opinions and took their comments seriously, making changes in his arguments when he felt they did not stand up to criticism, as in his early dealings with Fuller. Liddell Hart took the initiative and sent his writings on infantry tactics to Fuller, asking for comments. These two military thinkers then engaged in a pointed debate about the role of the tank. Liddell Hart did his best to defend the position that infantry would continue as the dominant force on the battlefield, with the tank serving as an adjunct. He soon began to realize, however, that Fuller, who argued otherwise, had the better case. He subsequently changed his position and accepted Fuller's.[7] Liddell Hart's early thinking about his relationship with Britain's military leaders complemented his analytic approach to developing new ideas about tactics and strategy. He viewed himself as a brilliant young thinker who would provide receptive senior commanders with the keys to military success. This relationship was to be a rational process where open-minded general officers would recognize the merits of his carefully developed ideas.

---

[6]Jack L. Snyder, *The Ideology of the Offensive: Military Decision Making and the Disasters of 1914* (Ithaca, N.Y.: Cornell University Press, 1984).

[7]Anthony Trythall, Fuller's biographer, describes this early exchange of ideas between Fuller and LH similarly: "In the twenties the two corresponded voluminously and met frequently . . . the correspondence centered on the tank itself, and it is interesting to note the way in which the pair of them batted back and forth the ball of argument to their mutual benefit in a sort of epistolary Socratic dialogue" (*'Boney' Fuller: The Intellectual General, 1878–1966* [New Brunswick, N.J.: Rutgers University Press, 1977], 93).

By the late 1920s, Liddell Hart was drifting away from analytic history toward a pattern of omnipresent history, largely because of his growing disillusionment with the British military, which was fueled in good part by his disgust with its conduct of World War I. His disenchantment eventually became so deep seated and all consuming that he devoted himself to assuring that the British army never again fought a land war on the European Continent. In other words, his thinking about World War I shaped his position on the Continental commitment, the most important grand strategic issue facing Britain. Whether Britain followed his advice, however, was to some extent dependent on his views about a number of important strategic issues: armored strategy, the capabilities of the French and German armies, and the shape of a future war. Unfortunately for Liddell Hart, his *early* positions on these strategic matters were more likely to draw Britain onto the Continent than keep her off. His claim that the tank would revolutionize warfare and provide the means to avoid a repetition of World War I was, for example, an argument likely to encourage British policy makers to go back on the Continent. To rectify this unwanted result Liddell Hart changed his position and argued that on a tank-dominated battlefield defense has a great advantage over offense. He had changed his views on each key strategic issue by the late 1930s. These important changes were *not* the result of new evidence or challenging arguments that cast doubts on his earlier positions, as in the 1920s. Instead he altered his military thinking because of the overriding importance to him of his thinking about the Great War. A key historical event shaped his views on grand strategy, which in turn, defined his views on strategy and tactics.

When Liddell Hart first began to alter his position on these strategic matters, he was probably aware he was being expedient. His writings, for example, suggest that had he been confronted in 1934 or 1935 with his early arguments about the blitzkrieg, he would have conceded their merit. With the passage of time, however, he moved to an extreme position that effectively ruled out any possibility of a blitzkrieg. All available evidence indicates that he had complete faith in the validity of this extreme position by the late 1930s. He was no longer the rational thinker about military affairs that he had been in earlier times. Otherwise how could an intelligent person like Liddell Hart have so completely misjudged the shape of events in May 1940—especially when his early writings were so prescient?

This same pattern is reflected in Liddell Hart's thinking about broader foreign policy issues. His principal aim throughout the 1930s was to fashion a foreign policy that would deter aggression in Europe but at the same time ensure that Britain not become involved in ground combat, should deterrence break down. Here, too, his views were largely governed by his view of World War I. The shift that took place between 1938 and 1939 in his assessment of the German threat illustrates this point. Liddell Hart apparently had a pretty good appreciation of Hitler's designs throughout most of 1938 and thus expressed serious reservations about the Chamberlain government's appeasement policy. When that government decided in early 1939 to threaten Hitler with large-scale British involvement in a European land war, however, the specter of World War I so distressed Liddell Hart that he began changing his assessment of the seriousness of the German threat. In 1939, when virtually everyone else in Britain was coming to recognize that Hitler could not be appeased, Liddell Hart began downplaying the seriousness of the German threat and calling for further appeasement.

There are also traces of the third pattern, selective history, in Liddell Hart's writings, where he describes a historical subject in terms relevant to his theories. Selective history, by definition, however, pertains to thinking largely unaffected by the past: no historical event has left a marked impression, nor has there been a serious effort to understand the present by carefully studying the past. Liddell Hart's military thinking was significantly influenced by history. This was true during the early 1920s, when he studied the past to find a sound battlefield doctrine for fighting the next war, as well as the 1930s, when omnipresent history obtained. When he used history selectively, it was to illustrate and support theories already shaped in good part by his understanding of history.

Selective history is often employed to protect a threatened organization. In military organizations, competition among different services as well as the dynamic nature of modern military technology constantly threaten organizational essence.[8] What is particularly interesting about Liddell Hart, an infantry officer during the early 1920s, is that his ideas about infantry tactics and his subsequent conversion to the position that the tank promised to transform the nature of the battlefield were not linked to bureaucratic or organizational politics. There is no evidence that when he and Fuller debated the future of infantry, Liddell Hart's defense of infantry was motivated by the desire to protect his branch of the service from the threat posed by the tank. This undoubtedly helps explain why he was able to accept Fuller's views about the tank and then request a transfer to the tank corps. Liddell Hart appears to have been remarkably free of service parochialism during his tenure as an army officer. This fact, coupled with his then positive view of

[8]Halperin, *Bureaucratic Politics.*

British conduct of the Great War, allowed him to behave according to the rational actor model.

What does Liddell Hart's story tell us about when the different patterns are likely to obtain? The story bears mostly on the circumstances likely to produce omnipresent history, a pattern commonly thought to be found when a person has been directly involved in a major event that leaves a deep and lasting impression; for example, a war (Vietnam), a crisis that threatens to turn into war (the Cuban Missile Crisis), or a major diplomatic development that does lead to war (Munich). Yet direct involvement in a momentous event need not result in omnipresent history. A person is most likely to become a prisoner of an important experience if three conditions apply: (1) involvement takes place early in life; (2) involvement with similar policy issues follows later; and (3) the original experience is very negative.[9] The first two conditions give the historical event special importance for life; the second and third conditions combine to foster a belief that repetition must be avoided at any cost. In the years immediately after the Great War, when Liddell Hart was very much a rational actor, what stands out is his generally positive view of the war; only the first two conditions for omnipresent history applied to him in this early period. In his case, condition three proved critical in determining his policy prescriptions. As his view of Britain's role in World War I changed from positive to negative, he moved from analytic to omnipresent history.

How Liddell Hart used history, or more accurately, how history used Liddell Hart, has implications for decision-making theory and also offers lessons for Americans who remember the Vietnam War. That conflict deeply affected many who were young at the time, which makes it a critical referent for analyzing contemporary national security issues.[10] Almost everyone considers that conflict an unequivocally negative experience never to be repeated. It is likely that future policy makers deeply affected by the Vietnam War will confront situations resembling the circumstances surrounding the decision to enter that conflict. All the ingredients for omnipresent history will be present. This is not to say that American policy makers are sure to make wrongheaded foreign policy decisions in the future, only that the legacy of Vietnam has potential to create trouble. Foreign policy makers will of course deny that they could ever be prisoners of a historical event.

[9]For a thorough discussion of when omnipresent history is likely to obtain that varies some from mine, see Jervis, *Perception and Misperception*, 239–82.

[10]See Ole R. Holsti and James N. Rosenau, *American Leadership in World Affairs: Vietnam and the Breakdown of Consensus* (Boston: Allen & Unwin, 1984); Melanson, *Writing History and Making Policy*, esp. chaps. 6–7.

Virtually everyone fancies himself the ultimate rational actor. Liddell Hart, for example, frequently claimed during the late 1930s (e.g., in the preface to *The Defence of Britain*) that he was a dispassionate analyst fully capable of rendering objective assessments on the most controversial issues. His self-delusion should serve as a warning to all of us.

The second broad lesson from this case concerns quality control in the marketplace of ideas. The process of making national security policy is deeply affected by the ideas and theories that shape the central debates of the day. Certain ideas obviously provide better answers than others, and some ideas are prescriptions for disaster. Given the grave consequences of adopting flawed national security policies in a nuclear age, we need a policy process that allows valid ideas to triumph over falsehoods. The Liddell Hart case is disturbing in this regard. He was able in the 1930s to make deeply flawed arguments to a vast audience without being seriously challenged. Furthermore, he was able in later years to distort the history of that period so that future generations of national security scholars and policy makers who looked to the past would base their ideas about contemporary problems on warped history.

How does an intellectual community, in this case the national security community, prevent future cases like this one? First, foster intellectual pluralism; welcome different viewpoints; encourage open and sophisticated debate. There is no assurance, even so, that false ideas will be discredited, but at least critical assessment maximizes the prospects of that outcome. Liddell Hart suffered for the absence of criticism, which permitted him to make questionable arguments and then repeat them over and over. Formidable critics might have forced him to qualify and sharpen his ideas, perhaps even change them. He certainly would have been more careful in presenting his arguments.

Second, hold people accountable for arguments they put forward in key policy debates. Defense intellectuals need to know that informed judgments will be passed on their views and their overall conduct and that charlatanism will be exposed. Absence of penalties for misbehavior means no brake on the spread of false ideas. Liddell Hart actually was held accountable at one point. The significant ebbing of his influence during and immediately after World War II was, in effect, punishment for offering flawed ideas about how to deal with the Third Reich. What is disturbing about Liddell Hart's case, however, is that eventually he was able to escape from this predicament by rewriting history. The national security community, especially its historians, need to be alert to historical manipulation for selfish reasons.[11]

---

[11]This point is nicely illustrated by Holger H. Herwig, "Clio Deceived: Patriotic Self-Censorship in Germany after the Great War," *International Security* 12 (Fall 1987): 5–44.

A third broad lesson concerns the need to keep national grand strategy integrated and the difficulty of doing so. A grand strategy is integrated if means are well chosen to support national ends. It is disintegrated when ends and means are poorly related, so that national goals are poorly supported by national military posture.[12] The difficulty of achieving and maintaining integration is clear in the case of Liddell Hart and his contributions to British strategic thought. Although he surely would have accepted the dictum that national grand strategy must be integrated, he was unable, despite prodigious effort, to devise an integrated grand strategy. The fact that his military ideas were accepted nevertheless illustrates how an inadequate national security debate can give rise to a disintegrated grand strategy and at what cost. Liddell Hart recognized that Britain had no choice but to maintain a balance of power on the Continent, but he was unable to find a military policy to achieve that end. He explored many military ideas during the interwar years, but none met his criteria while also promising to check the German threat to the European balance. The root of the problem was Liddell Hart's antipathy toward a Continental commitment. Britain's only hope of maintaining the European balance of power was to raise an army that could be used directly against the Third Reich. There was no other way to thwart Hitler's plans for continental hegemony. Liddell Hart, however, could not face the fact that Britain could not stay on the Continent politically but remain off it militarily. He was not forced by British security debate to see this harsh reality because the British security community was so small and Liddell Hart was so powerful within it.

This episode has an important contemporary analogue. Despite the decline of traditional great powers like Britain, France, and Germany, and the emergence of a superpower rivalry that spans the globe, Europe remains the most strategically important area of the world. The Soviet Union has concentrated formidable military assets there, and although Soviet intentions in Europe are not altogether clear, the United States, like Britain, cannot tolerate a situation in which a single power—be it the Soviet Union or Germany—controls the Continent. Therefore, the United States must maintain powerful military forces *in* Europe that can deter a Soviet threat in some future crisis.

Proponents of reducing or abandoning the American commitment to maintain forces in Europe are motivated by a number of concerns: desire to cut the American defense budget; fear of involvement in a European war; annoyance at Europe's alleged unwillingness to carry a

[12]For an excellent discussion of this matter, see Barry R. Posen, *Sources of Military Doctrine: France, Britain, and Germany between the World Wars* (Ithaca, N.Y.: Cornell University Press, 1984).

fair share of NATO defense burdens; distaste for the leftist tilt in the domestic politics of some European countries; and pique at European policies toward Israel. Many observers will think at least some of these concerns are worthy. The question, however, is not Would a force reduction have benefits? but Would a force reduction leave the United States able to achieve its fundamental goals? If not, advocates of reduction are repeating Liddell Hart's mistake by recommending a disintegrated strategy. They advise a posture that cannot protect core national interests. As the Liddell Hart case clearly shows, an insular power cannot exert meaningful political influence in Europe if it is not willing to stand and fight on the Continent. The United States runs a serious risk if it fails to premise its policy on this reality and should not make such a grave decision without facing its full implications.

Index

CPSIA information can be obtained
at www.ICGtesting.com
Printed in the USA
LVOW03s1924201017
553177LV00002B/153/P